Cities of the Jungle

It seems incredible that the Maya accomplished what they did. They began as a jungle tribe at ground zero. Within time their magnificent stone cities filled the jungle and the plains. Their work was so grandiose that the world, when it saw it the first time, thought it to be the handiwork, or even the work of one of the lost tribes.

The vast and complex structures that towered above the tangled verdure, the delicately wrought artifacts, the involved hieroglyphic writing, and their precious calendar that regulated their lives—all were developed in the confines of the land in which they began and in which they became extinct. Here in the country that composed Mayadom, a tribe of Indians numbering three million brought their civilization to a rare and brilliant Golden Age . . . abandoned their great cities . . . began again in Yucatán . . . and then lost all, forever.

Victor W. von Hagen explores the lost world of the Maya. Through his personal knowledge of the land, through archaeology and the use of ancient documents, he restores the picture of Maya society as it then was. He describes how their cities—such as Tikal with its zigguratlike temples and Chichén Itzá with its outsized ball courts animated with intricate carving —were built out of the work-service tax of the common Indian.

Von Hagen searches into the everyday life of the Maya —birth, marriage, sex customs, all of which were regulated by complicated rituals. He details the amazing Maya astronomical calculations, analyzes the mystery of their hieroglyphic writing, and pictures the high quality of their sculptural arts. He depicts the life of the theocracy and the nobles who moved about in a panoply of pageantry greater than anything known in feudal Europe.

Other MENTOR Books You'll Enjoy

The Aztec: Man and Tribe *by Victor W. von Hagen*
A noted authority on ancient Latin-America tells the history, daily life, religion, and art of the nation that ruled Mexico before Columbus' time. Profusely illustrated. (#MT618—75¢)

Realm of the Incas *by Victor W. von Hagen*
The history, culture, religion, art, social and economic life of a fascinating Indian race that achieved a fabulous empire before Columbus discovered America. Copiously illustrated. (#MT636—75¢)

The Conquest of Peru (abridged)
by William H. Prescott
The authoritative history of the Inca empire and its subjugation by Pizarro; abridged and revised with a new Introduction by Victor W. von Hagen. (#MD314—50¢)

Indians of the Americas (abridged) *by John Collier*
The first book to paint the full panorama of the Red Indian from the Paleolithic Age to the present. (#MP494—60¢)

WORLD OF THE MAYA

VICTOR W. VON HAGEN

ILLUSTRATED BY
ALBERTO BELTRAN

Mentor: Ancient Civilizations

Published by THE NEW AMERICAN LIBRARY,
New York and Toronto

The New English Library Limited, London

Library of Congress Catalog Card No. 60-14722

MENTOR TRADEMARK REG. U.S. PAT. OFF. AND FOREIGN COUNTRIES
REGISTERED TRADEMARK—MARCA REGISTRADA
HECHO EN CHICAGO, U.S.A.

MENTOR BOOKS are published *in the United States* by
The New American Library, Inc.,
1301 Avenue of the Americas, New York, New York 10019,
in Canada by The New American Library of Canada Limited,
295 King Street East, Toronto 2, Ontario,
in the United Kingdom by The New English Library Limited,
Barnard's Inn, Holborn, London, E.C. 1, England

PRINTED IN THE UNITED STATES OF AMERICA

To the great American chewing-gum chewer, whose insatiable demands sent the chicle-tree scouts into the jungles, where in the process of finding new gum sources they discovered, over the decades, uncounted Maya ruins.

Contents

PART ONE

The Historical and Geographical Background
of the Maya Civilization

11

PART TWO

The People

37

PART THREE

The Ruling Classes

112

PART FOUR

The Achievements

140

Bibliography and Notes

213

Index

220

Figures

1. La Malinche (Doña Marina), Cortes' interpretor.   14
2. Physiographic map of the Maya area.   20–21
3. The bee god swarming the hive.   24
4. Archaeological map of the Maya area.   30–31
5. Kukulcan, the Plumed Serpent god of the Maya.   33
6. The walled city of Mayapán.   35
7. The basic dress of Maya men.   39
8. Maya woman wearing the *kub*.   41
9. Maya marriage rite.   49
10. The Maya house, past and present.   52
11. The hunting methods of the Maya.   54
12. Methods of artificially flattening the head and creating the "squint."   57
13. The coming-of-age ceremony.   59
14. Ix Chebel Yax, the goddess of weaving.   70
15. Illustration of the spindle-whorl.   72
16. The sacred quetzal bird and a parrot.   75
17. Phases of Maya pottery.   81
18. "Thin-orange" period of late Maya history.   82
19. An important Maya trade center.   86
20. Sea animals drawn by a Maya artist.   87
21. Name-glyphs of the Maya months.   92
22. Maya musicians playing percussion instruments.   95
23. Maya musicians playing trumpets.   96
24. Ceremonial dancer.   97
25. The game of *pok-a-tok* played at the ball court at Chichén Itzá.   100
26. The *holpop* seated on a mat representing justice.   103
27. Ruling chieftain of the Maya.   113
28. Maya *batabob* conversing over a fill-dish.   116
29. *Batabob*, the functional officials of the hierarchy.   117
30. The farmer as agriculturist and warrior.   125

31. The *nacom* holding judgment over prisoners
     of war.   126
32. Techniques of war.   128
33. Types of Maya weapons.   130
34. The sky god and the god of corn.   133
35. The Maya high priest.   134
36. Sacrifices at the *cenote* at Chichén Itzá.   138
37. Stages of quarrying.   142
38. Maya men rolling rock-mass.   142
39. Erection of roughed-out stela.   142
40. The carving of Stela E at Quirigua.   143
41. Architectural form and structure of
     Temple V, Tikal.   145
42. Plan of the Maya acropolis at Copán.   148
43. Stucco figures from the façade of House D
     at Palenque.   151
44. Cross-section of the Temple of the
     Inscriptions at Palenque.   152
45. Plan of the ceremonial center of Bonampak.   154
46. Plan of the civic and religious center of Uxmal.   156
47. The Nunnery at Uxmal.   158
48. The Pyramid of Kukulcan, Chichén Itzá.   161
49. Plan of Chichén Itzá.   162
50. The Temple of Kukulcan, Chichén Itzá.   163
51. The diving god.   166
52. Maya artists painting murals.   173
53. The mechanics of the Maya calendar.   175
54. Glyphs for the Maya time periods.   177
55. Inland communications.   180
56. The *sacbe*-road complex about the Cobá lakes.   183
57. A schematic plan of the *sacbe*-road complex.   186–187
58. Maya roads and city planning.   188–189
59. Drawing of canoes, from the Temple of the
     Warriors, Chichén Itzá.   191
60. Glyphs of the Maya days.   196
61. Maya numeration.   198

Plates

1. Temple I at Tikal.
2. Carved sapota lintels in Temple III, Tikal.
3. A stela at Tikal.
4. Stairway of the Pyramid of Kukulcan.
5. The Pyramid of Kukulcan at Chichén Itzá.
6. The Monjas in the Nunnery Triangle at Chichén Itzá.
7. The Temple of the Warriors at Chichén Itzá.
8. The Palace of the Governors at Uxmal.
9. The north façade of the Nunnery Quadrangle at Uxmal.
10. Maya pottery.
11. Pottery from Honduras.
12. Head of the corn god.
13. Head of the serpent god from Copán.
14. Stela P at Copán.
15. The obverse side of a stela at Copán.
16. Figure of a man in Maya headgear and armor.
17. Detail.
18. The gateway and priestly residence at Labná.
19. The ruins of Xlah-pak.
20. The corbeled arch at Kabah.
21. The long-nosed rain god at Sayil.
22. View of Casa Cerrada at Sayil.
23. Slab of sculpture found at Jonuta.
24. A Jicaque Indian of Honduras.

PART ONE

THE HISTORICAL AND GEOGRAPHICAL BACKGROUND OF THE MAYA CIVILIZATION

1. Of Man, History and Fable

Maya was, naturally, not their name. No one knows what they called themselves or what the name of their language was. Nor do we know, with any degree of certitude, the names of their stone cities, which are now entwined with tree and vine much as Lacooön was enveloped by the tentacles of serpents. The Maya are as little known as the other side of the moon once was, despite the fact that their civilization has been subjected to an unusually intense study.

All this is very disturbing. For the Maya were the only people of America's high cultures who developed a glyph-writ language capable of recording events, yet so far as is known they have left us little or nothing of themselves beyond certain calendric dates. No other culture in the Americas, perhaps in the world, in so confined a space, has had so much attention paid to it from every possible angle of approach. Few lost civilizations have had so distinguished a list of investigators. From the time of Christopher Columbus,[1] the first white man to see them (1502), down to the present turbulent times, when the Russian Dr. Yuri Knorosow[2] claims to have a "key" to Maya glyphs, there has been a veritable parade of people drawn by the air of mystery that hangs over Maya. Conquistadors, priests, historians, explorers, adventurers, geographers, astronomers, engineers, botanists, epigraphers, not to mention a generous sprinkling of picaros, have walked the Maya earth and left their impressions.

A preliterate people can only be seen through their art,

11

for they are otherwise inarticulate. From the vague Maya beginnings, somewhere around 2000 B.C. down to A.D. 987, there
are no tangible records and no traditions . . . . nothing else
except (and this in an overwhelming degree) the evidence of
their existence contained in the remains of buildings, sculpture, murals, and pottery. All that which the Maya really
were is known only through inference.

This is why the literature gives Maya art so much attention.
It is easier to describe a monument or photograph a ruin
than to find the intimate details of a people's existence, that
sort of thing which really breathes life into the skeletal remains of a past people's handiwork. This is why this has been
a hard book to write, and why it may be even more difficult
to read. The Maya as people remain unreal. One finds oneself
because of this almost as exasperated as Prescott when he
was writing *The Conquest of Peru*: ". . . imagine making a
hero out of Francisco Pizarro, a man who couldn't even read
his own name. . . ."

It is not that there is any lack of literature on the subject. On
the contrary, there is wonderfully much and of wide variety.
It is often written with so much profundity that discussions
tend to go far into the empyrean. The simple Indian, creator
of it all, sometimes wholly disappears.

The Maya have been characterized as the "Intellectuals of
the New World" because of their highly developed calendrics,
their glyph-writing, and the ornamental complexity of their
architecture. For long theirs was considered to be the peer
of American civilizations. They were unique in their culture;
pacific, they fought few wars; they viewed life from their
jungle fastness with Olympian detachment, working out complicated calendric inscriptions that could push their history
back to 23,040,000,000 days.

This archaeological daydream has been shattered by the
new discoveries. The Maya were a feudal theocracy. They
were, apart from being "intellectuals," just as cruel and ruth-
less—that is, human—as any of the other tribes about them.
The murals of Bonampak, discovered in 1946,[3] have provided data for an analysis of Maya character, for here graphically is the full interplay of Maya life forces that most of
their sculptured monuments have only hinted at. They were,
may we thank Itzamna, human, all too human.

Moreover, the Maya were not the land-bound people as
pictured, living in the splendid isolation of their stone-built
ceremonial centers. They were seafarers; setting out in large
canoes that held as many as forty people, they cruised for
thousands of miles along the Gulf coasts around the Caribbean, one of the most dangerous of seas. They and they

alone of the great theocracies—Inca, Aztec, Chimu, Mochica
—regularly used the sea for maritime traffic.

This book is an attempt to portray the Maya as culture
and as people. The Maya will be treated here neither as "Intellectuals of the New World" nor as fossilized archaeological specimens. Instead they will be shown as they depicted
themselves or else told of themselves to others: feeling, moving human beings, as contradictory in thought and action as
we ourselves are.

Maya history began with Columbus. On his fourth and last
voyage, Christopher Columbus landed in 1502 at Guanaja,
one of the Bay Islands off the coast of Honduras. There the
Admiral of the Ocean Sea met an Indian trading party in an
immense dugout canoe. When asked wherefrom they came,
the Indians replied: ". . . from a certaine province called Maiam."

Some years later another Spanish navigator skirted the
coast and saw the well-constructed buildings. When he landed
and inquired in Spanish as to who had built the buildings
and who they themselves were, the reply came back: *"Ci-
u-than."* It actually meant, "We don't understand you," but
the Spaniards took it for an answer to their questions, and
with time's alchemy the land became "Yucatán." However, a
conquistador who wished to preserve the "true history of
things" wrote that the Maya "now say their country is called
'Yucatán,' and so it keeps that name, but in their own language they do not call it by that name."

In 1511 Captain Valdivia, sailing his ship from Panama to
Santo Domingo with 20,000 golden ducats aboard, ran onto
the reefs of the Jamaica shallows. Escaping in an open boat
without sails, oars, or food, he and his twenty men drifted
thirteen days until they came upon Cozumel Island. This was
within sight of Yucatán. The natives, who were Maya,
promptly put to death all the survivors except two and these
were traded as slaves to the Lord of Xamanzaná on the Yucatán mainland.

Gerónimo de Aguilar [4] of Ecija, Spain, was one of the two
first white men to live in Yucatán, and the first to learn
Maya. He kept a breviary which he continued to read in order
to keep track of Christian feast days. When rescued in 1519
by Hernando Cortes he became with the Indian woman Malinche ("the Tongue") one of those who helped to defeat the
Aztecs.

After the fall of the Aztecs it was the turn of the Maya.
The Spanish conquest of the Maya [5] had neither the terrible
fierceness nor the dramatic impact of the conquest of the
Aztecs. It went on for nineteen years in Yucatán, from 1527

to 1546, and was not completed until 1697 when the Itzás, who carried on the Maya way of life in the area of Lake Petén, were finally engulfed by time and man.[6]

Unlike the Aztec campaigns, these wars of extermination did not inspire the writing of first impressions by the Spanish captains who took part in it, but Hernando Cortes [7] gives in his fifth letter a general narrative of his almost unbelievable march through Mayadom; and the invaluable Bernal Díaz, who accompanied him in 1524, penned in considerable detail some wonderful factual accounts of Maya life that picture this as a still-living and functioning community.[8]

Once Yucatán settled down under the yoke of peace the priests took over. It was under the priests, who were at once destined to be the destroyers and conservers of Maya culture, that history was written. All or almost all we know of the living Maya—and so, by inference, of those who lived a

Fig. 1. La Malinche (Doña Marina), "the Tongue" of Cortes' conquest of the Aztec and the Maya, spoke both Nahuatl and Maya. She was given to Cortes at Xicalanco, the great trading center in Tabasco, in 1519.

thousand years before—comes from the writings of these God-inspired *frailes*. Much of their written material was in the form of *relaciónes*, a sort of informal history intended to instruct and guide the Spanish court. Like so many of the accounts of Spain in the New World, these were not published until 300 years had passed, and then under the title *Relaciónes de Yucatán*.[9] There was an occasional padre, such as Antonio de Ciudad Real, who could rise above the prejudices of his cloth and deal objectively with what he saw. The brief *relación* in which he describes his discovery "of the very renowned edifices of Uxmal" is a classic.[10]

But of all these creator-destroyers the most notable was Fray Diego de Landa. His small book *Relación de las Cosas de Yucatán* (On the Things of Yucatán), written before 1566, is the principal source of late Maya history. The details Landa gives of their lives, the description of food, history, and tribal mores, the delineation of the katuns of Maya history (which made possible the modern reduction of Maya dates), and his insistence that the Maya in his time were the very same people who built the stone cities found in the jungles (which even then were ascribed to Roman, Greeks, and Jews) have given him a unique place in Maya history. Landa was born at Cifuentes, Spain, of noble parents. In 1524, he joined the Franciscans, at the age of sixteen. He set off for Yucatán in 1549. In time he became adept at the Maya language.

Landa had prime informants, and his interests were broad. Considering what he had to do, he was amazingly objective. He is our one source of the habits and foibles of the Maya, and his immense historical value is attested by the number of editions of his little book.[11]

From the late sixteenth to the beginning of the nineteenth century the Maya were the specific charges of the *padres*. The earth during this time went about its appointed rounds and the great stone cities of the Maya were gradually grown over with jungle verdure; in time they were blotted out of human memory. There was, to be sure, an occasional chance discovery of a Maya city. In 1576 Diego García de Palacio on his way to Guatemala discovered the city-state of Copán. He sent a report to Philip II, "I have tried to find out . . . what people lived here. . . ." The report made no impress.[12] The Spaniards were making their own history.

If the final conquest of the Itzá tribe, which occurred in 1697, had been delayed until a half century later, the known history of the Maya might have been somewhat different. The interest in the antique which occurred in Europe around the middle of the eighteenth century began the fashion. As king of Naples, Carlos III patronized the excavations of Pompeii, and later as ruler of Spain he continued his royal interest. When Palenque was discovered in 1773 and a report sent to him, Carlos III ordered a royal commission sent to the ruins with artists and engineers, specifying that artifacts be gathered there so as to illustrate an *Ancient History of America*.[13]

Maya archaeological history began at Palenque. These ruins, buried in the jungles of Chiapas, would seem the least likely place for it to begin. No roads led to it. This city, once one of the great centers of the Maya, had been deserted since the ninth century and promptly reclaimed by the jungle. Palenque was discovered in 1773 by Indians who carried their information to a priest, who, upon visiting the ruins, promptly prepared a *memoria*. This excited interest and drew numerous expeditions. The account of one of these, that of Captain Antonio del Rio, was translated in 1822 into English and its inaccurate drawings were redrawn by one "J.F.W.," none other than Jean Frederic Waldeck, who later himself went to the ruins. The bibliography of Palenque is immense.[14]

The drawings of Waldeck set the Maya on the road to Rome, for he stated that Palenque was either Roman or Phoenician and even altered his drawings of the monuments to give proof to the theory. At the same time he gave aid to Edward King, Viscount Kingsborough. This gently mad Irish aristocrat was then compiling what was to be the monumental *Antiquities of Mexico*.[15] It was published in nine huge folio volumes at $150 the copy. One might read therein, in a potpourri of English, Greek, Latin, Hebrew, and Sanskrit, that the Americas had been peopled by the Lost Tribes of Israel. One shudders to think what might have been the fate of the Maya had John Lloyd Stephens, a well-traveled New York lawyer who had seen Roman and Egyptian ruins, not rediscovered the Maya ruins in 1840. Stephens had an excellent historical sense and, moreover, a facile pen. Catherwood, his English-born companion, had limned many of the known ruins in the Near East and had made detailed architectural drawings of the Mosque of Omar, where to effect entry he had submitted himself to circumcision. Although his illustrations have overtones of Piranesi, they are so accurate that scholars can read his renderings of the Maya glyphs. So the one with critical judgment and good clear writing and the other with superbly accurate drawings laid down the base of American archaeology. They established that the Maya were of indigenous American origin, and that the buildings found were built by them. So timeless are these books they are still being reissued today.[16] They were published at the same time as Prescott's famous accounts of the conquests of Mexico and Peru. And they had a marked effect on the literature of American archaeology, inspiring an interest among the Mexicans in their own past. Histories of Yucatán began to appear, and in Spain scholars were shamed into publishing manuscripts which lay moldering in the archives. In the following years this filled something of the void. In the first decades of the twentieth century the Mexican archaeologists worked mainly in the immediate Mexican milieu, but now much work is being done by Mexican archaeological explorers, who are well equipped with the intellectual tools to solve the Maya problem.[17]

The French have sustained an interest in the Maya for centuries. Their contributions have been mainly in scholarship, deduction, and literature, rather than in systematic archaeological excavations. From the time of Jacques de Testera, who came to Yucatán in 1539 and invented the "Testerian Hieroglyphics,"* to Waldeck, to Brasseur who discovered Landa's *History* moldering in Spanish archives and first published it, down to the present-day, controversial Jacques Soustelle (who is perhaps better known as L'Aztec, the "executor" of do-nothing French cabinets), an ethnographer known for the lucidity of his texts, the French have maintained a creative interest in things Maya.[18]

The English have been on these native grounds ever since the early seventeenth century when Thomas Gage, the English-American, first gave them insight and interest in the Maya. He was followed by Juan Galindo and then by Captain Herbert Caddy, who anticipated the famous trek of Catherwood to Palenque. Alfred Maudslay combined excavating with exploration and published well and effectively. He is in all respects the first Maya archaeologist. English interest has continued unabated; British museums contain some of the choicest documentation on the history of the Maya.[19]

Interest in the Maya has not remained the exclusive concern of any one nationality. The truly great figure among the German contingent was Alexander von Humboldt. Arriving in Mexico in 1803 after four years in South America, he spent a year there preparing what is now a classic and encyclopedic work on Mexico. He also gave much attention to American archaeology. His critical judgment stands as a landmark in this field, and although he himself did not enter Maya territory, he did reproduce and comment for the first time on several pages of the now celebrated Dresden Codex.

---

* Testera, a brother of the chamberlain to Francis I, on the king's order came to America in 1529; he and four others were the first to arrive. In Mexico he devised a method of putting the Catholic catechism into a picture writing similar to that used by the Mexicans.

While French interest in the Maya was literary and speculative, the German was geographical and exploratory.

Captain Teobert Maler, who escaped the debacle of the
Emperor Maximilian in Mexico in 1867, went down to Guatemala and became enmeshed in the mystery of the Maya.
Alone except for native carriers, Maler plunged into new
archaeological grounds, photographed, described, and published accounts of them for Harvard University. Then, un-
settled by his privations and convinced that money was being
made on his reports, he filled his letters with insults and
execrations, and bitterly withdrew into himself. His contemporary Eduard Seler, as thorough as Maler, made outstanding contributions, as did Sapper the geographer, Walter
Lehmann the linguist, and Forstemann, a librarian who
evolved a way to decipher the Maya "dates." [20]

The dominant names in Maya archaeology, however, have
been the North Americans. Ever since Stephens initiated the
Maya interest in 1840, the largest amount of field work, the
restoration of Maya ruins, and especially excellent and
solid publications have resulted from the American contribu-
tion. A list of the important work done and published is
long and impressive.[21] Most of all it has been the Carnegie
Institution of Washington. Ever since that institution entered
the Maya field in 1915, scarcely a year has gone by when they
did not have a dozen men representing various fields of research
somewhere in Mayadom. However, with the expanding atom
and the expanding universe, its interest has been stifled.

So out of this two centuries of frenzied activity has come
a bewildering mass of literature; it would be difficult to en-
compass all unless one gave it a lifetime. Much of it is
highly technical—specialist talking to specialist—so that the
general reader, unless he is as tough-fibered as General
Grant ("I propose to fight it out on this line if it takes all summer") may, out of sheer bewilderment, leave the Maya theater
all too early and never really come to see the drama of a people
crawling out of the primeval clay and by sheer will-to-cul-
ture finally conquering nature, raising tall stone towers over
the jungle.

Eric Thompson, one of our finest Mayaists and a graceful writer, said that his impression is that "travelers as well
as most readers of books on Maya civilization return from
their journeys, physical or mental, curiously unsatisfied. . . ." [22]

The monuments remain, the people have disappeared. The
whole human business is so inextricably bound up with pre-
history, conquest, epigraphy, astronomy, that the Maya story
by its very nature is disconnected. Thompson feels that he
and his fellow archaeologists are partly to blame for the

frequent failure of the nonprofessional to get a coherent impression of past civilizations: ". . . the very nature of the material that an archaeologist handles, exacting excavations, the shapes of cooking pots, the reduction of Maya dates, the abstract speculations of time and space," the minutiae out of which archaeological history is fashioned, is not meant for inspiring reading.

As the author of *The World of the Maya* I depend heavily, as will be seen, on this mass of technical literature; I would be the last to denigrate it or the privations and difficulties that were its birth pains.

My attempt here is to tell of the Maya as human beings. Speculations have been held to an absolute minimum; I have used my own experience as ethnographic explorer to test if what I culled from the literature had the weather tints of reality.

And so if out of this the Maya emerge from their fossilized archaeological limbo as sentient and living people, perhaps then the reader will not go "curiously unsatisfied." It has been said that the pleasure that art gives ought not to cost the slightest fatigue. Can this also be said for archaeology?

I hope so.

2. The Country

"Projecting northward into the Gulf of Mexico like a giant thumb between North and South America lies the Peninsula of Yucatán. . . ." The words are those of the late, great Dr. Morley. We might expand the simile to note that the Yucatán thumb broadens out to form a land something like the shape of a hand. This includes most of Mayadom.*

* Meso-America is the hybrid word now used by many to designate that portion of the world wherein the Maya kingdom lay. It lacks as much meaning as that other hybrid "Amerindian." Middle America is designated as that land that lies roughly between the Rocky Mountain system of Mexico and the Andean Mountain system of South America. This also has little meaning, since Panama, reaching to the border of Costa Rica, is historically, linguistically, and biologically South American. But if the specialists wish to speak of "Meso-America," this terminology must then be extended. North America would be "Proto-America" and South America, "Meta-America." This *reductio ad absurdum* is enough to show how undescriptive the term "Meso-America" really is.

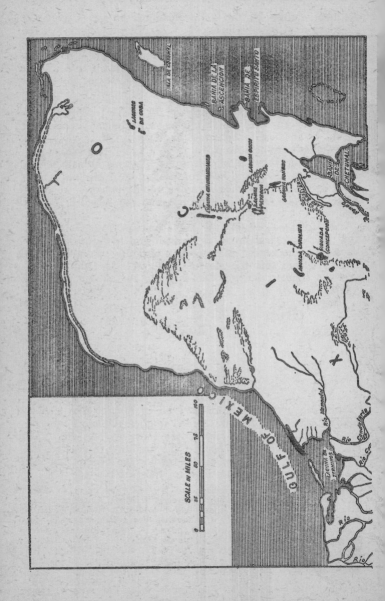

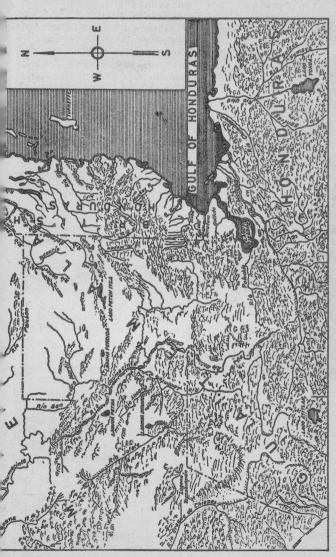

Fig. 2. Physiographic map of the Maya area. From S. G. Morley, *The Ancient Maya*, Stanford University Press, 1946, Plate 1.

Towering ranges of volcanic origin (Mount Tajamulco, at 13,809 feet, is the highest) lie along the Pacific slopes, and the climate here is variegated. The soil is cultivated from sea level to 10,000 feet. The whole area is characterized by deep valleys and pine-fringed mountains; there is an excessive dryness on the western slopes and excessive wetness on the eastern. In this high zone the Maya found volcanic stone to make the *metate* for braying corn. They also found obsidian, volcanic glass, which made mirrors, knives, and razors; from the streams came jade, as important to the Maya as life itself; in the high cloud forests there were the red-green parrot and the far-famed quetzal bird that yielded the jade-green tail feathers which decked the headgear and cloaks of the chieftains.

In the lowland areas—where the great temple cities were located—such as Tikal, Uaxactun, Yaxchilan, Calakmul—is El Petén. Here rain forests alternate with depressed areas, which are seasonal swamps called *skalches,* and high bush with alternating savannahs of tall grass. It is the least likely place one would choose for developing a culture, yet it is precisely here that the earliest-known Maya cities are found. The lowland jungles are set upon plateaus of limestone and are amazingly fertile, yielding valuable trees and plants which were of great use to the Maya economy. Giant cedars were fashioned into outsized canoes eighty feet long for navigation on the Caribbean. *Copal,* an odoriferous resin, as essential to the Maya as amber was to the Greek, was a commodity of "very great business for them"; it was burned on all priestly occasions. There was the brazilwood, used for dyeing Maya cloth ("for when thrown into the water it turns to red"); and the chewing-gum tree, which yielded a fine-tasting fruit as well as the chicle sap. Lignum vitae, as hard as iron, was "a specific against syphilis and buboes."

These jungles were rich in birds and animals: quails, woodpeckers, pheasants, and the ocellated turkey with feathers "as beautiful as the peacocks in Spain"; pumas, jaguars, and "wonderful many deer"; brockets (red deer) and tapirs were common and killed whenever possible.

The tropical jungles graduate into the "thumb" proper. In Yucatán this low, tortilla-flat limestone zone characterizes the whole northern part of the peninsula. "It is a country," remembers Diego de Landa, "with the least amount of earth I have ever seen . . . it all seems to be one living rock . . . this because there is only a small cap of earth over the limestone and in many places it is less than six inches in depth." Despite its apparent flatness, the land is broken up into limestone outcrops and depressions with a profusion of loose stones—*dzekel,* the

Maya called it—hillocks of limestone rubble. It was undoubtedly a good source of rock for the inner core of their buildings, yet most difficult for traffic. It is because of this that the Maya built their famed *sacbeob*, or causeways, in order to make trade and travel easier.

As slight as is the earthcap covering the porous limestone base, the land is amazingly fertile. Now only a high bush grows in most of Yucatán, yet there is evidence, botanical and traditional, that trees, and even jungles, once flourished there. There is a Maya folk tale—which might well be pure history—that in 1467 after the fall of Mayapán, the capital of coastal Maya, ". . . during a winter's night about six o'clock there arose a wind, a hurricane. . . . There followed a great devastation—villages, temples, game, trees, were all destroyed . . . and it lasted until noon next day . . . there were thousands killed." Another Spanish chronicler remembers that "Yucatán is heavily wooded but of so uniform a height it seems that the trees were all cut with scissors. . . ."

"So much was lost [on that night] and so much changed," said Diego de Landa, "that even the name of the land disappeared, that land which was once called *The Land of the Turkey and the Deer.*"

Turkey and deer and much other game besides; here were rabbits "large and good to eat"; the agouti, "a little animal, sad by nature"; and opossums and coatimundis (these last the women suckled at their breasts and deloused as they did their own children). Along the coast there was an abundance of birds: frigate birds, cormorants, herons and egrets. The Muscovy ducks, a source of plumes, were raised in the house from eggs and did not "run away." On the beaches sting rays were killed for their tails, which had razor-sharp bone used as saw-knives to cut and bleed the body for blood sacrifice; it was "the duty of priests to keep and have many of them."

Iguanas are everywhere along the shore; they yielded flesh that tasted like chicken. Turtles and turtle eggs were plentiful. As for *ain*, crocodile tails, they were considered a rare delicacy. In the lagoons, of which there are many along the coast, the Maya hunted for the manatee. These they killed with harpoons and from them had more meat "than a yearling calf."

Fish were plentiful and an important native industry. Chieftains of the sea towns in the Maya province, called *chikin-cheel*, were the "lords of the sea," and they controlled fishing rights. They used their slaves as fishermen. Fishing in these lagoons, with nets, harpoons, bow and arrow, was a vast operation. "Their fisheries," says Landa, "are on a very large scale."

And salt was had in great quantity. It was one of the lifelines of grain eaters such as the Maya. It had preservative qualities and was used as a tonic. The salt taken from long coastal lagoons about Ekab was "very white and highly concentrated . . . the operation was simple and salt was a great trade commodity."

In the interior the cultivated maize milpas gave other subsistence crops in addition to corn. Stingless bees were bred in tree hollows; "the land abounds in honey used for sweetening and, more important, for a meadlike intoxicant called *balche*." There was much cotton, "gathered in wonderful quantity," which was spun and woven into mantas. Cacao, the seed of which when dried, toasted, and ground is chocolate, was the Maya elixir. It was raised in the tropical extreme of Mayadom.

In the north of Yucatán was Campeche, a rolling country of forests and rivers, and beyond it the lushly tropical Tabasco, covered with swamps and quagmires, a network of bayous, creeks, rivers. The land was made for cacao plantations and the Indians planted little else, depending on the exchange of cacao for cloth, salt, and corn. South, at the

Fig. 3. The bee god as a bee coming in to swarm at the hive. Honey and wax played an important part in Maya lives.

other extreme of the Maya domain, was Hibueras—Honduras—also possessed of rivers. On the banks of these rivers there were "wide roads bordered with cacao trees."

Such was the geography and such the environment of natural riches of the Maya. The entire area was equivalent in size to the state of New Mexico.*

Water, however, was the one element the Yucatán Maya could not command. Although water was everywhere, there was often not a drop to drink. Great quantities of rain fell, varying from 39 inches a year in the driest parts of Yucatán to over 150 inches in the wetter zones. During January and February there were light rains. June through August were heavy rain months, and even September brought light rainfall. The temperature varied with the seasons, as low as 45 degrees in December, as high as 105 degrees in April. Still, there was no way to hold the rain. There are no rivers on the Yucatán peninsula.

To meet the water problem the Maya constructed reservoirs and cisterns. At their greatest city, Tikal, they hollowed out an immense reservoir between two temples, cementing the porous limestone so it would hold water. In northern Yucatán, where all the rain water percolates underground, Maya cities developed around natural wells.† At Chichén Itzá there were two, of these one for drinking, the other for watery sacrifices. Where the natural *cenote* (Maya, *dzonot*) did not occur and they wished to build a city, the Maya in Roman fashion made underground cisterns. These were called *chultunes*.

Water, or the lack of it, was the curse of the Maya paradise (it was equally so to the Aztec), and drought and its disastrous consequences play an important role in native Maya literature.

Aside from their periodic plagues with drought, the Maya lived in a land which might be characterized by the Biblical phrase "flowing with milk and honey." No other tribe in the Americas had so balanced a wealth of natural resources. Although the Maya were a neolithic society (they had neither metals nor the wheel nor dray animals, and needed none), they had a soil and climate that gave them maize in such awesome quantities that it allowed them leisure. A rich and

---

* The lands occupied by Mayadom totaled about 125,000 square miles and included Guatemala, Yucatán, Campeche, Tabasco, the eastern half of Chiapas, Quintana Roo, British Honduras, and the western section of the Republic of Honduras.

† These wells were formed by the collapsing of the friable limestone shelf, which exposed the subterranean water table. Some of these natural *cenotes* are 200 feet in diameter, with the water 100 feet below the surface.

varied flora and fauna yielded all they needed for food, clothing, and medicine. Limestone rock for temples and dwellings was easily quarried, even without metal tools. The same stone was burned and easily reduced to lime. The material for a durable stone-mortar masonry was everywhere available.

Some time, circa 2000 B.C., these who were to be the "Maya" filtered slowly into this land. Once in possession, they were to hold it for 3,700 years, in continuous cultural sequence.

3. The Coming and the Rise

The Maya, as culture, developed within the Americas; nothing came from without.

As man, the Maya developed out of the various peoples whose common ancestors were those mesolithic wanderers that century upon century poured across the Bering "land bridge" once connecting Outer Asia to Alaska. It is perhaps one supposition that finds support in geography and paleontology, and considerable inferential proof in anthropology. It has a closer relation to fact than those will-o'-the-wisp theories of the "diffusionists," who to explain the origins of such civilizations as the Maya, Aztec, and Inca would have whole peoples, with cultures already full-born, being wafted across the sea on rafts or canoes.

The author has elsewhere entered into the controversy over the origin of American Man that has raged since the discovery of the Western Hemisphere.[23] It is sufficiently diverting, but one must be on guard against seeing the obvious and missing the significant. And the significant thing is that Maya culture was an attenuated and in some ways a rarefied variation of a culture that was basically Middle-American-Mexican. Its characteristic elements are to be found in every culture which bordered it.

This one must insist upon, for since the beginning the Maya have been described as everything—Roman, Jew, Egyptian, Phoenician—but what they really are: *Maya,* a tribal group as "American" as the Sioux or the Pawnee, as "American" as the Inca or the Fuegian. Maya society is an American society. It was organized on a kinship basis. Like the other tribes that developed from the primitive hunting-fishing stages and turned farmers, the Maya became temple builders and myth makers.

In the beginning there were "other people" who lived in the lands that later became Maya. Around 2000 B.C. there lived a "longheaded" people in thinly scattered tribes over most of the land which became the Maya area. We know little more. They were rudimentary farmers and were perhaps the proto-Maya. Tribes using Mayance speech were widely scattered along the hotlands of the Mexican Gulf coast from Yucatán to Tampico and doubtlessly inland into the low, flat Tehuantepec isthmus; and certainly in the high hinterland, since they followed the Rio Usumacinta along the fringe of the tropical highlands of Chiapas.

At this theoretical date, 2000 B.C., the intellectual equipment of the Maya was certainly no better than that of any of the other tribes about them. Their agricultural traits were the same. Society was primitive and agricultural techniques were on the same level. Their society depended on the beneficent gods. They counted the stars in their balance, watched the seasonal rising of planets, noting the portents in the sky for rain or sun, and in this way gradually roughed out their primitive calendrics.

There is no tradition that can be taken as history, even in the Maya chronicles, about their place of origin. The latter-day interpretation of the *Popol Vuh* is concerned only with the coming of the Toltec-Mexicans in the ninth century. The theory—inspired by missionary zeal—that the Maya came from the eastern sea and expected for centuries greater gods and men to follow, is a part of the Maya mythos. The general reliability of tradition can be trusted if corroborated by archaeology. It is missing here.

There *is* linguistic evidence, however, that sometime early in Maya history—the date 2000 B.C. may, for convenience, be assumed to be it—a non-Maya-speaking group drove a wedge between the tribes, thus isolating the Huasteca (who speak a language definitely Maya) from the bulk of the others. It is presumed that by this time the Maya were scattered throughout the lands which became Mayadom in small tribes, various kinship groups which formed self-contained social units. They were corn-growing, pottery-making peoples. In appearance, although there is little skeletal evidence, they were not much other than they appeared a thousand years later.

What these people did, said, and wore can only be inferred. At the moment all we have of early Maya man is a collection of potsherds. These are fragments of a utilitarian pottery which is called "Mamom." * Their houses, circular and

---

* *Mamom:* "Grandmother." The term was suggested by the *Popol Vuh,* the sacred book of the ancient Quiché Maya. (See Chap. 14, on pottery.)

thatched with palm leaf, were of wood. A crude flat stone braised the maize for making unleavened corncakes. Open woven bags held beans and squash. Their crude beds, over which rush mats were thrown, rested on stilts. Until cotton was developed and the loom perfected, clothes were beaten from the bast of wild-fig fibers. The fire-hardened planting stick (never improved upon in 3,700 years by the Maya) they already possessed, and their weapons were spears and arrows tipped with flint or obsidian. For hunting they had the bark-less dog.

To infer more about these "before-people" would involve fiction. It would be pleasing to be able to embroider around these minor facts a wealth of the incident that gives history its sparkle. But the cultural sequence is missing, as is the archaeological evidence that shows the slow evolution of the primitive into the sophisticated. Strange, and yet not surprising. Even with exhaustive records, there are wide gaps in such histories. Suddenly, it seems, archaeology reveals mounds and small pyramids; there is a developed pottery and much other evidence that the Maya type of social organization is formed.

These Maya are revealed as people with wit, passion, and interest. Superbly painted polychromic pottery shows that the upper classes are already formed; society is stratified and inequality stressed. Man has set bounds to his fields, and he wars, hopes, fears. All this is Maya, but also it is essentially as old as man in the Americas. Similar communities are spread from the Pacific to the Caribbean. Trade is already advanced. Tribes are in touch not only with each other, but also with foreign ones in Mexico, principally through the great trading center of Xicalanco. Glyph-writing is known and used by all tribes, and each also has its calendrics based on the twenty-day lunar calendar.

Archaeology reveals that population centers, small, compact, and self-contained, were springing up over all these areas during the long formative period, that is, between 1000–300 B.C. Trade, language, and common culture, rather than political ties, hold them together as "Maya."

El Petén is the name given to a region which is composed of vast swamps, jungles, and savannahs, with a medial chain of lakes and grassland surrounded by tall tropical forests. It is here that the people begin to show the characteristics of their culture which define "Maya." The potters depict representational human forms on their bowls, painting and coloring are rich, imaginative, and polychromic. Much of the pottery is dated with glyphs. Thus far no one has traced the evolution of utilitarian pottery into aesthetic ware. It appears suddenly, full-born.

By A.D. 200 Uaxactún* is already on its cultural way; the oldest stela there is dated A.D. 328. Eleven miles beyond, the temple city of Tikal is being built. After this there is a quickening of building throughout the entire length and breadth of the land. The cities can be listed by their dated stelae in the order of their appearance in Maya history.

Still, this is not a unique performance. There was a fluorescence of cultures throughout Mexico and Middle America. The perfection of the calendar, the progress of glyph-writing, the perfection and use of paper, the ritualistic calendar, and dated monuments were common to all advanced peoples. Cultural exchange of ideas and techniques through trade had gone on since the beginning. So far as is known now—although this concept is subject to revaluation at any time owing to new and continuing discoveries in the Maya area— the early Maya city-states had a common trade, a common language, and similar cultural traits. There was a cultural union but not a political one. There is no known center or capital. These cities endured between the extreme dates of 500 B.C. and A.D. 1000.

It is believed through inference that they ceased to function after the year 1000. The archaeological evidence gained through the superb deductions of the epigraphers would indicate that after this date the Maya tribes within the area of the "Old Empire" no longer raised dated monuments, and so far as is known now, the cities ceased to function. This does not imply that the temple cities disintegrated at once; it was perhaps a long, slow process. The explanations for the decline and fall have been many; all explanations have been examined and none can withstand the catapult of criticism.

To us it seems illogical that a people numbering no less than three million would abandon stone cities which took them centuries to build. Yet the archaeological evidence shows that city-states as widely separated as Copán and Tikal "ceased to erect monuments at the end of successive periods— one of the fundamentals of Maya life," and gradually melted away.

These Maya temple cities (they number in the hundreds) were not in most cases abandoned because of conquest. The temples, the priestly houses, the pyramids, and the dated stone monoliths stand as they were left. There is no evidence

* However, Maya epigraphy no longer suggests that the Tikal-Uaxactún region was the immediate birthplace of Maya civilization; the art, architecture, and ceramics of the two cities are also indicative.

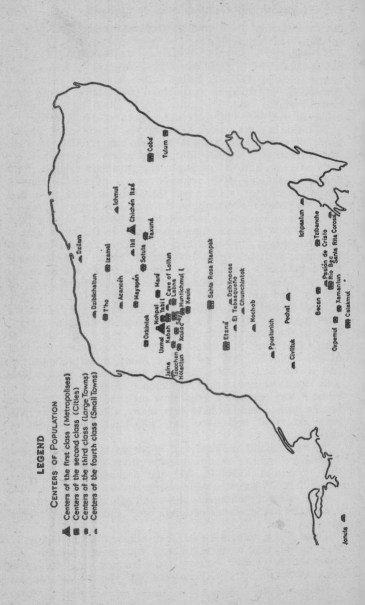

LEGEND

CENTERS OF POPULATION

◀ Centers of the first class (Metropolises)
▦ Centers of the second class (Cities)
▦ Centers of the third class (Large Towns)
▲ Centers of the fourth class (Small Towns)

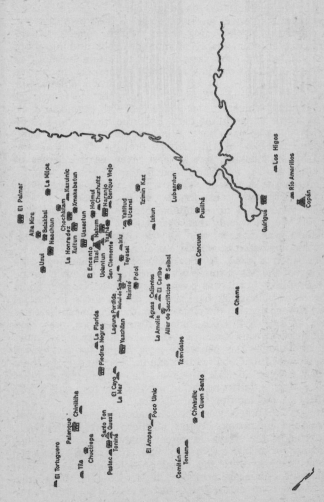

Fig. 4. Archaeological map of the Maya area. From S. G. Morley, *The Ancient Maya*, Stanford University Press, 1946, Plate 19.

of any cataclysmal climatic change or of diseases that had not appeared elsewhere in the Americas, nor is there evidence of large-scale wars. The cities, some of the most impressive monuments built by man anywhere, were just left to be enfolded by the tentacles of the jungle flora.

The Maya themselves have compounded their own mystery. Their involved glyph-writing, even though capable of expressing the abstract quality of numbers, tells nothing about themselves beyond such facts as that a certain building or stela was completed on such and such a date. Of themselves —nothing. They have not left a name, even of a chieftain or a city. Until formulas are found to decipher the remainder of the glyphs—which are not concerned with calendrics—we shall be a little longer in the dark. Even the Incas, who had no writing[24] and who have never been championed as the "intellectuals of the New World," left an oral history which, confirmed by archaeology, has at least given us the names of their kings and the epochs in their history.

Whatever the causes, the cities within a wide range of the humid forest were abandoned. What happened to the people? Where did three million people go? Or did they go at all? We know only that after A.D. 1000 the bulk of the population was concentrated in the Guatemalan highlands and in the northeastern part of Yucatán.

Once upon a time, in the language of archaeology, the centering of the Maya in the Yucatán area was known as the "New Empire." But it was neither new nor an empire. Some of the stone-built cities here are as old as those in the interior. Tulum, high on the cliffs facing the Caribbean Sea, has a date of A.D. 564. Cobá, inland from the sea, was connected by road with Xelha, a walled coastal city a few miles north of Tulum. This causeway runs inland for sixty-seven miles, connecting Cobá with Yaxuná. A stone stela there gives the date of A.D. 361. These and many other temple cities were existing in full panoply during the last four and a half centuries of the interior "Old Empire."

After A.D. 900 there was a concentration of the Maya tribes, for reasons unknown, in the northern part of Yucatán. This brought the Maya in direct contact with the Toltec Mexicans. From 200 B.C. to A.D. 900, the Toltecs, who even to their enemies were the classic people, maintained their capital at Teotihuacán, northeast of Mexico City. They practiced crafts such as weaving, had a calendar, used rebuswriting, and made paper. From A. D. 300 onward, the Toltecs carried on trade with the highland Maya. After the decline of Teotihuacán, the Toltecs concentrated about Tula (A.D. 900–1106) which lies sixty miles north of Mexico City. Tula, the capital of that strange and haunting man-god Quetzalcoatl, is bound up with the latter-day history of the Maya.

Quetzalcoatl, in various guises, was the cultural hero of the land. His motif, a plumed snake's head—an exact translation of his name—existed long before Quetzalcoatl as person took on flesh at Tula. There as priest, ruler, and demiurge he ruled for twenty-two years. Civil war forced him into exile. After various vicissitudes, which have been recounted elsewhere,[25] Quetzalcoatl himself, or another leader

Fig. 5. Kukulcan, the Plumed Serpent god of the Maya, who is identified with the Mexican Quetzalcoatl. Various symbols are included in the snake's body and in the god's head.

who had taken his patronymic, arrived at the-place-where-the-language-changes, that is, Xicalanco, the ancient trading center in Tabasco. This was the edge of Maya territory. The date was about 987.

Early in the tenth century a small army of Maya-speaking Itzás* had begun to move as a conquering horde across Yuca-

* Historically a Nahuatl-speaking people, Toltecs had been in Tabasco long before this date. The original inhabitants were of Maya stock and spoke Chontal, a Maya variant. The Mexican intruding peoples spoke Zoque and Nahuatl, and were called, at least by the Maya, "Itzás."

tán in a northeast direction. The leader was called Kukulcan, the exact Maya translation for Quetzalcoatl. They had
lived in the area about Chakanputún (now Champotón, in
Campeche) and were Maya-speaking. After wandering and
waging occasional battles, they came upon Chichén Itzá,
which had been abandoned in 692. They rebuilt it and it became their capital. ". . . the Itzás who occupied Chichén
Itzá . . . had a great lord who reigned there, named Kukulcan. They say he arrived from the west [i.e., Mexico] but
they differ among themselves as to whether he arrived before
or after the Itzás—or with them." 26

The Toltec-Itzás were exceedingly active. Under the aegis
of the Tutul Xiu dynasty they formed a league of Maya
states, erected a capital, and called it Mayapán. It became
the first known capital of the Maya.

It is at this point that the actual documentary sources of
Maya history begin. The Books of Chilam Balam 27 lay down
the katuns of Maya history. The sources of it are many and
widespread. Several chronicles, taken from Maya glyph-pic-
ture histories and written in Spanish characters, such as the
Tizimin manuscripts, give historically verified accounts.

The highland Maya were also subject to the Toltec invasion and clearly remembered it in their *Popol Vuh*, a chronicle set down in Spanish script in 1550.28 The Toltecs followed
the course of the Usumacinta River inland and upward into
what was the heartland of the Old Maya, and then on into the
Guatemalan highlands, where the Quiché tribes were established. The "priests," says the *Popol Vuh*, "as they journeyed
toward [Yucatán] took all their paintings [books] in which
they recorded all the things of ancient times [i.e., of crafts
and calendar and magic] and [Quetzalcoatl] gave to the
Quiché Lords among other things *u tzibal Tulán* . . . the
paintings of Tula, the paintings as those were called, in which
they put their chronicles."

This was the time of the Maya Renaissance; art and architecture flourished anew. There was an introduction of Toltec
motifs throughout the region of the Puuc and about Chichén
Itzá—the plumed-serpent caryatids, the prancing jaguar; the
eagle with unfurled wings, talisman of the warrior-knights'
cult of Toltec origin. A new architecture introduced wooden
beams, instead of the self-limiting corbeled arch, and buildings took on new graces. During this time Uxmal, the most
beautiful city of the entire region, was built. New or extended
rituals came into religion, including human sacrifice with its
bloody bath. New weapons made war more fearful, and the
Spartan principle for warriors stiffened the flaccid spines of
the old Maya. The old causeways were rebuilt and extended,

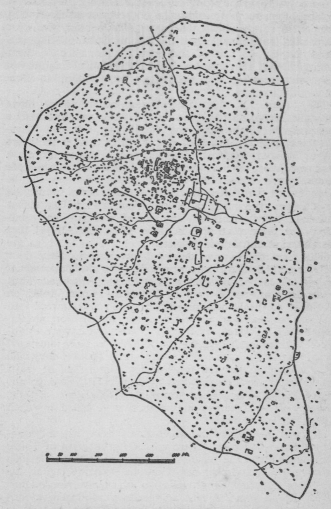

Fig. 6. The walled city of Mayapán, capital of the Yucatán (987-1441). The wall is five and a half miles around. More than 3,500 buildings have been located within it. From a survey of Morris Jones.

and cities were walled along the coast. Seafaring Maya moved as far as Panama and up into the Nicaraguan lakes. Trading posts were spread along the coasts, and contact was even made with the Arawaks from the isles of Cuba and Jamaica. Maya learning was revived and extended, painted books were multiplied, and the Dresden Codex, a beautiful example of Maya draftsmanship, was made into a "new edition" in about the twelfth century.

The League of Mayapán endured, according to Maya chronicles, from 987 to 1194. In the latter year occurred a civil war, the origins of which are obscure, between Mayapán the capital and Chichén Itzá, the larger and most famed city of Yucatán. Mayapán emerged as the leading city-state. Centuries later, in 1441, war again broke out between the "natural lords of the Maya" and the Itzás, who were the descendants of the Toltec invaders. A mass attack was made on Mayapán; the inhabitants were killed and the city sacked and destroyed. ". . . in this city . . . after it had been established for more than five hundred years [987–1441] they abandoned it and left it desolate."

These are the bare katuns of Maya history. They mark the rise of a people from, technically, the mesolithic age to one of the highest cultures of the ancient Americas. Thus, from 2000 B.C. to the fall of Mayapán in A.D. 1441, the World of the Maya was forged.

4. The "Lower Men": Appearance and Reality

Like all theocratic societies, in which god-men rule the roost, Maya society was a pyramid with the common man at the bottom. The precise generic name for him is not known, but early Maya-Spanish dictionaries interpreted *yalba uinicob* to mean the "lower men."

The common men were maize farmers. When war was upon them they were soldiers, acting as an agrarian militia. Their labor erected the soaring temples. They built the immense ball courts and terraces. They felled the trees, dressed and then transported the limestone blocks, carved the glyphs, and sculptured the Maya art. They built the raised causeways, the *sacbeob*, that bound city to city.

Like all Americans, the Maya belonged to a soil community. It is presumed, although we have no precise knowledge of it, that the Maya were a clan society. The prevalence of an exogamous surname marriage taboo (Landa says: ". . . they always called their sons and daughters by the name of the father and mother") suggests that there was a clan system and that each bore a totem name.

Each member of such a clan was part of an earth cell. The lower and higher man both were wedded to the soil. One's taxes were paid out of it; either a portion of the crops went to the *batab* (tax collector) or else the cultivation of the fields was in the form of work service tax. Agricultural surplus provided time that was used in the building of temples, palaces, and roads.

Around A.D. 800 there were more than three million people in Mayadom.*

* Since no one really knows, the estimates of Maya population vary; the lowest given is 1,250,000, the highest 13,000,000. I am in accord with Eric Thompson, who gives the figure of 3,000,000.

Although Landa called him "tall," the Maya's average height was five feet, one inch. Still, he was robust and strong. The Maya were brachycephalic, one of the most broad-headed peoples in the world. Even today their features closely resemble the faces on the ancient monuments. As soon as a baby was born his head was artificially flattened by being placed within two tied boards. This custom, as it was explained to Landa, "was given to our Maya ancestors by the gods. It gives us a noble air . . . and besides our heads are then better adapted to carry loads. . . ."

Earlobes were pierced for pendants and so was the septum of the nose. The left side of the nose was also pierced—as is the practice of certain peoples of India—and, the gods willing, a topaz was set into it. The hair was long, black, and lustrous, wrapped around the head, and "braided like a wreath, leaving the queue to hang down behind like tassels." Tied to the hair was an obsidian mirror disc. "All of the men wore mirrors," but the women wore none, and for one man to call another a cuckold, "he need only say that his wife put mirrors in her hair."

The hair on top of the head was cropped short, singed in fact, so it looked like a monk's tonsure. Facial hair was disliked. Mothers stunted the hair follicles of the young, and therefore beards were scant. Such hair that appeared was pulled out with copper tweezers. Despite this, old men had straggly beards, which are often represented in Maya sculpture.

"They tattooed their bodies . . ." (which has been confirmed by archaeology, since quite a few sculptured stone heads show tattooing) "the design being pricked in the skin with a sharp bone into which pigment was rubbed, accompanied with great suffering." For this reason, the more tattooing one had the more one was thought brave and valiant.

Maya eyes, dark and lustrous, appear to be more Mongolian than those of most "Americans," because the eyes being placed obliquely in the face emphasizes the epicanthic fold that gives them the "slant." Many were cross-eyed. In fact, to be so was considered both a mark of beauty and distinction. Itzamna, god of the heavens, is always featured as cross-eyed, and so are some of the other gods and personages that appear on the carved monuments. Bishop Landa wrote: "Maya mothers hung a pitch-ball in front of their children's eyes so close that both eyes focused on it and in this way began to cross." The practice must have been widespread, for Bernal Díaz in the early days of the conquest "took prisoners . . . many of them cross-eyed."

Maya skin varies from the color of café au lait to dark copper; the men for some unaccountable reason seem lighter than the women. At least such was the opinion of Landa, who had much occasion to see both bathing in the nude. Painting of face and body was general among the men. Black was used by young unmarried men and those enduring a fast. Red was used by warriors, and blue by priests and those about to be sacrificed. Warriors painted themselves red and black "for the sake of elegance"; and when captured, the greatest deg-

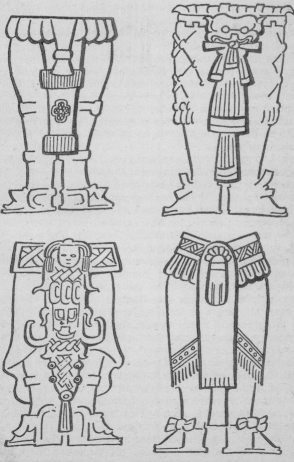

Fig. 7. The basic dress for all Maya men was the breechclout, elaborately decorated. These are redrawn from sculptured monuments.

radation was for a warrior to be "despoiled of his insignia and smut." One could gauge the social condition of a Maya by the color of his paint.

Men dressed for the climate. The basic dress was the *ex* (pronounced "eesh"), a woven-cotton breechclout which the "women made with great care." This was wound around the waist several times and passed between the legs. The ends hung down in front and back. This is the most common article of Maya dress and is pictured from the earliest times. Men wearing the *ex* are found on painted pottery, and certain sculptures dated A.D. 600 show the ends of it elaborately embellished and decorated.

Around their shoulders the Maya wore a covering like a poncho (*pati*); it was elaborated according to one's life station. The same piece was used as a covering for the night's sleep. If this sounds rustically simple, it must be remembered that the classic Greek wore no more; he also used the sheet in which he had slept as clothing, shaping it elegantly around himself in the morning when he set out to face the world. Sandals were the final item in the attire of the lower men. Almost all wore them (especially in Yucatán, because of the roughness of the terrain). These *xanabkeuel* were made of either tapir or deer hide and tied to the feet by two thongs.

The women were comely. Diego de Landa, that observant bishop, thought them better-looking "generally . . . than Spanish women, larger and better made." Maya women were small, in fact, dainty. Their average four feet, eight inches in height is not much taller than a fair-sized nymphet. They pierced their ears, as did the men, and tattooed their bodies "but not their breasts." They had their teeth filed to points by old women using pumice stone as an abrasive. They thought this dental style very elegant. The hair was worn long and intricately braided. The outsized necklaces and richly woven dress that one sees modeled on the clay statuettes from Jaina indicate the high position of women in Maya society.

They bathed often, using the same *cenote* wells as the men. The bishop also noted, and it has been since his time confirmed, that the women have an irregularly shaped bluish-purplish mark near the base of the spine, just above the buttocks—the "Mongolian spot." This is prevalent throughout Asia and the Americas, but is especially marked in Yucatán.

The women painted their faces. Red, obtained from the seed of the *achiote*, was a blood symbol. It was mixed with the highly perfumed *ix tahte*, the liquid amber resin that was "odoriferous and very sticky." It was supposed to be a prophylactic against sun and insects. In reality, it was a blood surrogate. Women were fond of perfumes and they "anointed their breasts, arms, and shoulders" with it. In addition they walked abroad with nosegays of flowers, "arranged with great care," which they smelled from time to time.

Dress was the *kub*, a single piece of decorated woven cloth with holes for the arms and a square-cut opening for the head (the original chemise). The style, which one sees on the famous murals of Bonampak, has survived for 2,000 years; it is still worn throughout Yucatán. Underneath, the women wore a lighter white petticoat, decorated and fringed. About their shoulders they draped a stole (*booch*). They walked barefoot.

Women married young. They bore from seven to nine children, of which unfortunately only half survived. "They had children early and many," Landa comments, "but they were excellent nurses because the continued grinding of tortillas constantly agitated their breasts, and they do not bind their breasts as we do in Spain and so they have large ones that have a good deal of milk."

Bishop Landa found the women "marvelously chaste" and correctly estimated them the "soul" of the household. Good housekeepers, they worked to pay the tribute tax. Good managers, they worked at night at their weaving and raised ducks to obtain plumes for feather weaving. They reared deer, monkeys, and coatis, which they suckled at their ample breasts. They worked in the fields and when needed were

Fig. 8. Women wore the *kub*, and their hair was elaborately dressed. The woman's husband sits next to her. Late Maya figures from the island of Jaina, Campeche.

the transport animals; they educated their children and in leisure time spun and wove cotton in the company of other women. They had a robust sense of humor. They danced only among themselves, and they got properly drunk with other guests, but not so much as to be unable to carry home their drunken husbands. They were "prudent, polite and sociable . . . and not given to any erotic practices and they had no gods of love."

The women's goddess, Ixchel, which some scholars had hopefully thought was the goddess of desire, was in reality only the patroness of pregnancy.

5. Maya Speech

". . . in this country there is but one language." Landa, who first studied it, stated this as bald fact, and time has borne him out. The Maya did not always fully understand one another, but a lowland Maya generally could understand a highlander, just as a peasant from Naples can understand a peasant from Milan. Since there was common trade between the diverse areas—coast, highland, jungle—and common communications, and the same glyph-written language was used in cities that might be 500 miles apart, it is presumed that there must have been a basic common tongue. Although more than fifteen dialects were spoken (such as Yucatec; Chontal, which extended across the humid center of Maya-dom; and the dialects in Guatemala, Tzeltal, Ixil, Quiché, etc.), languages must have been, as Eric Thompson suggested, closely related to one another as are the Romance languages. The modern conclusion is that one can properly speak of at best only two Maya languages, highland and lowland Maya, the dialects being only variants of these.

Although Maya speech is not closely related to any other language of Central America or Mexico, this does not imply that it is derived from "something" outside of America. Walter Lehmann, the German linguist,[29] believed from his study of all the known Maya vocabularies that the language is related to Mixtec-Zoque-Huave speech, which in turn was derived from some common parent language.

There were linguistic links between Maya and Mexican on the north coast, especially at the great trading center of Xicalanco, and archaeology in the Guatemalan highlands has shown the close contact that the Maya there had with the cultures of Teotihuacán. When the Toltecs made large-scale penetrations into Mayadom in the tenth century, they were Maya-speaking.

Upsetting this neat linguistic package, however, are the Huasteca. All Maya-speaking peoples lived contiguous to one another, with the exception of the Huasteca. This tribe dwelt 300 miles northeast of the nearest Maya and was separated from them by five distinct tribes—Nahuatl, Popoloco, Totonac, etc.—and they spoke, and still speak, a language which is definitely Maya. Yet their cultural sequence (archaeologists have found ceramic sequence of more than 2,000 years) has no Maya characteristics at all (in dress, hieroglyphics, architecture, etc.). This suggests that before the formative period of Maya culture a "cultural wedge" of people of another linguistic stock split the primitive Maya who once, by this implication, occupied a large area along the Gulf coast. It is the only way to explain the linguistic schism.

The precise name of the Maya speech is unknown. "Mayathan" was that language used by the Maya of the League of Maya-Pán in the area controlled by them in Yucatán. There was undoubtedly a certain unity of speech among the lowland Maya as there was among the highland Maya; that the name-glyphs were uniform throughout Mayadom did not mean that the language itself was without variants. In the eighteenth century one who spoke Low German could read Schiller, but in verbal contact with a Hoch Deutscher, he could have hardly understood him. We know that in the seventeenth century a priest in Yucatán, when talking to Cholti-speaking Itzá Maya peoples gathered about Lake Petén, needed Indian interpreters who understood both dialects. This shows the great divergent linguistic evolution which had taken place within Yucatán in 200 years. Despite his statement that "in this country the language is but one," Diego de Landa admitted that there were some differences in usage between the speech of the coastal inhabitants and that of the inlanders, and that "along the coast they are most polished in their language and behavior."

It is not possible here to give more than an idea of Maya speech. Maya is spoken today by most Indians and many white people throughout Yucatán and Guatemala (just as Quechua is spoken by both whites and Indians in the Peruvian Andes). The bibliography on Maya speech is most voluminous. Most authorities have found it "musical and pleasant." Several letters and sounds used in our speech are absent, that is, *d*, *f*, and *r*. The speech, which is low-pitched, has many glottal stops and fricatives, and its pronunciation is not easy to learn unless one has been reared in Yucatán. The Maya wrote simple sentences. It is doubtful, even after scholars have translated 60 per cent of the corpus of the still-untranslated Maya glyphs, that we will find the Maya had glyph-affixes to express verb tenses and pronouns. The Maya were weak in verbs, and made much use of the verbal noun. Thompson has given us an example of it.[30] A literal translation of the glyphs would read like this: "His influencing the maize, the death god heaped up death."

Transposed into our literary forms thus fractured Maya would read: "Much death will be the result, for the death-god now rules the growing maize."

Maya	English
(Figurative Pronunciation)	
Báax a kati? Baaxi?	What do you want? What is it?
Túux cahanech?	Where do you live?
Bix u kaba le dzuló?	What is the name of that man?
Yan in bin ta ueteleex.	I must go with you.
Yan c-bin.	We have to go.
Ten dzictech.	I give it to you.

A short vocabulary:

man	*xib*	corn	*nal*	tortilla	*ixim*
woman	*chhup*	door	*hol-na*	manta	*nok*
boy	*pal*	maize	*milpa*	deer	*ceh*
girl	*chhupal*	cornfield	*col*	sandals	*xanab*
house	*nā*	roof	*yoc-na*	jaguar	*balam*
water	*ha*	sky	*caan*	dog	*pek*
rain	*chaac*	stars	*ek*	wild pig	*citam*

6. Social Organization

Maya society, like that of all other theocratic states, was composed of man higher and lower. There was a noble class, *ahmehenob*, from which all officeholders—and there were many—were selected. The broad base of the social pyramid was sustained by the *yalba uinicob*—the lower man—as well as by multitudes of slaves. This much is certain, but it is readily admitted that "we have no direct evidence as to the type of government and social organization prevalent among the Maya." The evidence gathered from art, sculptures, murals, and painted vases shows the nobleman in full command. Maya lords are shown being carried in litters. Armies are led by superbly accoutered leaders in panoplies of jade and quetzal feathers. Chieftains are seen laying down laws, the captured warriors being judged and put into slavery. Yet these vignettes refer only to limited aspects of the social organization. The Aztecs had a well-known clan organization wherein the land was communally owned and communally worked. The Incas developed the *ayllu,* which was collectivistic in principle, as their basic social unit. The Maya are thought to have had some similar form of organization, yet its name and precise form are unknown.

The Maya were not an empire, as the Incas were, with one ruler controlling vast lands maintained by tribute tax. Nor did they have a complex tribute-gathering organization like the Aztecs, who had domination without dominion over vast lands. There was, so far as we know, no center of Maya organization, no capital, no Cuzco, no Tenoch-titlán, no central ruler.

Explanations are needed, since what we now know about this stirs the curiosity without satisfying the reason. There was a common Maya culture, language, and religion. There was a system of roads, some the finest constructed in the protohistorical Americas, binding coast and highland together. Trade was general and far-flung. Why, then, did not someone of imperial ambitions force the whole into a single imperial state? Perhaps because of the hazards of geography? Yet this did not prevent the Incas, whose empire was geographically far more complex than that of the Maya, from uniting Andean South America under one realm.

Maya society has been likened to that of the city-states of Greece. The comparison is most apt. Although Sparta, Athens, and Corinth had, like the Maya, a common language, culture, and religion, they were fiercely independent and often warred with one another, sometimes even supporting foreign invasions against other Greek cities.

The Greek word *polis* is translated "city-state." It is, thinks a recent writer,[31] a bad translation because the *polis* was more state than city. Plato's ideal *polis* had a population of 5,000. The largest Greek *polis* in his time was Syracuse, with a population of only 20,000, approaching in numbers the smaller city-states of the Maya. Like that of the Greeks, Maya society had a household economy and was self-contained. Writing of the Greeks, H. D. F. Kitto says, "the nature of their society was that the group is socially more important than the individual. The individual is a member first of the family, then of his polis. A wrong done to him is a wrong done to his family or his polis." This was also the case among the Maya. And it is the nature of the clan society everywhere.

The temple-city organization is well known. The archaeological evidence of the Near East shows that farming peoples living in a neolithic economy brought their agricultural offerings to a center. It might be formed about a rock outcrop or a lake, or a *cenote* as in Yucatán. This is a waste from an economic point of view, but if the location of such a temple city is chosen for religious reasons it becomes a *huaca*, as in Peru, and a temple is built on the site and the priests make contact with the gods. The first fruits of the harvest are brought to the temple. The people knew, of course, that the produce did not go directly to the gods. They were aware that it was eaten by the priests. All of the early peoples, who were farmers, believed that they were dependent on the favor of the gods and that they needed the hierarchic priesthood to secure it for them. The priests maintained the temples and were themselves maintained by the products and the work service of the farmers. As the local shrine grew into a temple and the temple into a city or a ceremonial center, houses were grouped about it.

Because a high culture must originate with an aristocratic class, for only such a class has the time and energy to create it, there developed a corporation of priests who acted as god-contacts. They saw to it that all rituals were followed. In this way the lower man, whose tribute and work service help to build the temple city and maintain it, finds the temple-ceremonial center to be useful. His maize grows better. He is told the time to plant and harvest (the priest is also the astrologist-astronomer), and the nature of mysteries is explained to him. Generations repeat this performance and, since useful habits, when repeated, finally become invincible, this type of life becomes in time virtually instinctive.

Out of this develops the clan organization. The lower man is convinced that the gods are the owners of the land and that the priests in parceling it out are acting on behalf of the gods. The various clans are allotted areas of land by the temple-city councilors (among the Aztecs actual maps drawn on *amatl*-paper gave the rebus names of the owners), and the councilors presumably officiate at the division of the land. Among the Maya, each family was assigned a piece of land of 400 square feet, a *hun uinic*, measured with a 20-foot measuring tape. We are ignorant of further details. Whether the land was held in trust by the ruler, as among the

Incas, and was returned to the clan on the decease of the user to be reallotted, or whether it belonged to the *calpulli* as among the Aztecs, we just do not know. At least no more than Diego de Landa says: ". . . each married man with his wife . . . sow a space 400 square feet . . . which they call a *hun uinic*, measured with a rod of twenty feet."

The land was worked communally: ". . . the Indians have the habit of helping each other in all their labors . . . they join together in groups of twenty and do not leave the communal property until everyone's own is done." This would indicate the existence of a clan organization. Clans are the closest bond, the most intelligible relationship. The Maya were held together by supernatural bonds, that is, blood bonds, "for to be of the same blood is to possess the same vital principle and in this sense all who are of like blood make one single living being. It is in this that the clan relationship really consists." [32]

That the Maya were organized into clans can also be inferred from Landa's remarks on the prevalence of an exogamous surname marriage taboo: ". . . they always call their sons and their daughters by the same name of the father and the mother . . . and this is the reason why the Indians say that those bearing the same name are all of one family . . . and on this account when an Indian comes to a place in which he is not known and he is in need . . . he at once makes use of his name and they receive him with kindness. . . ."

7. Marriage

"There are no monogamous animals save those who love once in their lifetime." [33] The Maya were well aware of this and tried, as do all other civilizations, to make rules so that permanent marriage could be maintained. Yet mating, the most natural of functions, has never been treated by human beings, civilized or primitive, as either natural or normal. Marriageable ages were considered to be eighteen for the Maya men, fourteen for the girls. One of the stringent taboos was that a man could not marry a woman having the same surname as himself. But he could marry any woman stemming from his mother's line, even a first cousin.

The Maya had a professional matchmaker; she was called *ah atanzahob*. To the Maya it would have been "mean-spirited" for men to seek wives for themselves. Sometimes fathers arranged marriages between sons and daughters in infancy and treated each other even before formal marriage as "in-laws."

For this reason, among others, Diego de Landa thought that the Maya married without love. But, despite the bishop, the Maya were fully aware of the force of romantic love, though perhaps like the Greeks they believed passion to be a destructive thing. Besides, primitives are always superstitious about marriage; go-betweens acted, they believed, as the first barrier to defilement. Still, it is amply true that the ancient Maya were not lascivious.

Aldous Huxley, after viewing Maya sculpture *in situ*, concluded with a certain amount of irritability: "There is no sex in the art of the Maya!" He reasoned that perhaps it was because the native's nervous excitability was less than ours and their sexual imagination very sluggish.[34] He also noted the infrequency with which the female form appears in Maya art.

Had Huxley traveled in that region of Yucatán called the Puuc, where lies the superb stone city of Uxmal, among others, he could have seen enough evidence of "ithyphallic traditions." On the façade of the building called, ironically, the "Nunnery" there are sculptured naked male figures with full emphasis on the ithyphallic. In front of the Governor's Palace, at the same site, are the remains of a gigantic phallus in full and glorious beatitude. Throughout the Puuc and extending to the ruins of Chichén Itzá, the phallic symbols stand about like toadstools to shock or amuse the visitor. There is enough evidence that the Maya had, in some yesterday of his tribal life, a full share of libidinousness.

There was sexual liberty—whatever that means—among the Maya. Young men, who lived apart from the old, had in each village "a large house, whitened with lime, open on all sides," where they met for amusements, dice, ball and bean games. Their bodies were painted black as was the custom for a man before marriage. They slept together, but, says Bishop Landa in a quick aside, they did not practice the "abominable sin," that is, sodomy.* We do not know whether they, like the Greeks, regarded homosexual love as a

---

* Bernal Díaz said, however, that he saw on the island of Cozumel in 1516 murals in which Indians were shown in the act of sodomy. He is contradicted by Landa's contemporary Padre Ciudad Real, who wrote that there were three things for which the Maya should be commended: "The writing of books, absence of cannibalism, and their lack of interest in the abominable vice of sodomy."

normal thing and treated it as frankly as heterosexual love, but we do know the young men brought public women (*guatepol*) into their quarters. "Although the women received pay for it [a handful of cacao beans] they were besieged by such a great number of men—one after the other—that they were harassed almost to death."

Monogamy was the rule among the lower men. "The Yucatecans never took more than one wife." When a young man thought of marriage and his father put the thought into action, he took good care, writes the bishop, to seek a wife in good time and of good quality. An *ah atanzahob* matchmaker was engaged, a dowry (*muhul*) and marriage settlements were worked out. To ward off the evil spirit that hung over marriage they consulted a priest, an *ah kin nec chilan*, who read the astrologic book-of-days to determine whether their birthdays, their names, and the date of the contemplated union fell on unlucky days. The mothers-in-law then wove new garments for bride and groom, and the bride's father prepared the house for ceremony and feast.

Marriage customs here are not as detailed as among the Aztecs, nor is there any data on the Maya practice of *jus primae noctis* in which the father-in-law or other male relatives partake of the bride during the first nights of the marriage to prevent the bridegroom from being menaced by malign influences. Many tribes do not allow husband and wife to live together until several months have passed, so as

Fig. 9. The Maya married early—women at fourteen, men at twenty. The marriage broker stands at the left, while the priest "purifies" the couple with copal vapor.

to avoid the evil influence that marriage brings—since to all primitives new experiences, and marriage is certainly that, are regarded as dangerous. In primitive society virginity is not generally highly valued. A Maya girl could not be overzealous about a mere hymen, a thing which she shared in common with a rabbit. But the evil thing that might come from improper consummation of marriage was something else again, and she and the whole clan could be menaced by it.

Marriage for the Maya was matrilocal: that is, the son went to the father-in-law's house and worked for him, as part of his family, for about five years. It was called "marriage in service." As such, Maya marriage was fundamentally permanent and women played an important part in society. This much can be seen without the help of Bishop Landa, for the murals found at Bonampak show women taking part in important affairs, and the grace that the sculptors gave to women in the statuettes found at Jaina, Yucatán, show the respect in which they were held.

Women were jealous. Fights often occurred among them over men, yet Landa found them "marvelously chaste" because they turned their backs on men whom they met on the road, or stepped aside to let them pass. They had a great desire for children, praying to their own goddess for many and asking Ixchel, goddess of pregnancy, to ease their pains. And with reason. A man could repudiate marriage if there were no children. Just as among the Greeks, a "childless union could be dissolved at the instance of the wife's relatives." [35]

Although Maya women were "marvelously chaste," adultery was common. This is evident from the place it holds in their code of crime and punishment.

Woman could not hold public office. That she had some property rights is evident, but she was not allowed within the precincts of a temple. But then Greek women, too, were not enfranchised, nor could they hold property; and from birth to death they were, so to speak, the ward of their nearest male relative.

The best reputation a Maya woman could have was not to be spoken of among men for either good or evil. If women were accused of adultery they had to be found *flagrante delicto*; then they were disgraced. They seem to have undergone no other punishment, except that the husband could, if he wished, repudiate the erring wife. The aberrations of marriage are understandable. In all societies, primitive or civilized, the couple is natural, but the permanent couple is not. Man the world over and at all times has become monogamous with difficulty. In all human societies there is a radial polygamy that is concealed behind a façade of monogamy, and "nothing," says Rémy de Gourmont, "so favours marriage and consequently social stability as the *de facto* indulgence of temporary polygamy; the Romans well understood this and legalized polygamy."

But the Maya were not Romans. A Maya of the lower orders found engaged in "temporary polygamy" with another man's wife had his arms bound behind him and was brought before the husband, who had the right "to kill him by throwing a large stone upon his head from a great height."

Divorce was by repudiation. If the woman was barren, or if she did not properly prepare the husband's daily steam bath, she could be repudiated. She might also take similar action against the man; though that was not as easy. When a couple was divorced the younger children stayed with the mother. If older, the sons went to the father, but the daughters always remained with the mother. Divorce was common in Diego de Landa's time (1550–1570), though the elders of the tribes did not countenance it and "those of better habits condemned it." Men left wives and wives left husbands, and there seemed to be no proscription against remarrying. However, when death put an end to marriage, it was something else again. The widowed husband could not remarry for a year after his wife's death. He was not supposed to have any women during this time, and the Maya community had little regard for him if he did. A widow was bound with taboo; remarriage for her was complex and problematical.

Death, like sex, complicated everything.

8. Nā, the Maya House

The house of the lower man was like that of the eternal peasant everywhere, simple and practical.

After marriage a Maya built first a small house opposite the dwelling of his father or father-in-law. Later, his larger house was built with the aid of the community. The house could be constructed round, square, rectangular, or, as it is best known in Yucatán, apsidal, rounded at both ends. Its frame was made of withes and rested on a stone foundation.

The withes were then covered with adobe. Later the house was colorfully painted. The high-pitched roof was made of trunks and saplings and wonderfully thatched, then as now, with palm (guano) "of very good quality and in great abundance." In ancient times (A.D. 500) the Maya house was usually square and mounted on a low substructure. Maya houses, while not always the same, tended to resemble one another in specific areas.

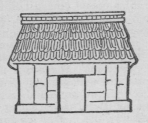

Fig. 10. The Maya house, past and present: *above,* the *nā* of the common Indian immortalized in a stone frieze at Uxmal, and *below,* the present-day Maya house.

The interior of the house was divided by a wall. One part became the kitchen, and the other contained the sleeping racks. "They had beds made of small saplings"* says Landa, "laced together by withes which . . . gave way to the movement of the body like a mattress." This was covered with a woven grass mat. They used their cotton mantas as blankets.

There was one entrance, and it had no door. Across the entranceway was placed a light string from which hung small copper bells. One brushed against these to give the owner

* Whether the hammock later used by the Maya was known to them before the arrival of the Spaniards, who brought examples of it from the island of Hispaniola, is doubtful.

notice of arrival. People seldom entered a house without permission, for "they considered it a grave crime to harm the houses of others."

This functional house has varied little in 2,000 years. The terms for various parts of the structure are the same in various Maya dialects and may be thought of, writes an archaeologist, as "linguistic paleontology." [36] The roof purlin is called "the road of the rat," the entrance "the mouth of the house," and the main roofpost "the leg of the house."

The common man built the houses of the nobles, which were larger and more spacious than the others. Some were made of sculptured stone. "The slope of the roof comes down very low in front on account of their love of sun and rain" (i.e., as protection against the sun and the rain). The walls of their houses "were painted with great elegance," which observation has been confirmed by archaeological excavation. The single entrance, also without a door, could be closed with a drapery, usually a woven hanging of great elegance. Certain structures that are now found in the temple cities may have been nobles' homes, although no buildings have been found which can be definitely associated with the ruling class.

A house endured for little more than a generation. The excavations of the house mounds reveal a "complete ceramic period." As the inhabitants of a house died they were buried beneath the hard mud floor ("they bury their dead inside or in the rear of their houses"). After several burials the house was abandoned and was then treated as a sacred burial plot.

9. The Round of the Maya Day

The woman rose first, between 3 and 4 A.M., rousing the flames from the smoldering ash in the *koben*, the three-stone hearth; if a household had a slave, he or she carried out this task.

"Their principal food is maize [*chim*], from which they make various foods, also drink . . . in the morning all they ate was maize-water [*pozole*]." The evening before, the woman, with the aid of daughters or slaves, had prepared the dried maize. It was boiled with ash until softened and then husked, after which it was brayed on a stone grinder until reduced to a thick paste. From the ground corn, or *zacan*, the women prepared tortillas, or as the Maya called them, *uah*.

When the Maya farmer departed in the early dawn for the fields, he took with him several apple-sized balls of ground maize wrapped in leaves. Steeped in water and flavored with burning-hot chili peppers, these became his lunch, to which he added perhaps a piece of dried venison. His diet, mainly carbohydrate, was less than 2,500 calories per diem, yet many waxed fat on it, as Maya wall paintings and ceramics reveal. But then, gluttons are many on this terraqueous globe.

The farmer returned early in the afternoon. The women, by custom, had a hot bath ready for him. In the large centers such as Tikal and Chichén Itzá, there were communal steam baths. Where these were not available, the common man contented himself with a crudely made steam bath or hot water in an improvised tub, with a dip later in the local well.

The evening meal was the only elaborate one of the day. The menfolk sat in a circle, some on low wooden stools, the others on woven-grass mats, and were served by the women. Stews were prepared of deer-meat, wild or tame fowl, or fish, fresh or sun-dried; sometimes this was supplemented by the flesh of a tapir, *tzimin*. Deer were plentiful, as were rabbits and agoutis. Armadillos (*zub*) were considered a great delicacy. There were also iguanas, turtles (*ac*), and on occasions flesh of the *baclam*, the manatee or sea cow, which "yielded much meat . . . more than a yearling calf." Fowl was varied and many. Yucatán had been called by the Maya "The Land of the Turkey and the Deer." Foremost was the wild ocellated turkey, famed for its gamey flavor. Its feathers were used for making cloaks and headdresses, "as beautifully feathered as the peacocks of Spain." The domesticated turkey shared the house and the land with young ducks (*axix*), "which when home-raised do not fly away." The muscovy was raised more for its feathers than for food, "and as well a certain white mallard-duck." Doves were reared in cages. Almost as abundant as the turkey was the yellow-crested curassow.

Fig. 11. The deer caught in a snare shows the hunting methods of the Maya. From page 45 of the Codex Tro-Cortesianus.

All these found their way into the Maya *olla podrida*. Yet eating was disciplined; they ate well when there was food and could endure hunger when there was none. Washing preceded and followed meals. A natural detergent was used, the roots of the soapberry tree (*Sapindus saponaria*), "from which they washed their bodies and clothes like soap."

Maize, the "principal sustenance," was supplemented by several varieties of beans (*buul*), squash, and pumpkins. The *chayote*, a vine bearing a squashlike fruit, was found everywhere. The pale sweet potato appeared on the warm coasts. Fruits were many. The avocado was cultivated, as were the papaya and sapote. Mulberries and melons were gathered, and the vanilla bean of the orchid was found in the jungle. Maya boys ate the fruit of the "chewing-gum tree" (*cha*), and chewed its gum.

"The land," said Bishop Landa, "abounds in honey." Then as now, it was gathered from the hollow of trees, and easily extracted because the bees were stingless. Fermented, the honey became mead, an intoxicant. Mead is one of the world's earliest beverages. It was nectar, the mythical drink of the gods. An illustration of an upper-paleolithic honey collector has been found in the Cueva de la Araña, Valencia, Spain. Maya honey mead was fortified by the addition of an alkaloid-yielding bark called *balche*.

Like the Aztecs, the Maya were enthusiastic drinkers of chocolate. "They made it of cacao and ground maize . . . a foaming drink which is very savory." As it was grown in the humid lands on the periphery of the Maya country, it was expensive, so much so that the beans served as money.

Yet—turkey, chocolate, or fish notwithstanding—the principal sustenance of the Maya (as with all of the Central American and Mexican tribes) was—maize. Maize was eaten on every occasion. During the main evening meal each male would consume upward of twenty large-sized tortillas. Water was never drunk pure but always with the addition of maize meal. Does the type of food suggest the civilization? Does the bon mot of Brillat-Savarin—"Tell me what you eat and I will tell you what you are"—correctly gauge a people?

The diet of the Greeks and the Romans was mainly farinaceous. Until 600 B.C. the Greek ate *artôs,* a coarse leaven bread baked in ashes. When baking became a profession a form of porridge, groats made from *emmer,* was the basic food of the Greek common man. Flavored with honey, salt, and olive oil, it was not much different from the Maya maize *pozole*.

Greeks only rarely had meat and fish, and only the well-heeled could afford and obtain game. In general, meat was eaten freely only at sacrifices. The people of ancient Rome ate mostly unleavened bread dipped in milk, relieved by onions, peas, and turnips. Only those in close contact with the sea had fish; and only the farmer had meat, which consisted mostly of goat, pork, and lamb. While Oriental fruits—cherries, peaches, apricots, and the like—were introduced into the Roman diet in the first century B.C., active citriculture did not develop until the fourth century of the Christian era. It was only after the fall of the Roman Republic that the rich lived in the Lucullan fashion; they constructed refrigerators, kept cold with snow and ice, to preserve foods. In the year 1000 man in Europe ate like a poor poll when compared with the Maya of the same period. The diet of the masses was vegetarian and frugal, and they usually ate but two meals a day.* The impression given by medieval chroniclers of colossal meals washed down with quantities of wine, mead, and beer, was true only of rare occasions in the lives of nobles.

The classical archaeologists, seduced by the honeyed words they have used to conjure up the classical past, still turn up their noses at the thought that the Maya (in culture, art, or mathematics) could be dimly compared to the early Greek or Roman, and this is often because of their belief in the bucolic savagery of the Maya life and diet. As seen above, the Maya had a list of available foodstuffs which most Europeans of their time would have thought "paradise enow."

At sundown a breeze springs up from the sea, churns up the Caribbean, and wafts across the Yucatán flatlands and up into the highlands. At this hour the Maya man retired to his home and had his principal meal. Then, in Yucatán, he sat in semidarkness and worked wood, jade, or cotton into articles of trade, or made weapons. His wife spun cotton and wove mantas. In the highlands they made light with pine splinters, as bright as candles.

Time was found for love and children were born, early and many. Seven to nine offspring from each marriage were considered the norm, although only half survived. Women made pilgrimages to the island of Cozumel, a hazardous twenty-mile trip in an open dugout canoe across the wind-whipped channel separating it from the Yucatán mainland, so as to worship at the shrine of Ixchel, the goddess of pregnancy. It is an act of devotion that outstripped that of those pregnant women of the eighteenth century in Europe who were wont to put the printed hymns of Saint Marguerite

* A medieval bon mot had it that "angels need to feed but once a day, mankind twice, beasts thrice or more. . . ."

as a poultice on their extended bellies to ease the pain, "as it acted better than when recited."

Within five days after birth, which was attended by a midwife, the head of the child was placed between boards and bound so that it would become "flattened and molded as was the custom of all." The child was bound into a rigid

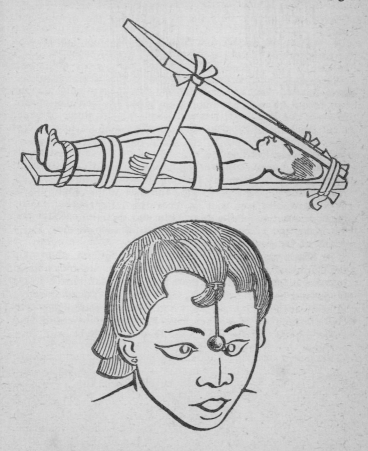

Fig. 12. *Above*. The method of artificially flattening the head. The custom is ancient. ". . . it was given to us by the gods and gives us a noble air." *Below*. The "squint," a Maya beauty feature, was created by hanging a ball of wax in front of the eyes. The concept is ancient.

cradle, over which balls of pitch were dangled to cause it
to become cross-eyed. Later, when released from the cradle,
the baby was carried *hetzmek*, that is, astride its mother's
hip. This caused its legs to be bowed. Children were weaned
at four. In their first years the young Maya were "pretty
and plump, good and frolicsome, running about naked
as they played at hunting games." Later the boys put on a sort
of G-string, and the girls tied a shell over the mound of
Venus.

Names and naming were of cosmic importance. Each Maya
had four names: (1) the given name, *paal kaba;* (2) a patronymic; (3) a combination of his father's and his mother's
family names, *naal kaba;* and, like everyone everywhere, a
nickname, (4) *coco kaba*. Names were magical; a name could
be worn out by excessive public use; only intimates knew the
real one. If a doctor wished to use the name of his patient
to call the soul back, he chose the private name which possessed strength, rather than the social one, which was hack-
neyed and worn from use.

Influence began, they believed, as soon as the woman was
pregnant. The position of the planets, the advent of the
unlucky days played a part in the fortunes of the child-to-be.
All primitives believed that an enterprise must be begun on
an auspicious day—days exert favorable or unfavorable or
even malignant influence. Much attention was given to the
suprasensuous realities.

The Maya were not far wrong. After long-term study of
prenatal factors, modern researchers have reported that *there
is* some connection between seasonal conception and birth
and mental disorders, and that there is a greater possibility
of mental deficiency in children born in winter as opposed
to those born at other seasons. Children conceived in summer
reduce the protein intake of a pregnant woman.

After birth, the priests consulted the horoscope for the
best time to name the child, taking into consideration when
it was conceived. Names were given only on lucky days; the
ceremony could be put off until an auspicious time. Names
once given were the Maya badge. Masculine given names
(*paal kaba*) began with the masculine prefix "ah," the
feminine with "Ix."* The *naal kaba* name, which was taken
after marriage, was made up of the prefix "Nah," the mother's
matronymic, and the father's patronymic. Landa mentions
as example a man named Na Chan Chel—Chan was his
mother's maiden name; Chel, his father's family name. Thus

---

* Some typical names for boys: Ah Kukum (feather), Ah Cuy
(owl), Ah Tok (flint knife), Ah Balam (jaguar). For girls: Ix Chan,
Ix Can, Ix Kukul.

the names of the families of both father and mother were perpetuated.

As mentioned earlier, the Maya believed that all people bearing the same surname were of the same family, which points to the clan origin of the system. Each Maya of the same name was treated as part of the clan family even though he could not work out the precise genealogy. Name exogamy still holds true in Yucatán, and there still remains a taboo for marriage between people of the same name.

Inheritance was patrilineal; the sons inherited and divided what the father had accumulated, the mother acting as guardian, and when not the mother, then the deceased father's brother. When the boys were of age they received their inheritance before the town officials, which illustrates the primitive's system of "legality by publicity."

At the age of puberty (girls, twelve, boys, fourteen) there was a coming-of-age ceremony. This custom, *emku,* was

Fig. 13. The coming-of-age ceremony (girls, twelve, boys, fourteen). The rope is held by four *chacs,* who restrain "evil" while the children are purified by a priest.

seen by Diego de Landa, who describes it minutely—except that in his unsullied innocence he thought it was baptism. Those parents who had pubescent children banded together to share the costs, just as today socially ambitious mothers introduce their daughters to society by means of a collective cotillion. On a lucky day, old "honorable men," *chacs*, were chosen to help the priest, *chilan*, to officiate. Food and sexual abstinence before the ceremony were required of parents and officials. The courtyard in front of the local temple was swept clean and spread with leaves. At the four corners sat the *chacs* holding a cord. Within the square so formed were the children.

The *chilan* purified them with copal and tobacco smoke, and they were asked to "confess their sins." This is Diego de Landa's interpretation and as there is no one else to gainsay him, it must stand as given. If any present confessed an "obscene act" he or she was dismissed from the circle. To the primitive, confession was imperative. If one was "unclean" and did not confess it could cause social misfortune. But confession made the evil nonoperative. So before the primitive undertook anything hazardous, he confessed and overcame social defilement.

Water is the great purifier, not only among the primitives but also in our own "civilized" religions. At the end of the long ceremony, after the children had been admonished and the *chacs* had recited age-old homilies of respect to parents, society, and so on, the priests put on their feathered robes and headdresses and anointed each child with "virgin water," "showing," says Landa, "exactly the same gravity as the Pope shows in crowning an Emperor."

Then the boys took off the white bead which had been stuck to the top of their tonsured head since birth. The mothers then knelt down and removed "from their daughter's midsection . . . the little shell which all wore as a symbol of their purity." It was, Landa insisted, "a very dishonorable thing for any man to take this off before the ceremony." It was not less so to the Greeks—it was death to man to remove the aegis, the goatskin chastity tunic worn by Libyan girls, at least without the owner's consent (hence the prophylactic Gorgon's mask set above the chastity belt). After the shell had been removed the girls were allowed to "marry whensoever it pleased their fathers." Today's matron who presents her daughter to society is practicing an exquisite archaism; she is figuratively kneeling down like the Maya mother and removing the little shell—but then people everywhere make gestures that are explicable only on the hypothesis that they once had a different intention.

Young men had great respect for their elders; boys listened to their fathers, worked with them. Companionship was very real. Fathers helped them choose their brides and counseled the sons in marriage. At an early age the boy followed his father to the maize *milpa*. Education was by imitation, by rote; knowledge followed by observation. The boy hunted and learned of nature. He was told and believed that everything had soul. To the gods of the earth, who were very much alive, he addressed his prayers. When hunting he learned to whisper a prayer before killing: "I have need." And when he killed he made an amulet of the slain animal so that other animals in the future would allow themselves to be killed to fill his need. Rather than eat his kill, he gave it to others, who then returned part of it. All this so that the animal would not feel that he was lacking in respect. How ancient this code is can be seen in the Austrian Tyrol. There too the hunter does not eat his kill, but takes only the horns and head and, symbolically, the loin of the chamois. Some of the hair is made into a *Gamsbart* and put into the hunter's hat. The head and horns are mounted and kept as a trophy, which could be said to have the same significance as the amulet of the primitive.

Maya morality was a group morality and co-operation of the individual with everyone in the community was "virtue." Custom demanded that the Maya be hospitable and provide guests with food and drink. A boy learned through custom that when he visited he must always bring a gift. He must be humble and repeat over and over again a person's title, especially if he addressed a lord. Another custom ordained that while listening to someone he must make a soft affirmative sound in his throat, as if to say: "Indeed," "you don't say," "you do tell me."

Because everything in the Maya world was alive, sentient, and possessed of soul, an object made by a person took on something of the soul of its creator. Theft was an aberration (unless decreed by tribal war, in which, as in our own world, everything was then permitted). Maya scribes have asserted: "Before the coming of the Spaniards there was no robbery or violence. The Spanish invasion was the beginning of tribute, the beginning of church dues, the beginning of strife." *

This moral code was essentially as old as the Maya him-

* The Maya wrung tribute out of the defeated and practiced slavery. Yet in the face of the new threat from without this was forgotten—which reminds one of the validity of Nietzsche's apothegm: " 'I did that,' said my memory: 'I could not have done that,' says my consciousness, and remains inexorable. Eventually the memory yields."

self. Clan co-operation, respect for family, and personal discipline brought about what Eric Thompson believed to be
a living form of the Delphic motto: "Nothing in excess." This
idealized portrait of the Maya does not agree with the violence
and unrestraint shown in the murals of Bonampak. They
were no freer than other people from paroxysms of savagery.
It is much to be doubted that the Maya was any more con-
servative than was the Greek was wrote the motto and invented the "mean." It did not, as a modern author stated,
"imply the absence of tension and lack of passion, but the
correct tension."

Daughters were the images of their mothers, disciplined
from the beginning and made to repeat useful actions. They
were lectured, too, pinched on the ears, and when really in-
tractable had red pepper rubbed into their eyes. They learned
to make corncakes, to spin and weave cotton, and they
learned those prayers which were concerned with their part
of the Maya world. Instinctively, when they were born they
were already old, more rooted to earth than man. Man made
history but woman is history, and Maya women knew that
the great Maya calendar had first been based on her menstrual cycles. She was the producer, the fundament. As with
the Aztec, so with the Maya: when woman died in childbirth
she was honored among the heroes.

She was not allowed to go into the temples or to take part
in the ritual of religion; still, she was the seeress.

Like all women everywhere, her principal conquest was
man.

10. Maya Agriculture

Corn was the epicenter of the Maya world.

The cornfield, the *col*, was their preoccupation; "the greatest number of them were cultivators . . . who applied themselves to harvesting maize," said Diego de Landa. These
observations are confirmed by another priest in a sixteenth-
century document written in the Maya highlands: "If one
looks closely he will find everything these Indians did and
talked about had to do with maize. . . ." The grain is ancient—the latest dating through maize finds in the Bat Caves
of New Mexico places it as a cultivated plant before 2000 B.C.
Dr. Paul Mangelsdorf, whose studies on the origin of corn

in the Americas are classic (and never given to undue speculation), believes that "the present-day races of maize in Mexico . . . are the product of 4,000 years or more of evolution under domestication." [37] Its place of origin within the Americas is still undetermined.

The Maya had corn as a developed plant. In their mind there had been, since time immemorial, something sacred about growing corn. It was symbolized by a young, beautiful corn god, to whom prayers were offered. The head of Yum Kaax,* found at the ruins of Copán, is among the most sensitive in primitive American art.[38]

Methods of agriculture seem not to have changed much since the earliest times. The Maya felled trees and brush with a stone ax (*bat*) and burned them during the dry season. The earth was turned with a fire-hardened digging stick (*xul*). Each Indian was allotted by his clan organization a portion of cornland, a *hun uinic*, of 400 square feet. Land was communal property, ". . . the land was held in common and so between the towns there were no boundaries or landmarks to divide them except when one [city-state] made war on the other. . . ." [39] The technique of corn culture was the same everywhere in the Americas: the felling of trees, burning, fencing, planting, weeding, bending the stalks at harvest (so as to deter the birds), harvesting, and shelling. The Maya preserved the corn in storage bins; "they kept it in fine underground granaries called *chultunes*."

As was mentioned earlier, water was, among the Maya, always a problem. Those in the hinterland built huge reservoirs. At Tikal an immense one was located in a deep ravine, the porous rock cemented and held by a masonry dam. The sites of Piedras Negras, Palenque, and Yaxchilan were located on rivers. Cobá, in Yucatán, was set felicitously between two lakes, but most of the cities in Yucatán had as their only permanent source of water the well, the *cenote*. A Maya farmer tried to locate his milpa as close as possible to the wells, which were located between two to fifteen miles from the city or village. As new fields were needed, there was a tendency for the Maya farmer to move farther and farther from a given center. This in time undoubtedly loosened his connection with the city-state. Agricultural decentralization could well have been one of the factors which loosened the social structure of the "Old Empire" and contributed to the disintegration of cities.

Between January and February, at the time of light rains, trees were felled. From March to May was the hot and dry

* Yum Kaax, believed to have been the corn god, is always represented as youthful and wearing an ear of corn in his headdress.

season; the living trees blossomed and the cut trees were burned. The larger unburnt logs were dragged to the edge and built into a crude but effective fence against deer and other animals. Ash from the burned plants was turned over with the digging stick, and the land was cultivated. From June through August, the rains fell heavily.* These were the planting months.

Planting was ritually controlled. Maize, the gift of the gods, was sacred, and planting had to be done with the proper ritual. The rain god Chac was properly propitiated and those days selected to plant when rain should fall, in order that the newly planted seeds sprout. Astronomy was mostly astrology. But the almanacs for planting were based on empirical observation. In one of the Maya codices it is stated: "This is the record of the year-bears of the *uinal. . . ."* Actually, this was weather forecasting based on observation of previous years. In the ninth month, Chen (Moon), and the tenth, Yax (Venus), planting was to be done during certain lucky days. Typical interpretations of the Maya planting almanac were these: "Cimi, the 5th day of the 11th month Caz [i.e., July] . . . bad day for planting . . . with rain incantations there is a good downpour . . . The month and day of 9 Caban [August] . . . good day, lucky day, heavy rains, good for planting everything."

For every detail of planting, sowing, and harvesting there was ritual, yet much of it was based on the shrewd observations of the earth-bound man, who related them to the priest-scribes. The priests in turn set it all down in glyph-script so that it could be remembered. Dr. Morley found during his excavations at the ruins of Copán, in Honduras, that two stone time markers were placed four and a half miles apart in such a position that the sun set directly in line with them on April 12 and September 7. It is thought that April 12 was the date chosen for burning the brush in the fields around Copán.

Chac was the rain god. He is represented in the Maya glyphs in books, on sculpture, and in painted murals as the long-nosed god. His eyes, T-shaped, suggest tears and, symbolically, rain. His importance in the Maya pantheon can be gauged from the fact that the Chac name-glyph occurs 218 times in the three surviving Maya codices. Chac was

---

* Rainfall is heavy in the jungle regions, 80 inches a year. In El Petén (near where the first great Maya cities, Tikal, Uaxactun, etc., were located) it rains 65 inches a year; in Yucatán, 46 inches. There is a high incidence of rain but water is not held by the shallow soil; it percolates down through the porous limestone into the *cenotes* 100 feet below the surface. Some water remains in pockets called *aguadas.*

a benevolent deity and considered to be man's friend. The Maya farmer always evoked his name when planting. He was *the* god. So in the months of Chen and Yax there were great festivals to honor him. (See the chapter on religion, p. 133.)

Planting was simple and effective. All that was required was a bag to hold the maize kernels and a fire-hardened planting stick. A hole was made in the soil, 4 or 5 inches deep, and into it three to six kernels were dropped. After that, Chac willing, the Maya frequently weeded the fields and waited for the maize to grow. "And when it rains," exclaimed Diego de Landa, "it is marvelous to see how maize grows." September and October brought light rains; they were also the hurricane months. In November, when the weather was cool and dry, the corncob was bent downward to keep it from the birds. Dry, it was harvested.

What did it yield? From exhaustive studies made in Yucatán over a ten-year period an idea has been gained of how much maize was harvested. How many fields, of 400 square feet, the Maya farmer planted we have no precise idea. "They plant in many places, so that if one fails, the others will suffice." The yield of corn from a given field would vary. Production was higher in the humid areas than in Yucatán, where the statistical studies were made. The present-day farmer in Yucatán plants an average of 12 acres. A hundred and ninety days of the year are given to preparing the field, burning, planting, weeding, harvesting. The average cornfield produces 168 bushels a year. An average family of five consumes 6.55 pounds of maize per day, 64 bushels a year, including that fed to the livestock. From the fruits of his 190 days of labor the Maya feeds his entire family and still has a corn surplus of 100 bushels, which he uses to buy the luxuries that he cannot produce. It is presumed that since the Maya in ancient times cultivated less land than at present, and kept no dray animals, his farm labor consumed only 48 days of the year. In the surplus time of nine to ten months a year, he built the great city-states.

The Maya cultivated much besides maize. In the same cornfield, using the maize stalk for support, the farmers planted beans; on the ground, squash and pumpkins. Chili peppers were grown at the edge of the fields or in the houses as an ornamental shrub. In separate fields in the warmer areas the Maya grew the pale sweet potato. The sweet cassava (*dzin*) was known, as was *chicham* (from the Mexican *xicamatl*), a root shaped like a turnip. They had one good green vegetable, the *chayote*, the fruit of a herbaceous vine that when cooked tasted like summer squash.

Around the gardens which surrounded their houses the Maya planted papayas (*haaz*) "which they esteemed very highly." The avocado (*u cheel*), a "very large and fresh tree with fruits of great delicacy," appeared in groves, while the soapberry tree "they put near their houses to obtain the roots from which they wash their clothes like soap."

The fruit of the *achiote* tree, mentioned earlier as a source of color, was also used in food, giving "color to their stews, like saffron." The gourd tree, which produced large, unedible melon-sized fruits, gave very thin but durable drinking cups that, as Diego de Landa observed, "they paint very handsomely." The *balche* tree was planted; its bark yielded the strong alkaloid used in making honey mead.

Hemp was raised for its fiber, "from which they made an infinite number of things," sandals, ropes, twine, bowstrings, fishing line, and so on. Cotton was of two kinds; both were grown "and gathered in wonderful quantity." It was of great economic importance because of the manta cloth woven from it. The ceiba (*piim*), a sacred tree that was supposed to hold up the Maya heavens, yielded a fine cotton that was made into pillows for Maya heads. The sapodilla, or "chewing-gum tree" (*ya*), the source of our modern chicle, is a large tropical fruit tree growing to a height of sixty feet. The Maya boiled its sap to a sticky mass and used it in making blowguns and for adhesion when a strong glue was needed. It was an article of trade; Maya boys chewed it, calling the stuff *cha*. The search for chicle to fill modern needs has done much for archaeology; many of the Maya ruins were discovered by *chicleros*, who spend the rainy season searching for sapodillas.

Copal, which yielded a resin burned in all religious ceremonies, "was a commodity and is very great business," wrote Landa. Cedar (*kuche*, which meant "tree of God") was used for the large dugout canoes. Brazilwood, the famous dyewood called *cachte*, "when thrown into water turned it red." It was used for dyeing cotton cloth. Palms were many, and their leaves were used for thatching house roofs. Cacao was grown on the two extremes of the Maya domain, Tabasco to the northwest and Honduras to the southwest. It was a Maya passion and farmers in Tabasco grew it exclusively, even to the detriment of the traditional maize, and traded "that gold of the country" for their needs.

One fruit was not native to Maya land: "There are many bananas . . . the Spaniards brought them; for before this there were none."

Droughts were frequent and of great intensity and their "disastrous consequences play an important role in Maya literature." As explained in an earlier section, rains were usually heavy, but the greater part of the lowland is only a thin soil cap laid over a limestone outcrop (". . . the country with the least earth that I have seen," says Diego de Landa). The rain trickled through the porous limestone and down into natural cisterns. The Maya tried to combat this; at many of the city-states they built artificial cisterns. During the rainy season water was gathered from the roofs by means of cemented run-offs and was directed into wells, which were elaborately roofed to prevent evaporation in the hot weather. Tikal, although in one of the wettest zones, suffered repeatedly from drought. There the engineers cemented up an entire ravine of porous limestone around the principal plaza, to create giant-sized reservoirs. Over these passed causeways which served as both dams and roads. All this was to no avail for the maize fields. When rain did not fall at stated intervals, the soil quickly dried up, cracked, and became cement-hard.

When this happened (and it is obvious from the frequent appeals to the rain gods that it happened often), the Maya abandoned their cities, went into the jungles, and were reduced to eating the bark of trees. The old, who were unable to come, were left to die. Human sacrifices to the gods were frequent on these occasions. Other Mexican tribes suffered in the same measure from drought, and the Aztecs sacrificed thousands to the rain gods.

One of the enigmas of the Maya is that neolithic mental block which prevented them from devising a way in which to obtain the water which lay immediately below the land surface. Landa noted that there "are few places where one digs down that water cannot be found, sometimes within one meter." Irrigation techniques are inseparable from a developed agriculture. The pre-Inca civilizations in Peru, whose rainless coasts were more of a challenge to the primitive mind than the situation which faced the Maya, solved their problems by the construction of an elaborate system of irrigational aqueducts, water often being brought down for hundreds of miles.

Although they were able to perfect a calendar as good as the Greek or Egyptian and raise stone cities from the jungle, the Maya used the wheel only in toys for children. It would not have been beyond Maya technique to install a treadmill that dipped into the giant *cenotes* and raised the water to the surface, conveying it then, by means of an aqueduct, to their fields. In arid Numidia and Mauretania (present-day Algeria and Morocco) the Romans used reservoirs, ponds, and underground cisterns, linking them with canals and aqueducts to convey water to field and home. The water tunnel widely used by the Achaemenian kings in Persia (circa 600 B.C.) and later introduced into arid Egypt was a product of the intelligent use of gradients and the natural flow of water into waterless areas. It could easily have been worked out by the Maya. The giant wheel built by Augustus in A.D. 113 in the town of Fayum, in Egypt, lifted water from the Nile by a human tread method and fed it into reservoirs, which in turn flowed to fountains, baths, a brewery, and even to two synagogues. Such a device was not beyond the means of the Maya.

There was a mental block against the principle of the wheel in the Americas, where man was the dray animal. None of the practical uses of the wheel, in whatever form, were known: pulley, arch, roller wheel, rotary quern, potter's wheel, or water wheel. Had the Maya had the latter in that terrible year of 1464, when there was drought followed by a locust swarm so thick that the weight of it broke the limbs off large trees and engulfed the land until "nothing green was left," they might have survived and weathered the great hurricane that followed and destroyed houses, trees, and fields. "After this the land of Yucatán remained so destitute of trees that . . . casting one's eyes over the country from some high point it looks as if the whole land had been cut by scissors. . . ."

II. The Tax

Only the gods seem to have been able to create something out of nothing. That something cannot come out of nothing is the reason for taxation. The Romans called it *taxare*, meaning "to be touched sharply," and most people of all times have felt it to be a burden. To the Maya, whose closest approach to money was the cacao bean, the tax burden was in the form of work service.

Little is known of its details. With the Aztecs we have some idea of how each clan or *calpulli* was collectively taxed. Aztec charts give a precise idea how tribute (which was a form of tax) was levied from the conquered. That other great theocratic state, the Inca realm, had a form of work tax called the *mit'a*, in which every able-bodied man was obliged to give a stated amount of work service to the state, which service was recorded in their knotted-string *quipu*. Though it is possible that the Maya had such records, they have left none behind.

The Near East civilizations, such as the Sumerian and Mesopotamian, kept precise tax accounts in cuneiform writing, and it is thought that this necessary business stimulated the invention and perfection of writing. This was also true as regards the Aztecs. From the name-glyphs in their tribute books, we know the precise towns that lay within the Aztec orbit. If such lists existed among the Maya, the overzealous padres must have destroyed the evidence.

Maize was the first tax. Part of a farmer's surplus was turned over to the tax-collecting *batab,* who brought it to the "state" depositories. Then, as a form of work-service tax, the personal maize fields of priest and nobility were cultivated and harvested. Writes Landa: "They [the common men] improved the lands of the lords . . . planting them with wine-trees [*balche*] and they sowed cotton, chili peppers and maize."

Construction was also a part of personal tax. The houses of the directing classes were built by the common people, at their own expense. The causeways were built as part of the work service; it was carried out by *corvée* by the clans that lived near the road. The nobility were carried in a litter, as were the Aztec "kings," who allowed themselves to be carried short distances. The Inca nobles used the litter as a conveyance and picked groups of hardy tribesmen who carried them for thousands of miles. It is not known whether the litter convoy was used among the Maya, but "if the lords went out of their fief, they took with them a great many people."

Public building was the principal labor tax. It is fully evident that immense religious centers, temple cities such as Tikal—a city covering many square miles, complete with reservoirs, giant causeways, and ball courts, whose façades are intricately carved—presupposed a complex social organization and effective use of work service. The Indian could always be counted on willingly to work on the construction of a temple city, since in the long run it would benefit him. All wished to gain favor with the gods. It would be wrong to believe that this was slave labor. It greatly differed from the labor to which the Maya was later put by his white conquerors. The latter benefited the Spanish, not the Indian.

Many in Maya society were exempt from taxes. The nobles, priests, and civil and military officials lived on the tax tribute of the lower man. In addition a sizable number of artisans, who decorated the temples, carved the stelae, and directed if not actually carved the wooden lintels and the masks for the actors, were supported out of the accumulated surplus brought to the official storage chambers by the tax-paying Maya.

The gods, no matter in what guise they came, have always cost Mexico dear.

12. Weaving

Ix Chebel Yax, daughter of the goddess of pregnancy, was the patroness of weaving.* Because weaving was done exclusively by the woman and because she was almost continuously pregnant, the association was perhaps made in Maya minds between the two otherwise unrelated activities.

Fig. 14. Ix Chebel Yax, the goddess of weaving. She was the daughter of Ixchel, the goddess of pregnancy and the wife of Itzamna, the Maya god of learning. From the Codex Tro-Cortesianus.

Weaving was both for home consumption and for trade. The women wove *huipiles* for themselves, and breechclouts for their men. Unfortunately we have no examples of these

---

* Eric Thompson believes that Ix Azal Uoh, the wife of the sun god, was the goddess of weaving, that Ix Zacal Nok was the "lady clothweaver," and that the figure shown in the codex Tro-Cortesianus (102, b, c, d) may represent the moon goddess spinning. If this be true I am fully willing to bow to Dr. Thompson, who has spent more time than any other living man exploring and writing about the Maya.

garments beyond the representations of them on murals, pottery, and sculpture. So far as we know, Maya weaving was secular. They did not, like the Incas, appoint "chosen" women to live and weave in the sacred precincts.

Spinning invariably has been *woman*. The very tools are symbolical: an unmarried woman is a *spin*ster; and the female is "on the distaff side," since the yarn was always spun from a distaff held under the woman's arm.

The spindle whorl is universal. The Maya spindle was a stick ten to twelve inches in length, with a pottery balance ring three inches from its end. It was spun about in a small ceramic dish. These pottery whorls are all that survive of Maya weaving.

Cotton was "gathered together in wonderful quantity and grows in all parts of the land . . . there are two kinds of it." One type was an annual; ". . . they sow it every year." The other was a perennial, a sort of tree cotton (*Gossypium herbaceum*), as its classification suggests, "and this lasts five or six years and bears cotton every year." Tree cotton* was known and used by the pre-Inca cultures; it grew in the coastal drylands about Piura.

Dyeing was done before weaving. Colors, vegetable and mineral, were symbols. Black was the symbol of war, since obsidian tipped arrow and spear; black was obtained from carbon. Yellow, the color of ripe corn, was the symbol for food. It was extracted from hydrous iron oxide. Red was a blood symbol; it came from several sources: red iron oxide and, from the vegetable world, *achiote* and brazilwood. Cochineal, *mukay*, was highly prized, "the best in the Indies coming from the dry land." It was obtained from the insects that Maya boys "herded like cows" on cactus pads.†

Blue was the color symbol of sacrifice. That particular "Maya blue" which one sees so vividly on the murals of Bonampak came from a mineral which has been identified. "Colors of many different kinds were made from dyes of cer-

---

* Cotton and its distribution are fascinating botanical and anthropological problems. The origins of the Greek word for cotton point to India, 2500 B.C., but cotton must have been known earlier than this. It became familiar to the Greeks through the conquests of Alexander the Great (d. 323 B.C.). Theophrastus reported that Indians planted cotton in rows, and his contemporary Aristobolus said seeds were separated from the capsules and the fibers combed. Cotton did not appear in the Nile valley until 500 B.C. (it appears in Peru as early as 2000 B.C.) and was known as "tree wool." The Romans made cotton goods on a large scale in Malta from cotton grown in Egypt.

† In the sixteenth century cochineal found to yield a good color was extensively cultivated in Italy and Greece; it replaced all other sources of red dye.

tain trees." The Maya also used the juices of the wild tomato, the blackberry, and the green-black avocado. The most
prized, because it was difficult to obtain, was the deep purple
obtained from a mollusk *(Purpura patula)*. It is almost
identical with the famous Tyrian purple derived from several
species of mollusks, murex and purpura. Dyes were pounded
in stone mortars, which are sometimes found in graves. The
dry colors were undoubtedly kept in small bags, which one
does not see among the Maya, but their counterpart in Peru
has been preserved.

Fig. 15. The spindle-whorl is universal. The spindle
stick was rotated on a small pottery dish as shown here
in an illustration from a Mexican codex.

Independent invention is an archaeological fact. Peoples
living under similar geographical conditions will resemble
one another in various practices. Like the Maya, the Egyptians used carbon for black, and got their purple from the
Purpura mollusk. Ancient weavers needed a mordant to fix
their dyes. The Peruvians used copper. The Maya first used
urine, as did the Aztecs and the Egyptians. That it was so
used in Egypt is attested in a papyrus dated 2000 B.C.:
". . . his hands stink [referring to a dyer working in the
urine vat] and he abhorreth the sight of cloth." When the
cloth trade was extended, the Maya obtained alum from the
Mexican highlands, using it as a mordant for dyers, an astringent, and a preservative for leathers.*

The Maya loom was identical with that of all the other

* The whitish astringent alum came from Aztec-held territory and
was brought to the trading center of Xicalanco by the trading dele-
gations. (The people of the classical lands always used aluminum
sulfate, to cause the dyestuffs to adhere to textile fibers. It was
called "alum of Yemen" and loomed large in trade from the earliest
times. Alums were extensively used as mordants in Europe in the
Middle Ages.)

American tribes. The backstrap loom had a horizontal rod that was attached to a post or tree. The warp was then fastened to the lower wooden rod (*xunche*), which had a thick hemp cord (*yamal*) that went around the ample rump of the woman weaver. The essentials of weaving vary little, be it Aztec, Inca, Egyptian, Greek, Roman, or Maya. The weft is interlaced with the warp. But the arrangement of colors and pattern is the art, the genius of weaving. The designs of the cloth produced from these Maya looms must have been fantastic, judging by the scant evidence which is shown on their murals, sculptures, and vase paintings. There were fabrics made of the imported rabbit-wool yarn from Mexico, others with bird plumage tied in to form feather mosaics, and tough manta cloth padded with cotton and soaked in salt brine for body armor. Designs and colors ran riot, and yet all we know of them are from the scant, tantalizing illustrations. All of the art of those looms has perished with war and conquest, time, and the elements. Except for the fragments found at the bottom of the wells of Chichén Itzá, there is no other evidence. It is a great loss to the history of art, for we know from an analogous source—the weavings of Peru, where dry desert conditions have preserved many superb pieces—how wonderful it must have been. Since, as said an old report, "the traffic of this land is in mantas of cotton," and this cloth was produced over an immense period of time, 1000 B.C. until A.D. 1670, the amount produced could have certainly stretched around the world.

From the simple manta woven in strips eighteen yards long, used for trade, came the colorful *huipil* for women, and breechclout for men, the robes of the priests and chieftains, the cloth for dressing idols, the portieres for temple doors, and the body armor referred to above.

All this has perished.

13. Feather Mosaics

The art of featherwork was highly developed. It was equally so in the other great American theocracies, Inca and Aztec. Only that of the Incas has been preserved, owing to the enveloping sands of the dry coast of Peru. Of the Aztec work only two feather pieces have been preserved, and those by mere chance.* From the Maya, nothing.

Since the Maya did not have a centralized capital, we have no knowledge of craft guilds within such a center. The Aztec had feather weavers (*amanteca*) and a centralized aviary where birds were raised for their plumes. This was not necessary for the Maya; in their lands the birds were abundant. In Yucatán there was the motmot (*toh*), with its iridescent tail, and the blue Yucatán jay (*paap*), which traveled in flocks and yielded a wide variety of blue plumes. There were the modest-plumed quail, woodpeckers, pheasants, and the yellow-crested curassow, whose blue-black feathers were made into a feather mosaic for high priests. The ocellated wild turkey gave feathers which were used in Maya rituals. Along the seashore were ducks, egrets, herons, and the sun bittern. In the tropical area of El Petén there were toucanets, parrots, and trogons, and further up, in the high, cold forests of Guatemala, were the long-tailed green and red parrots and the fabled quetzal, a bird the size of a pouter pigeon, which yielded two long, golden-green tail feathers. The quetzal lives in the highlands and breeds in the cloud forests, above 4,000 feet. "In the province of Verapaz [in Guatemala] they punish with death him who kills the quetzal bird, the one of the rich plumes . . . for these feathers were of great value. . . ."

Birds were caught in bird lime or else felled with clay pellets propelled from a blowpipe,† a method of capturing a bird without killing it. The author used this means when he caught, photographed, and studied the quetzal bird for the first time in its history.

* When Cortes dispatched the first treasure ship to Spain in 1519, Charles V was in Flanders; the ship followed him. Though astonished by the golden ornaments, he was involved in war, and ordered them melted down into bullion to pay for his troops in the lowlands. The headdress and shield given to Cortes by Moctezuma were later given to Archduke Ferdinand of Tyrol, who sent them to his chamberlain. Preserved at the Hapsburg Castle at Ambras, they were discovered and identified only at the end of the last century. They are now among the archaeological treasures of the Museum für Volkerkunde at Vienna.

† This blowpipe, *dzonche*, was an effective instrument. Diego de Landa, who saw it in action, said that an Indian using a blowpipe (with a pellet the size of a marble) could knock down a bird however large. Moctezuma had dozens of blowpipes, made of gold, which he used for hunting. He gave one of them to Cortes. The same type of blowpipe is still used among the remote tribe of Jicaques in Honduras, who once bordered the Maya. The ingenious method of manufacture, with a botanical identification of the plants involved, the making of the pellets, and the methods of hunting have already been described by von Hagen.[40]

Fig. 16. *Above*. The sacred quetzal bird from a relief found at Palenque. Only the feathers are formalized.
Below. A parrot, drawn realistically.

The technique of preparing a feather mosaic began with
the preparation of the loom as in cloth weaving. The feathers
were then laid out in the desired pattern by the weaver. As
she wove, the quill of the feather was tied into the warp and
weft of the weaving.

The Maya made much use of the feather mosaic. The ends
of the man's breechclout which hung down, fore and aft,
were decorated with featherwork "with a great deal of care
and beauty." The priests and chieftains wore woven cotton-
mat helmets ornamented with the magnificent golden-green
feathers of the quetzal. There were feather fans for actor-
dancers, and for the nobles, long fans mounted on poles,
which kept away the insistent insects. One sees these on the
murals of Bonampak. For the festival of Xul five magnificent banners of woven feathers were presented to the temples by various artisans. Warriors dressed in featherwork,

which made them look something like Papagena in *The Magic Flute*. There were feather shields similar to the one made for the Aztec "king" Ahuizotl (d. 1503), which is still preserved at Vienna. In many dance ceremonies feather dress was used, as Diego de Landa saw and noted: ". . . one woman clothed in a feather dress danced for the people . . . and the lords of the land went clothed in certain *xicoles* of cotton and feathers woven into a kind of jacket . . . and the very lofty in fine feathers, especially the quetzal feathers, which are so valued . . . they are used as money."

14. Mats and Matting

Pop was the word for the woven-grass mat.

The mat was the symbol of authority to the Maya as it was to the Aztecs. The *holpop*, he-who-sits-at-the-head-of-the-mat, was the title given to an official of the directing classes who sat in the place so designated. In the sixteenth-century Motul Maya dictionary, the word *pop* means both "throne" and "mat." More, *pop* was the first month of the eighteenth-month Maya year.

The importance of the rush mat to the Maya may be seen in the varied uses of it. In ordinary houses the mat was used as a floor covering. Food was served on the mat, and mats were used as mattresses for beds. On one of the temple walls, at Tikal, where some Indian circa A.D. 700 doodled the things of his life (one sees a man being ceremonially killed with an arrow, a jaguar with tail at the alert, a throne, a lord being carried on a litter), there are two sketches of the woven rush mat. The same type of decoration appears on the stone Stela "J" at Copán and again on Stela "H" at Quirigua, not far from Copán. At Chichén Itzá, on the small truncated platform in front of the great pyramid, the woven-rush mat shares the decoration with the symbol for the planet Venus.

Mats were woven by men and women in their homes, during the round of the day. "They have in the fields and forests many different kinds of osiers," says Landa. The woven mat undoubtedly antedates weaving. Mat weaving and basketry are found in all of the neolithic cultures dating as far back as 5000 B.C.

No examples of Maya matwork have survived.

15. Basketry

Basketry was highly developed. There seem to have been four types, but time has effaced them all. We know the Maya basket only from wall paintings, pottery, and sculpture. The Maya used reeds, rushes, sedges, grass, and vines for making baskets. "They have a certain plant [*Cyperus camus*] which they raise or grow in their *cenote*-wells and in other places from which they make their baskets . . . and they are accustomed to dye them in colors, thus making them very pretty."

The drawings show some baskets to have been twilled, others in a design of stepped frets and small squares. Inca baskets, as the hand of the maker left them, have been found in the preserving, desiccating sands of Peru and give a good idea of how well developed basketry was in the Americas. The techniques of basketmaking have changed little throughout the centuries; the earliest found in certain neolithic sites in Iraq (5000 B.C.) are almost identical with those found in the Americas.

16. Rope and Ropemaking

As master builders and seafarers, the Maya had much use for rope. Rope was plaited out of the tough fibers of the *henequen*, or hemp. It is one of the *agaves;* a genus of the large and important amaryllis family, with spined fleshy leaves. They were all of considerable economic use to the American Indian tribes. The Aztecs had 317 uses for the *agave*, which included the fabrication of a beverage called *pulque* from its fermented juice. The Incas plaited the same *agave* into thick cables, "as broad as a calf's body," and used them for sustaining the suspension bridges which they hung over Andean gorges. The Maya used it for a number of items: sandals, bowstrings, fishlines ("they tie their harpoons with buoys at the end"). They used it as cordage for sails on their long coastal sea voyages. One of the most frequent uses for rope was in temple building.

We may assume that the use of rope cables was analogous to that of the Egyptians (*henequen* was superior to their date-palm fiber ropes). Rope and ropemaking were of the greatest importance to theocratic empires. Rope was a basic source of power, for men with ropes suspended from their shoulders pulled huge rock masses into place. A bas-relief at Nineveh (c. 700 B.C.), at the Palace of Sennacherib, shows legions of men, bearded in the Hittite fashion, pulling huge carved monuments on wooden sledges. At the Tomb at Thebes (c. 1450 B.C.) there are scenes of ropemaking. Men are seen plaiting palm fibers into wrist-thick cables.

Unhappily for us the Maya were so preoccupied with the hierarchy of numbers and so intoxicated with time's flight, that they forgot to record all the daily events of their lives. They have left us no illustrations of the craft of ropemaking.

17. Pottery and Pottery Makers

Monsieur D'Asterac, the gently mad alchemist of Anatole France's *Reine Pédauque*, said that "Jehovah's artifice in making man did not go beyond that of a very able potter capable of molding beings such as we are, in clay. . . . We are, in fact, nothing but animated pottery."

The ancient Maya themselves are now not much more than animated pottery. Because pottery is a chronological frame upon which to gauge historical perspective, so Maya potsherds have been studied to the point of delirium. The preoccupation with pottery design and techniques is ofttimes carried to extremes.[41]

In the study of prehistoric cultures art is given undue attention because it is far easier to photograph a temple than to detail a form of life. Moreover, the Maya are inarticulate except through their art. So those Maya, anonymous and communal, who raised the stone temple cities and out of the chaos of the jungle built a concourse of roads, have now been reduced to a sequence of pottery. My friend Eric Thompson bemoans the fact: "There is not a little danger that the fate of Maya archaeology . . . might emerge as an interminable catalog of changes in the designs and shapes of pottery."

The Maya were pottery makers of the highest quality.[42] The imagination, design, and form are as good as anything of the Greeks, far surpass the Roman ceramic arts, and are superior to the pottery of almost any of the cultures of the ancient Near East. All these wonderful Maya pottery forms— too varied to detail—were done without the potter's wheel. Pottery was done by coiling. The technique is almost as old as man. Clay was molded into long coils—sort of outsized spaghettis—then laid down in successive rings and worked and pressed into a single form with the hands. The clay form was then smoothed with a shard. If the vase was large—and some were gigantic—the pottery maker walked around the vase, becoming himself the potter's wheel. This technique was not limited to the Maya; all the tribes and cultures covering the wide area of the Americas employed it, and many used it in Africa and the peripheral Asiatic world.

These time-consuming methods have changed little since the earliest neolithic times. The pottery wheel would have simplified the process but we have seen that the wheel was unknown to the cultures of pre-Hispanic America. The potter's wheel presented mechanical problems not easily solved unless a people were fairly advanced in metallurgy; it must turn true and tight on a bearing. It is not, however, to be supposed that because the Maya and other American potters used the primitive technique that their pottery was primitive. The wheel brought, as in the Greek vase, repetitive forms. Maya potters achieved greater individuality in their work because of a lack of mechanical devices.

Pottery was turned out in mass. They had molds for pressing designs on finished pots. Excavations have turned up such molds with decorations in vertical, horizontal, and pinched stripes for rouletting and comb markings, and molds of baked clay to impress patterns. There is no technique (other than the wheel) used by the best "mechanical" potters of the classic era that was not known and employed by the Maya.

After being decorated, the pottery was fired in an open kiln (wood- charcoal- or grass-burning) and baked at a heat of 450° upward. All Maya pottery was made in this fashion, simple utilitarian bowls and cooking pots, decorated dishes, pitchers to hold chocolate, beakers to be filled with the heady mead. Braziers were made (to warm a chilly room or to burn copal). There were plates to hold sacrificial urns the ashes of the dead ("the nobles had their ashes pla great urns"). They made man-sized jars, as large knotted and corded jars found in Knossos, Crete; the used immense ones for underground water storage. Those found at Tabasco had an elaborate appliqué decoration. Life-sized idols were fashioned from clay, and each of the 20,000 houses in Mayapán had one such. Even in Landa's time "they earned a great deal by making idols of clay."

The most beautiful of pottery, decorated with scenes of Maya life, was made for the dead. Those found at Jaina, Campeche, are clay figures, freely molded yet exquisite in detail, and show Maya chieftains elegantly dressed and women richly clothed with necklaces and elaborate coiffures: "an extraordinary mastery of handling, realistic knowledge of form and movement; they are elegant and refined, majestic and monumental . . . excellent examples of the Maya aesthetic ideal." Their pottery has left us many details of Maya life—especially that of the women—which are never indicated in the carvings on the monuments. Clay modeling was in a large sense a secular art; the clay figurines show Maya man as he saw himself. They were the expression of the lower man and the world about him—not an art form designed for the dominating elite, grandiose, elegant, and remote. The modeled figures give a picture of appearance and habits, the dress of men and soldiers, houses and games. Those that came from the coast of Veracruz much influenced the latter-day Maya. They show the Indian as gay; the laughing heads and soft modeling of bodies emit a sort of contagious happiness and embody sophisticated elements. The God-obsessed Maya, austere in their religiosity, were considerably influenced by the art of the figurines; they borrowed much from it for their Puuc-style architecture.

Pottery was woman. All we see of the remains of the Maya ceramic art was done by women. It is a fact that should be stressed. In almost every place where pottery making was on an archaic level—Africa or Melanesia—pottery was woman-made and its design woman-inspired. Throughout the area of the Amazon, pottery was a woman's task. Women were the potters, so far as we know, in ancient Peru. Early Greek and early Egyptian pottery was also woman-made until the introduction of the potter's wheel. Sir Lindsay Scott is "certain" that it was only after the introduction of the potter's wheel that pottery became—as the drawings on the walls of Thebes show—exclusively masculine. This suggests that all the superbly beautiful patterns found on pottery (as well as weaving) were conceived by woman.

Perhaps then, Art *is* a woman.

Pottery is a time marker. For the archaeologists who reconstruct the history of a preliterate people, the most important evidence is the shape, decoration, and temper of

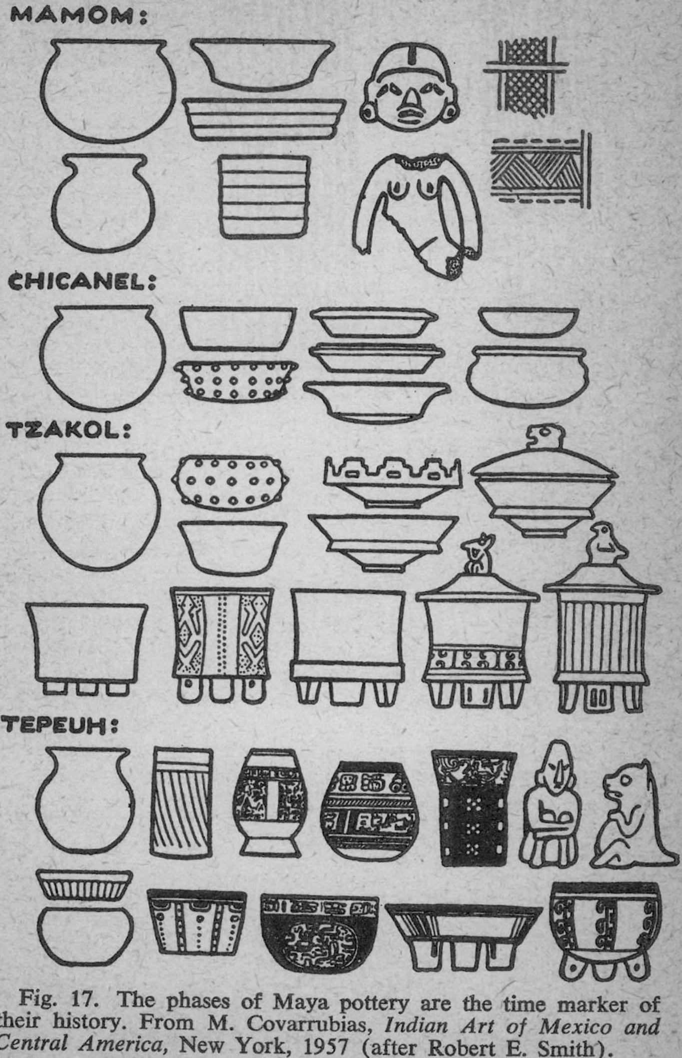

MAMOM:

CHICANEL:

TZAKOL:

TEPEUH:

Fig. 17. The phases of Maya pottery are the time marker of their history. From M. Covarrubias, *Indian Art of Mexico and Central America*, New York, 1957 (after Robert E. Smith).

pottery. Ceramics record stylistic and therefore social development.

Very primitive pottery is little known in Mayadom. When pottery appears it is already fairly well advanced. Archaeologists have given Maya pottery, and therefore Maya history, five phases and to each (except the fifth) a name drawn from the *Popol Vuh*.

1. *Mamom*, "Grandmother" (2000–500 B.C.). Pottery is strictly utilitarian; it has been discovered at the lowest levels in El Petén (where the earliest dated records begin). Most in evidence are the rounded cooking pots, *cum*, which remain relatively unchanged throughout the length of Maya history. They are simply decorated, grooved and incised. Naked clay figurines and flat eating dishes also appear.

2. *Chicanel*, "Concealer," is the Maya formative period (500 B.C.–A.D. 300). There now appears some of the superbly painted polychromic Uaxactun pottery. The human form is given literally, and it is often glyph-dated. Between this and the Mamom phase there has seemingly been no evolution of form; Chicanel suddenly appears full-born. The Chicanel

Fig. 18. "Thin-orange" pottery of late Maya history, from the region of Chichén Itzá.

styles vary widely throughout El Petén and Yucatán. The shapes are low, flaring; bowls have an orange color, decorated by what has been called the *abatik* process. It is also the beginning of the culture of Maya cities.*

3. *Tzakol*, "The Builders" (A.D. 317–650), is the period of the rise of the great ceremonial or temple cities throughout Mayadom. The pottery is sophisticated and polychromic. "Thin-orange," a very delicate pottery, appears. Distributed widely far outside the Maya area, it was developed from some

* The oldest dated stela thus far found (A.D. 328) is at Uaxactun.

unknown center. This period, archaeological stratification proves, lasted about three centuries.

4. *Tepeuh*, "Conqueror" (A.D. 650–1000), is dominantly Maya. All the traits that are "Maya" appear. Pottery is facile, sophisticated. One senses that the potter has now full control of clay and design, and it turns into decorative baroque. The arts, technically perfected, seem to lose their original creative vitality. The same flamboyance appears in Maya sculpture (which is less sensitive to periodic change than pottery). It is an ornate phase in Maya art. There is a change from static to dynamic composition; the richly dressed personages in the sculptures are presented in "anecdotal scenes," and there is an unrestrained elaborateness, an exaggerated love of ornament. The greatest temple cities, Tikal, Copán, Palenque, Piedras Negras, have all been built, and there follows what most have called a period of decadence—the mass of building stops and grinds to a halt. There seems to be some relation between this "baroque" period and the abandonment of Maya cities. The ceramic arts, at the same time, show a shift in frame of reference; decoration becomes secular, religious motifs no longer hold, and the artist becomes increasingly concerned with the world about him. The overelaboration of sculpture, the tendency of the lower man to concern himself with secular subjects, the cessation of building, the ruinous destructive methods of neolithic agriculture, the disintegration of central authority —all combine to show that "something" is happening in Mayadom. It is rash to base a theory of disintegration on flamboyance in the arts. Still, the condition of a people's art is often a symptom of its society. "Vulgarity is always the result of some excess. . . ." "Wherever artists find some technical difficulty in imposing form on brute matter, art tends to be simple . . . luxuriantism and consequently vulgarity become possible only when men have acquired complete mastery over matter."

If all this is not explanation enough, in the Tepeuh period, the "Conqueror" phase, "something" caused millions of people to abandon their cities.

5. *Maya-Toltec* (unnamed in the *Popol Vuh*) (A.D. 1000–1500) is the final phase. It begins with the introduction of new styles in architecture and pottery—the effect of the Toltec incursions—and ends with the occupation of Yucatán by the Spaniards.

Although the *cum* cooking pot retains its shape and function through all these periods (a confirmation of Spengler's "eternal peasant" theme), new ideas, new shapes of pottery, and especially new design and ornament appear in northern

Yucatán, which was invaded by the Maya-speaking Toltecs. *Pumbate,* the only glazed pottery in the Americas, appears. Manufactured perhaps at Soconusco, close to the Chiapas border, it is decorated with Aztec-like gods and animals. In the Puuc a new form of Maya architecture develops and along with it a hard, gray, slatelike carved pottery. Fragments of it from the ruins of Uxmal show pottery to have been as limpidly beautiful as anything out of early Egypt. Toltec motifs, themes from the military orders of the Jaguar and the Eagle appear, as well as variations on themes of the cult of the plumed serpent. Tradition and known history are confirmed by pottery and it by archaeology. Thus, pottery is an "index fossil" of Maya history.

18. Trade

"The occupation to which they [the Maya] had the greatest inclination was *trade.*"

This inclination toward trade had early manifested itself among the Maya; they were the only one of the three great American theocracies who maintained it by sea as well as by land. Ever since man has appeared on the earth, he has traded. Wars ceased so that man might trade. As man was willing to go vast distances for things he lacked, the early trade roads were luxury routes. He went vast miles, from the Mediterranean to the Baltic, to obtain amber, "that special act of God." Camel caravans traveled even greater distances through hostile lands to effect trade and bring in luxury items. Trading areas throughout the world had rights of asylum. Few were hindered in passing through hostile tribes when trade was the object.* Strabo stated that wayfarers whose object was business went under divine protection (Mercury was the god of travelers). In the Middle Ages, Edward the Confessor gave travelers protection on the four main Roman roads in England, declaring them "under the truce of God." It is then not surprising to find that the supreme occupation of the Maya was trade.

The trade routes date from the origin of the Maya. The Guatemalan highlands were linked with both coasts by trails

---

* Trade was sacrosanct. One does not have to go to ancient Greece for confirmation of this. Today it means imprisonment and perhaps death for anyone to pass into East Germany—yet daily trade missions cross over the border with complete freedom.

and later by man-maintained roads. The *Popol Vuh* speaks of "where the four [trade] roads joined." * The one great river of the Maya—the Usumacinta, which rises in the high mountains—was navigable to above the city of Piedras Negras; traders went up and down the entire distance of 240 miles. Trade traffic on land used a well-developed system of roads and causeways (*sacbe;* plural, *sacbeob*); many of these connected with the interior Maya cities. (See the chapter on land communications.)

Early trade routes have been traced by articles found in Maya graves. In Maya Guatemala, at the site of Kiminal-juyu, there are artifacts which derived from Teotihuacán, in Mexico—which shows that early Toltec trade lines moved along the Pacific side. Graves in the temple city of Tikal, deep in the jungle, have yielded sting-ray barbs (used for blood sacrifice) that came from the Caribbean Sea. Social surplus stimulated trade. The highland Maya traded in obsidian (all the active volcanoes yielding obsidian were on the Pacific side). Jade, a Maya symbol and passion, came from the highlands (although the geological source has not been found), as did the feathers of the quetzal. Copal, an incense, was an export item, along with flint, alum, and cochineal. These were exchanged with the lowland Maya for cotton, salt, cotton yardage, honey, wax, *balche,* cacao, dried fish, and smoked deer. So trade flowed in both directions. It brought with it new influences. New ideas accompanied the march to market—patterns for weaving, deadlier weapons, new foods, all these followed commerce.

The routes are best detailed in Yucatán, for here the Maya were concentrated in the last centuries of their cultural existence, and here they were conquered by the Spanish, who chronicled the details of their lives. Christopher Columbus was the first man to make a record of Maya trade. His caravels, on his fourth and last voyage to the Americas, met a Maya trading canoe on the isle of Guanaja in 1502. The canoes were forty feet long. They brought obsidian, razors, copper hatchets, and cotton draperies of many different colors, and the Maya chieftain explained that they had come to this island, which lay twenty miles off the coast of Honduras, to trade for green parrot feathers and crystal.

When Cortes was in Xicalanco in 1524, seeking the route to Honduras, one of the Maya traders there gave him a well-made map, painted on finely woven cloth, showing the entire inland routes through Mayadom, from Xicalanco in Tabasco to Nito, Honduras, a distance of 400 land miles.

* "One of the four roads was red, another black, another white . . . and the black road said to him, I am the one you must take." Colors were direction symbols.

Fig. 19. Xicalanco was an important Maya-Mexican trade center.

All sea or land communications led to the great emporium of Xicalanco. To the Aztec it was Anáhuac Xicalanco and called "the place where the language changes," that is, the tribes to the southeast of Xicalanco spoke Maya.

Xicalanco lies a few miles inland from the Laguna de Terminos. Into this outsized lagoon debouch four rivers; the largest of which is the Usumacinta. At the northeast end of the forty-mile-long lagoon there is a smaller one, the Laguna de Pom; on its shore was Xicalanco. It was strategically placed. To reach it traders coming southward had to use canoes. It was surrounded on three sides by bog and swamp. On the northeast side there was a causeway leading to Veracruz and Aztec Mexico. Xicalanco was a meeting place of Maya, Aztec, Toltec, Mixtec, and Totonac.

Merchants brought salt, dried fish, cotton yardage, copal, honey, wax, corn, beans, and feathers woven into cloaks, shields, and caps. Certain tribes of the Maya had a virtual monopoly on salt. "There is a marsh in Yucatán worth recording," says Diego de Landa, "more than 70 leagues long and entirely of salt . . . here God . . . has made the best salt." The lagoon beginning at Ekab (which was the first town seen by Grijalva in 1518; he called it "New Cairo") was a large commercial trading center with an extensive canoe trade dealing mostly in salt. Only certain Maya clans were allowed to gather the salt, and the lords of Ekab demanded a royalty on it.

Salt has been important in the history of most peoples. Rome's first formal stone road was the Via Salaria, built to obtain salt. In Colombia the landlocked Chibcha grew rich because of it; they had mountains of salt at Zipaquira (8,500 feet in altitude). Salt cakes in ceramic dishes were one of the most familiar trade items in pre-Hispanic Colombia. With emeralds, it was a Chibcha monopoly. Salt routes are found all over the world. There are many about the "fertile crescent"; grain eaters had great need for salt.

Fish, turtles, turtle eggs, and large conch shells (used for trumpets, and for making cement lime, the conch shell also became the symbol for zero in Maya arithmetic) were brought into Xicalanco from the sea. Cotton mantas were widely exported. Maize was sent in sacks. The Maya lacked metal, but flints were used for knives and were a large trade item. "God," said Landa, "provided them with many outcrops of flint . . . and so flint served for metal."

The Maya merchants, called *ppolm*, belonged to an honored profession. Like the Aztec *pochteca*, they were counted among the more "important people." They had their own god, Ek Chuuah, and their own rules of social conduct. They were nontaxpaying Maya, with special social privileges. The merchants operated canoe fleets, and maintained warehouses for exchange along the Gulf Coast, as well as deep into the interior of Mayadom. Hernando Cortes, in his famous trek across Mayadom in 1524 to punish a revolt, found evidence of stone-laid roads with "rest-houses along the entire way," and beyond Lake Petén he captured a high-placed Maya who told him he was a merchant trader and that he with his slaves had voyaged to these parts in his ships.

At Xicalanco large, palm-thatched, stone-built warehouses awaited the cargoes. The merchants gave and ex-

Fig. 20. Sea animals drawn by a Maya artist: Realistic turtle, sting ray (much used in Maya blood rituals), crab, barracuda, snail and, in the lower right-hand corner, a spheroid mollusk that the Maya used for the symbol of zero. From the murals of Chichén Itzá.

tended credit, solicited terms and payment dates.* Trade
was on a truly vast scale. Post-Hispanic tribute lists record
that 26 villages in the Maya province of Maní paid an
annual tribute of 13,480 cotton mantas, each 16 yards long
by 24 inches wide. This was 215,680 yards of cotton fabric
from this small area alone!

There was a considerable trade in luxuries—cacao, stone
beads, green stones called *tun*, "emeralds" (*popzil tun*),
topaz nose beads, cochineal for dyeing, alum, and, from the
distant Maya-speaking Huasteca, bitumen, which those
tribesmen gathered from oil seepages around Tabasco, now
Mexico's primary oil fields.

On the upper reaches of the Usumacinta River were the
large city-states of Piedras Negras, and Yaxchilan, and near
to it, on a small tributary, was Palenque. Traders from them
brought down copal, the odoriferous and magical resin. It
was used as incense throughout Central America and in
much demand in Mexico. Pelts of jaguar and puma, fruits,
vanilla beans (to season the chocolate), wood, lime, and clay
were items in the trade picture. In Cortes' fifth letter to
Carlos V dated 3, September 1527, telling of his awesome
trek of 400 miles through Maya territory, he spoke of the
province of Acalan:[43] "Of great size, containing many people and towns . . . many traders with slaves to carry their
merchandise from here to every part [and Xicalanco] . . .
cloth, colors for dyeing, candlewood for lighting [long splinters of pine], so full of resin they burned like a candle."
Most of this went overland to the Usumacinta, then by canoe
down the river. There are firsthand reports on how trade was
carried out.

After cacao, slaves. An excellent market for slaves was in
Tabasco, where Xicalanco was located. It was here in 1518
that Cortes on his way to the conquest of Mexico was given
the famous woman Malinche, "The Tongue," later honored by
the Spaniards for her part in the taking of Aztec Tenochtitlán, with the title of Doña Marina. She was "from the
town of Paynama, 8 leagues from Cotzacoalcos in Tabasco,"
writes Bernal Díaz. Her father had been the chieftain of the
town. When her mother remarried, her presence was found
inconvenient and she was given into slavery.

Slaves (*ppentacob*) were big business and the Maya traf-
ficked widely in them. The basic cost of a slave was 100 cacao
beans. They were used for heavy manual labor, as fishermen,

* Trade credit was given, taken, and extended. Contracts were
oral—there were no written documents. Deals were closed by public
drinking, emphasizing "legality through publicity," a system of the
Maya. Yet failure to pay or dispute over oral terms often led to
wars.

paddlers, and cargo carriers. Women slaves helped to draw water, grind maize, and dye cloth. Men slaves had their hair cut short and were given ragged mantles to wear. Slaves can be seen in ancient Maya sculpture.

Since there was always an acute labor shortage in theocracies, slavery was practiced throughout the whole of classical antiquity. All great states in history—be they Egyptian, Hittite, Greek, Roman, English, Spanish, American, or in our time, German and Russian—had slaves. Slavery was accepted as a social institution throughout antiquity. There is no basis for the oft-given assertion that slavery impeded the use, development, and evolution of the machine. In Rome, free and slave worked together, and the manumission of slaves had much influence on business and politics whether it concerned a Greek philosopher like Epictetus, an Aztec chieftain like "king" Itzcoatl, or a Booker T. Washington in America. Among the Maya, the Spaniard, Gonzalo Guerrero, who was first a slave, rose to captain when freed. He led the Chetumal Maya against the Spaniards.

Maya traders, who were given a high status in their society, purchased slaves by the hundreds in Xicalanco. They were tied together, as Bernal Díaz saw them in Mexico, by their necks to long poles, "just as the Portuguese bring Negroes from Guinea." Slaves were often treated well and considered as part of the family. Yet when times were out of joint, that is, if it did not rain, they were sacrificed and pushed into the *cenotes*. At Chichén Itzá, their skulls have been dragged up "somewhat inordinately battered."

19. The Maya Market

The North Star was the protector of the travelers. Under it, loaded down with luxury goods, they converged at stated times on local Maya markets. Travelers *(ah ppolom yoc)* were expected to burn copal while moving over the roads. Merchants stopped at the rest houses used only for that purpose. They were expected to stay no longer than a single night or one trading day, and when there they paid for their own food and entertainment as part of "business expenses."

Concerning markets the only details that have come down to us are from northern Yucatán, where the Maya were mostly centered at the time of the Spanish conquest. Along the coast the market towns were many and included Cachi, Chaunche, and Ekab, the first Maya centers seen by the Spanish explorer Grijalva when he skirted the coast in 1518. Juan Díaz, chaplain of the fleet, remembered that Cachi, which he visited, "had a large market square and beside it was a building which houses the court where disputes were settled; it also had a place for execution for those who dealt badly in business." There they were summarily tried and summarily executed.

Of all the market places known to the Spaniards, Chichén Itzá was the greatest. This sacred city, with its sacred wells and imposing buildings of Maya-Toltec origin, was a place of pilgrimage with an extensive market. "Pilgrims came from foreign parts to trade as well as to worship. . . ." Within the court of the thousand columns of the Temple of the Warriors is a large area which Landa called the *mercado*. Open on four sides, it had a thatched roof supported by tall stone Doric-like columns, which still stand. There are also remains of a stone dais, on which the official sat to administrate sales and trading. In the open courtyard, squatting under white cotton awnings, men and women bartered the goods that they created in the surplus time allowed them by the cultivation of maize. In appearance it probably did not differ from the Aztec market so often described. Each product had its place. There was a section where fish, deer meat, and birds were sold. Cloth and cotton dealers had their precise area, as did those who traded in plumes, arms, and the other items of commerce.

The lords who had accumulated a surplus of maize, beans, shells, salt, and cotton, through tribute tax and "gifts," offered this in trade to other merchants who brought cacao, gold, obsidian, feathers, or jade—things they needed to uphold the dignity of office or adorn their persons. Local merchants traded their surplus for the things they had acquired in other lands, principally slaves and cacao. They did business in gross. The goods in turn were traded to the lower man, who then resold or traded them under the shadow of the cotton canopies.

It is strange that the Maya did not use their highly developed glyph-writing for writing contracts. It seems generally agreed so far as the Near East is concerned that trade, tribute, and taxes gave rise to the scribe, "that agent of its acquisition," and that writing was perfected out of the need for exact transactions. Some of the earliest writings left us are contracts in Hittite-written cuneiform, pressed into clay tablets and fired for permanence. If the Maya used writing for trade, evidence of it had disappeared by 1500. But the Aztec used their writing for this purpose. Books of tribute have come down to us. Bernal Díaz saw "great houses full of these books" on the coast of Veracruz and in Mexico itself.

"Cacao was the gold of this country . . . and it serves for money in the plaza . . . of Chichén Itzá," wrote Bishop Landa. The cacao tree grew on the periphery of Mayadom, for it had need of much rain and thick jungle loam. It is a thick-trunked, low-growing tree that produces oval pods the size of small papayas. The pods when matured are allowed to rot and the seeds ferment. Cacao seeds are almond-sized and -shaped and when dried in the sun they become dark, chocolate-colored, with a dry, parchment-like skin. It is these beans that were used as money. A rabbit was worth 10 cacao beans, a pumpkin 4, a slave 100 (the same amount of cacao that would make about 25 cups of chocolate), and so on. Maya public women, always about the markets, "gave their bodies for a price. . . . he who wants them for his lustful use can have a run for 8 or 10 cacao beans. . . ."

Cacao-bean money had its counterfeit. There were traders who cleverly took off the thick cacao skins, filled them with earth or sand, and mixed the spurious beans with untampered cacao. For this reason wily Indians always pressed each bean to make sure it was solid, just as elsewhere in the world people would bite a silver coin to see if it had been minted of lead. Cacao-bean counterfeiting was one of the offenses most frequently judged by the Maya courts.

There is little data on the revolving Maya *yaab* market. Among the Incas the *catu* markets were regularly held but staggered between cities so that the trader could have time to attend them all. In Mexico the Aztec *tiaquiz* market was always in motion and others were held about it at different times so that the merchant had time to make the rounds. Of the Maya practice we know little.

20. Festivals

The festivals were religious in nature. To the Maya, religion was man and man religion; much, if not all, they did had a magical or religious purpose.

The month of Pop, which would fall in our calendar in

July, was the Maya New Year. It was the time for renewal. They put on new clothes, destroyed their old pottery and fiber mats. There was a sense of new dedication. It was a solemn occasion.

Uo, the second month, was a period of festivals for all the special patron gods, those who served the fishermen,

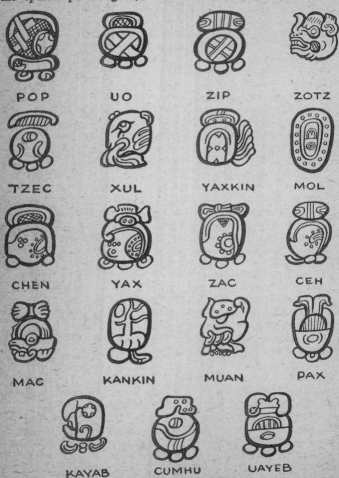

Fig. 21. The name-glyphs of the eighteen Maya months, including the five-day unlucky Uayeb period. Altogether, these totaled 365 days.

hunters, travelers, and so on. The Maya gods seemed innumerable to the Spaniards, for most gods had different aspects. Uo was the month of vocational festivals; it ended in drink, dance, and fornication.

Part of month five, Tzec, was the bee god's turn. All those who kept bees—and there were many—joined the festival. The object was obvious; they wanted to cajole the bee god into increasing the flow of honey. Honey, with its by-product, wax, was a trade item, and as mentioned earlier, the principal drink, mead,[44] was made of it. In these months all participants became uproariously, albeit ceremonially, drunk.

Xul, which fell in November, was the sixth month. This honored Kukulcan, the plumed-serpent god. In Chichén Itzá it was believed that he, or another of the same name, had rebuilt the sacred city and given it new laws. Rich gifts were exchanged. Featherwork, principally headdresses and shields and cloaks made of quetzal feathers, were displayed by the Maya lords in gala array. There were also processions of priests—and clowns. Although the ceremonies were most solemn, clowns carried on buffoonery; there was much burlesque.

So it went, month to month. Each had its special festivities. On Chen, the eighth month, new idols were finished, paid for, and presented. Yax was the renovation month. All over the land hunters made amends for shedding the blood of the animals they had killed. To the Maya all animals possessed soul force, and when they were killed the hunter had to show them respect. If this was not done, other animals of the same species as the one insulted would not allow themselves to be killed. So the feelings of the animals had to be humored and nothing done to offend them; antlers, jawbones, and wings were hung in the houses.

All festive months had dances prescribed for them. The month of Mac fell in April and part of May. It was the time of rains, so the choreography of the dance had to do with rain and crops. In the sixteenth month, Pax (so different in meaning from the Latin word!), war was celebrated. People poured in from all the smaller Maya settlements to the large ceremonial temple cities and there witnessed their *nacom*, the elected war chieftain, make obeisance to the god of war. He was carried in a litter. There were five days of dancing and drinking. Landa was horrified when he saw it: ". . . in the month of Pax the rites of which were paid by the wealthy, the Indians made wine-skins of themselves . . . and at the end of the five days the *nacom* were escorted back in their litter." Everyone (except the *nacom*, for whom it was taboo) got royally and ceremonially soused.

In the last three months of the Maya year, Kayab, Cumhu, and the five-day Uayeb there were also festivals, except that most pleasures were of a private nature. There was much drinking and—judging from the frequency with which it is discussed—considerable adultery. "They had no fiesta," says Landa in clerical disgust, "in which they did not get intoxicated, drinking a kind of mead into which a certain root was added by which the wine became strong and stinky."

The nobles gave many private parties. Those who accepted an invitation to one were expected to give one in return. On arrival each noble presented to the host a beautifully woven manta and a ceramic vase "as beautiful as possible." Food was offered in plenty—turkey, deer, duck, chocolate—and all were served by the most comely women. The guests separated in pairs or in couples of four, and dances were performed. Drink was brought by the cup bearers, who themselves were not supposed to get drunk. Women drank little, for they were expected to "get their drunken husbands home." There were scufflings and fights, and sometimes the "violation of conjugal rights followed," said the bishop, "the poor women thinking they were receiving their own husbands, whereas . . ."

21. Music, Dance, and Drama

Maya music was group music, and as with the Aztecs, percussion instruments were important. There were no string instruments in pre-Hispanic America, and music and song were one.

Drums gave the group a hypnotic feeling of oneness. The *tunkul* was an upright kettledrum, coming up to the beater's chest. It was made of a hollow log of light decorated wood, with a deer membrane stretched across it. It was beaten with the hands. Another rested on the ground and the drummer sat on it while it was beaten. A third was like the Aztec *teponzali*, horizontal and hollowed of wood, with two wooden tongues; it was beaten with "beaters tipped with rubber." If beaten when the wind was right, the drums could be "heard two leagues off." When dancing they held a small drum, called *pax*, "which they played with the hand and there was another drum made of hollow wood with a heavy, sad sound." Still another type of drum was made from the shell of the

Fig. 22. Maya music was percussional. In the center, the upright *tunkul* drum, to the left, musicians scrape the hollowed-out carapace of a land tortoise, to the right, gourd rattles. From the murals of Bonampak.

small land tortoise, the carapace carved and lacquered. This same type of tortoise drum is used by many other Mexican peoples. "They strike it with the palm," wrote Landa, "and the sound is doleful and sad."

The Maya also used an ingenious ceramic drum (called *huehuetl* by the Aztecs) shaped like two connecting vases; across one end was stretched a membrane. This type of drum still exists among the primitive Maya-speaking Lacandones, who called it a *kayum*. That it is very ancient is confirmed by its appearance in the Dresden Codex,[45] where an illustration shows musicians playing about the head of the corn god; one of them plays the *kayum*, and musical speech-scrolls pour from the mouth of the drum.

Trumpets were of various kinds. The large conch shells found abundantly in the waters off Yucatán were made into trumpets that emitted one full awesome sound and were used to call down the gods. Similar horns were used by the Incas as well as the Aztecs.

Trumpets carried "melody." The largest of them were of wood and ceramic, five feet in length. One can see these instruments painted on the murals of Bonampak. They were always made as twin trumpets and blown in unison, although each part was set in a different key.

Fig. 23. Trumpets were of wood, ceramic, or conch shell. Twin trumpets set in a different key always played together. Behind the trumpeters, the leader sets the beat with whistle and rattle. From the murals of Bonampak.

Flutes were of wide variety. The six-noted flute was made from a human leg bone, a deer's femur, reeds, or baked clay ("they had whistles made of the leg bones of deer—and flutes made of reeds"). The five-noted Panpipe, almost identical with the Old World type, was known to the Maya; it also was used extensively in South America. The place of its origin is unknown.

Bells of copper and of gold or silver, tied on legs, waist, or wrist, gave sound to the dancer's prance. There were *raspadores*, various grating instruments similar to those used widely in present-day Cuban music. These were made of bones—deer, tapir, or human—which, notched and ribbed, were grated by means of a stick. They gave rhythm for the dance. Archaeologists have found many types. In Monte Albán, 150 miles inland, was found one *raspador* made from the rib of a whale.

In the vivid murals of Bonampak there is depicted a twelve-piece orchestra. The music is scored for two matched ceramic trumpets, one kettledrum, three turtle-shell drums, and four musicians shaking gourd rattles. Music was ritual and sacred; all instruments were kept by the *holpop* official ("to his care the drums of *tunkul* are entrusted as well as the other musical instruments"). Punishment was meted out to those who did not keep time. The leader was the principal singer; he set the key and the rhythm. "This man they venerate."

There was no such thing as "pure" music. The song was a recital of "their fables and their lore," and the dance was in great part a ritual to cajole the gods into giving rain, sunshine, or whatever was needed at the moment. There were so many dances that an early Spaniard who witnessed some thought the Maya dance repertory could reach a thousand. There was a shield dance—presumably for warriors—who used their fighting shields as props; a monkey dance; a grandfather's dance-song; and one called "The Shadow of the Tree." [46] There was an erotic dance (*Nuaul*), called "bawdy" by a shocked friar. In one of the New Year ceremonies the dancers performed on high wooden stilts (an illustration of this appears in the Codex Tro-Cortesianus).

Fig. 24. A ceremonial dancer, representing a bird with extended feather "wings," holding rattle and banner. From the murals of Bonampak.

Landa saw 15,000 Indians come from miles around to attend the dances. There were two dances which he thought "worthy of seeing": *Colomche*, the Dance of the Reeds, was performed in a large circle of 150 dancers, who moved to the rhythm of drum and flute. At a signal from the leader two performers leaped into the center of the living wheel; one was the hunter, the other the hunted. The hunter threw rubber-tipped reed lances at the other, who caught them "with great skill." All the while the circle moved and kept time to the music. The other, which he does not name, was performed by 800 dancers carrying cloth, paper, and feather streamers. The choreography was a deliberate warlike step. They kept time (punishment was meted out if they did not), and danced the whole day without stopping, for food and drink was brought to them without breaking formation.

For the most part men danced with men, women with women. The only dance which men and women performed together was the one that Landa thought "not very decent."

Dance was a mystical communion between participants and the onlookers. The object of the dance was by group participation to gain victory over the unseen powers. To the Maya, drumming, singing, hand clapping, and ululation exercised a mystical influence. Formed a social bond in which they all felt in contact with the supernatural.

Dramatic presentations in which actors took part, their actions set to musical stresses, were also performed by the Maya. Landa tells us that "their players act with a great deal of wit," and one of the most learned of the Maya scholars unhesitatingly says that there were "professionals."

Stages were both indoor and outdoor. At Chichén Itzá in 1560, Landa saw "two stages built of stone with four staircases . . . and paved on top; here they recite their farces . . . and comedies for the pleasure of the public." These two-stage platforms, now restored, can be seen at Chichén Itzá. One is the "Platform of the Cone," a twenty-foot-high stage with four stone staircases on a direct line between the Pyramid and the *sacbe* roadway. It has a flat space on top for performances. The other referred to by Landa is the *Tzompantli* stage, decorated on all its sides with, as its name implies, stone-sculptured human skulls. It is in front of the Great Ball Court.

The actors were graceful, witty, and elegantly costumed; generally they were masked. This is confirmed by the murals of Bonampak, which show actors impersonating birds, animals, and sea life. One has his face incased in an alligator mask; another has the long tentacles of a crab. They seem relaxed, as if waiting their cue to enter the stage. Another has water lilies dangling from his earplugs (the water lily is the symbol for abundant earth) and yet another is a god-impersonator, wearing a mask with a *T* for the eyes (the *Ik* sign, symbol of fertility and germination).

This is pictorial confirmation of all that has been said of their cleverness, for the costumes were well made and imaginative. We can well believe Landa when he says that the actors had so great a wit and so wonderful a sense of mimicry that the Spaniards often hired them "to make jokes and burlesque of other Spaniards." Maya terms found in the old dictionaries show that there were humorous parts in their repertoire—parts for the parasite, the pot vendor, the cacao grower—which parodied phases of their own life and made fun of their own foibles.

To the primitive, the moment that an actor is masked he actually takes the place of the thing he represents. If he plays a god, he *is* that god. It is magic and magic "is a counterpoise to a state of unrest . . . really a waking dream," as Lévy-Bruhl pointed out in reference to other primitive societies.[47] "Life is a lying dream," says one of the characters in a Japanese Nō play, "he only wakes who casts the world aside."

Drama was all part of the collective hypnotism.

22. Games

Boys played at "beans" on a board something like our parcheesi, and they played the game of the young everywhere, hunter-and-hunted. Landa remembered that the children "never stopped going around with small bows and arrows and playing with one another." But the passion of the adult Maya—which they shared with most Indians from Nicaragua to Arizona—was the game played with a hard rubber ball and known to the Aztec as *tlachtli* (*Taxco* derives its name from it). The Maya called it *pok-a-tok*.

No one knows where the game began. Rubber came from Tabasco among the Olmeca Indians, who are believed to be precursors of the Maya, or at least contemporaneous with the cultural rise of the Maya. The word for rubber in Toltec was *olli*, and the Olmecas were called the "rubber people." All of the larger Maya temple cities that have been found have their ball court. Those who have visited the ruins in Mexico or those of Copán or Chichén Itzá will remember its appearance: long and rectangular in shape, like an *I*, with tiered seats on both sides for the spectators. In the exact middle on either side of the court, ofttimes as high as thirty feet from the floor, a stone ring is set, not horizontally as in basketball but vertically.

Because *pok-a-tok* was no longer being played by the Maya in Landa's time, we must fall back on a description

of the game as played by the Aztecs, written by the friar
Bernardino de Sahagun (who chronicled that people as Diego
de Landa did the Maya): "the balls were about the size of
bowling balls [i.e., six inches in diameter], and were solid,
made of a gum called *ulli* . . . which is very light and bounces
like an inflated ball." [48] In playing, both players and spec-

Fig. 25. The religious game *pok-a-tok*, played with
a rubber ball in the form of a basketball, was the principal sport. This is the immensely large ball court at
Chichén Itzá, 545 feet long by 225 feet wide. A ball is
aimed at the basket, which is "shaped like a millstone."

tators placed enormous bets, "gold, turquoise, slaves, rich
mantles, even cornfields and houses [which reminds one
that Cardinal Mazarin lost an entire château in a single play
of bezique]. . . . the court called *tlachtli*, 40 to 50 feet in
length with walls 9–10 feet high, had in the middle two
stones like millstones opposite each other . . . at other times
the lord played ball for his pastime . . . he also brought with
him good ball players who played before him, and other
principal men played on the opposite team, and they won
gold and *chalchiguites* and beads of gold, and turquoise and

slaves and rich mantles and maxtles and cornfields and houses, etc. [feathers, cacao, cloaks of feather] . . . the ball court . . . consisted of two walls, 20 or 30 feet apart, that were up to 40 or 50 feet in length; the walls . . . were whitewashed and about 8½ feet high, and in the middle of the court was a line which was used in the game. . . . in the middle of the walls, in the center of the court, were two stones, like millstones hollowed out, opposite each other, and each one had a hole wide enough to contain the ball. . . . And the one who put the ball in it won the game. They did not play with their hands, but instead struck the ball with their buttocks; for playing they wore gloves on their hands and a belt of leather on their buttocks, with which to strike the ball."

Though no such detailed description of the game as played by the Maya has come down to us, the *Popol Vuh* chronicle refers briefly to the sport:

"Let us play ball, said the lord of Xibalba.

"Then the lords seized the ball and butted directly at the ring of Hunahpu." [49]

Chichén Itzá had seven ball courts. The largest one, the greatest seen in any temple city in the Americas, is one of the exciting features of the site. It was built by the Toltec Maya and decorated with motifs derived from Tula, 800 miles away. It is 545 feet long, 225 feet wide, and the millstone "basket" is decorated with an open fanged snake, 35 feet above the playing field. It is so high, in fact, that the rule of the game cited by the friar—that the player could not use his hands, but only butt the ball through the "basket" with elbows or hips—cannot possibly hold for this court. As in Aztec Mexico, the Maya lords wagered high on the game, and if the player put the ball through the hole—a feat that seems rare enough—he had the right to demand as forfeit all the clothing and jewels of the spectators present.

With the Maya, as with present-day Americans, games were sometimes given more consideration than serious matters.

23. Crime and Punishment

The Maya "were governed by laws and good customs and they lived in peace and justice." That is the opinion of Torquemada. What is meant is that, while war was waged with other clans and tribes, there was still "peace and justice" among those living in the same tribe. There is no doubt that the Maya had a highly developed sense of justice—but definitely the form of justice meted out by a preliterate people. After 3,000 years or more of living within the same area, tribal mores had become dicta. What is done, *is* done; and what is not, is *not*. Any infractions of this brought retribution. It was executed rigorously. Crimes to the Maya were basic—theft, homicide, adultery, lèse majesté—and punishment often "fitted the crime," like being punished with like.

Theft, of course, was antisocial. Since all the clans within the tribe were of one blood, it was considered distinctly unethical to take something not of one's own. Maya houses had no doors, no locks, only a drapery or a string of bells to inform the owner that someone had entered. For theft the punishment was slavery. The thief had to "work off" the theft; or should his immediate relations feel the social defilement brought on by it, they paid off the debt. Second offenses could bring death. Theft perpetrated by any member of the directing classes brought disgrace; his face was scarred by deep tattooing and carried notice of his crime throughout life. There was no social atonement for theft. The thief did not pay "society," the Maya having no form of imprisonment except for sacrificial victims. The culprit paid the victim.

Even if accidental, homicide carried a death penalty—unless the relatives were willing to pay the victim's survivors. There was no such thing as accidental death; homicide was treated as willful murder. "The penalty of homicide," says Landa, "even when death was accidental, was to die in the snares set by the victim's survivors."

To their mystic mentality (this is true of primitives everywhere) there was no such thing as chance or accident; what we call "accident" was to them purposeful. It revealed that evil influences were at work even before the "accident" and that the intended victim had been "selected"; it was a sign of malignant influences. We acknowledge "accident"; they thought about the supersensuous realities of the incident.

Any form of death was defilement. The greater social uncleanliness came from the shedding of blood. The Maya had even to atone for the killing of an animal. That is why he hung up something of the animal and usually pierced his own tongue and/or penis and spread a few drops of his own blood over the recently killed animal. Killing an animal was the same as homicide, and anyone who took life and shed blood brought about social defilement; he was subject to tribal discipline.

Loss of property by accident was treated the same as if it had been caused deliberately. If an Indian knocked over another's beehive, he had to pay the owner. If it was proven that an Indian committed suicide because of blameful commission or omission on the part of another, the latter had to pay.

Adultery brought death. The only legal loophole was that one had to be caught *flagrante delicto*. If so caught, the wife's paramour was brought bound to the *holpop* judges, was heard, sentenced, and handed over to the "injured" husband—it being not so much a violation of virtue as of property. The adulterer was summarily executed by the husband,

Fig. 26. Justice was dispensed by the *holpop*, he-who-sits-at-the-head-of-the-mat. The mat (*pop*) on which he sat was the symbol of justice.

who "dropped a large rock on his head . . . from a great height." Or should the case involve the woman of a noble, the adulterer might have his navel cut open and his intestines pulled through it until he died (an illustration in one of the Maya codices shows an Indian being slowly executed in this manner). Among those of high rank, adultery was much detested because "there was no need," that is, the noble was polygamous and had ample women to satisfy his longings.

Crimes of malice were always satisfied with bloodshed. If complex, the case was heard by the *batabob*, the town rulers. Nothing was written down; everything was verbal. In complicated cases, speakers who took the part of lawyers were chosen and they "argued" the case. Accused and accuser alike brought "gratuities" to the judge. The Maya were talkative; a case could be prolonged by talk-talk for days. A suit, criminal or civil, might be so involved that it could run the gamut of sound, with complicated legal abracadabra such as Bridge-goose uses in the third book of Rabelais' *Pantagruel*.

24. Cures and Curers

Among the Maya, illness arose from a mystical cause. The one who cured disease and the one who brought it, *ah men*, were identical to their minds; "the physicians and the sorcerers . . . are the same thing," observes Landa.

Magic and medicine have always been bound together. One has only to call to mind the magical panaceas of the Middle Ages or, for that matter, some of the curatives of modern times to be made aware of this. Disease is caused by a someone rather than a something. It may be brought on by the malevolent influence of someone in the community, by someone who has broken a taboo, or by someone who failed properly to observe the rituals of life. This idea was interwoven into the deepest fibers of the Maya mind. The Maya was aware of the connection between disease and cure. Sacrifice—the tearing open of human bodies, the flaying of skins, the removal of skulls from the dead—had given the Maya some idea of anatomy and function, yet he was not able to turn this knowledge to account, for the Maya mind was orientated in another direction.

Illness, like death, was brought on by supernatural causes. When ill the patient called the *ahmen,* who diagnosed the malady by divination. He evoked the goddess of medicine *Ixchel* (who was also the goddess of pregnancy), placing her image before the patient. Copal incense was burned and tobacco smoke blown across the patient. The *ahmen* brought along the appurtenances of his trade, "the bundles of medicine." This fetish bundle might contain roots, jawbones, or anything that was deemed magical. The divine stones were rolled out in front of the patient to find the prognosis of the disease. Priests have been found buried with these *am*-stones. An illustration in a Maya codex shows an Indian tossing six stones, and in another there is a divination conference between two doctors. The patient had to combat the mystical forces which caused his disease with power of the same kind. Divination was, and still is, one of the accepted forms. After all, the Romans consulted chicken livers before battle to look for good augury and the Incas looked at the lining of llama stomachs for signs of good or ill fortune.*

Maya cures were effected by extensive questioning of the patient along mystical lines; and only after this, when the doctor believed he had found the cause, the physical cure began.

What were Maya diseases? There was asthma, rheumatism, stomach worms, and ankylostoma ("It is difficult to make love on an empty stomach," wrote Aldous Huxley, "and still more difficult to make it on a duodenum that is full of ankylostoma").

Pneumonia was frequent among Indians who were often soaked by the rains and later scoured by the winds. It was usually fatal. A Maya herbal, addressing the doctor, says: ". . . you will not be able to cure him of this because he will die vomiting." Malaria, termed "nightfever," was present; chills recurring every three days were the symptoms. Diarrhea and dysentery, which must have been endemic, are often mentioned. The Maya was subject to jaundice, cancer, tumors, and skin diseases of various kinds. Erysipelas was known graphically under the name of "hell eruption."

As the Maya diet was excessively starchy—beans and maize—they suffered from flatulence, vertigo, depression, nightmares, and epilepsy ("He is speechless and will fall," says the Maya herbal).

Yellow fever undoubtedly was present. Spider monkeys in the area about Tikal have been found to have it. It was called *cil*, "blood vomit." It appears historically about 1480, twenty years before the first Spanish contact with the Maya, and is mentioned in a Maya chronicle. "On 4 Ahau [1482] the pestilence, the general death swept over the land. . . ."

Syphilis is not described nor is there any disease mentioned by them that would seem to be syphilis (it is graphically described on Mochica pottery in Peru). The Maya do mention "a bubo of the groin" which arose when one "overcopulated."

Despite the generally good condition of Maya teeth—which women brought to early ruin by their custom of filing them to points, because it "looked well"—there was decay

* If one thinks that this is so primitive, he should think back on how long the tomato was regarded as a poisonous "love apple" and not eaten. The potato at one time was not accepted as edible because it was "liable to cause disease." In 1764 a Prussian edict signed by Frederick the Great forced it upon the Germans and then not as food but only as a source of starch.

and toothache. Said the Maya herbal: ". . . now to cure this, take the bill of a woodpecker. . . ." Teeth inlaid with jade have been found in graves. The inlaying was done not to fill cavities, but because it "looked well."

When bones were broken the patient got a specialist called a "bone-binder" (kax bac). The Maya seem to have been able to diagnose cancer. "There is a crab called ah buk . . . take its claws and powder them and apply this to the cancer . . . or else . . . [and the archaeologist should mark this well] powder a potsherd, which is not so bad. . . ."

No matter how advanced the Maya were in architecture, in working out their calendars, or in glyph-writing, regarding illness they were not much different from the most primitive of tribes. They did have cures and remedies and, in glyph-writing, "books" on astronomy, divination, prophecy, and incantations. It may be that among those hundreds that were destroyed there were herbals. It is true that there is none now extant comparable to the De la Cruz-Badiano Aztec herbal, written in 1552 by an Aztec who knew Spanish and Nahuatl (it was illustrated with pictures of the precise plants used in the remedies). None of the known Maya herbals, with which Ralph Roys worked to produce his Ethno-Botany of the Maya,[50] are much earlier than the eighteenth century. In his study of them Roys believed that the ah men doctors who survived the calculated massacre of Maya "intellectuals" had copied these from some glyph book and then dictated in spoken Maya.

Cures, as seen by the remedies proffered by the Maya herbals, were often worse than the disease. Many were sensible, some just ridiculous, and not a few, as will be seen, exceedingly harmful. Pleurisy, "extreme pain that attacks the ribs," could be relieved by drinking turkey broth, or balche mead containing the ashes of dog excrement that had been burned. Dysentery (kik-nak) was called rightly a "blood flux." For its cure an extended pharmacopoeia was offered: the sap of the rubber tree, a fungus, a euphorbia (which was perhaps better than anything else prescribed). Kik-nak was also cured by "taking the tender tips of the guava-plant mixed with the excrement of a dog, adding a little tapir dung as you boil it and after resting until dawn, adding a bit of honey." The herbal states that the kik-nak "will cease by these means." There is little doubt that the patient would cease also. Ta-kik-zok, blood in the feces, could be cured by putting a freshly killed bat into a balche brew. (As the blood-sucking vampire bat emits a bloody stool, one can see that here like was being treated with like.) The description of yellow fever, xe-kik, is given thusly:

*U cacale yitz xpomolche, chactez, u macil u capil kaxil-
koch, xtuzil, chac-kan-cab, chac-piliz-mo, chac-piliz, chac,
cicib, macap-lum huchbil, macoc zum, kankan u top y
kuxubcan y xanab-mucuy ukbil y cacal. U cacal xe tik tu
tamil ca chabac cincan y xcantacii y chilimcan y u yalaelel,
chacmuc y canchacche ak ca chacac hunppel akab ca ukue
lai ppiz y zappal yalil hun ppul cabin chacace.* Translated:
blood vomit.

The remedy includes the gum of a species of Jatropha,
the pith of the Cecropia, the *ix-tuzil* (moth), a certain reddish
earth, the feathers of the *chac-pillil-mo* (a certain small red
parrot), and of the Yucatán cardinal, the *macap-luum* ground
up with the *mac-oc,* yellow are its shoots, and the euphorbia.
The remedy is to be drunk.

An epileptic was described as a "man who falls to the
ground among the plants." The Maya herbal states that
"this is the cure for one who falls on the ground, waves
his arms and froths at the mouth . . . seek the horn of a
deer, powder it, drink it, or else the testicles of a cockerel
which has been shredded in cold water . . . if all this fails
. . . have him remove one sandal, urinate in it and drink it."
Nosebleed could be stopped by administration of a drink
made from various roots and plants, "but if this fails, then
the cure-doctor should bleed his foot." The nosebleed might
cease, but there may be another complaint, that is, "the
foot may continue to bleed."

There were ten types of scabies, *kuch,* and each was
treated with a different plant. The plant one used depended
on the type of scab. There was the contagious scab, the be-
hind-the-ear scab, and there was one that "looks like the
rectum of an old turkey hen." Smallpox was included by
the Maya among the types of scabies; it was called *cim-ex.*

Women had their problems which, then as now, were
usually combined with the menstrual period or pregnancy.
The Maya herbal stated that the type of womb "which
rises and falls and cuts off menstruation" was easily cured:
". . . an old leather sandal should be burnt under her nose,
or even better, the feather of a woodpecker." For delivery
the Maya women employed a midwife, *ix alanzah,* but if
there were complications she called in the *ah men.* "To
deliver the foetus which was already dead in the womb" it
was recommended that "the best was to take dog's milk and
mix it with *balche* mead and after she drinks it set a smoking
dish of coals under the woman so that it would reach her
inside womb to smoke her out."

There were frequent mentionings of infections of the
kidney (blood and pus in the urine) and gallstones. All this

suggests that the excessive drinking of *balche* took its toll on Maya health.

However, when the patient recovered from these diseases through the various specifics proffered by the doctor (which speaks more for the rugged Maya's constitution than for these un-Homeric simples stuffed down him) and his thoughts turned to love, the doctor could offer him one of several aphrodisiacs, such as the heart of a hummingbird or the testes of a crocodile (the headhunting Jivaros in the Upper Amazon extract, dry, and scrape the penis of a crocodile and offer it to a woman candidate in a bowl of manioc beer). As the average Maya was as libidinous as a two-toed sloth, he had need of it. They lacked sexual imagination, which is the only aphrodisiac; and Aldous Huxley, as we have seen, gave them up completely.

Finally, if one survived illness and cure, and escaped the witchcrafts which caused the illness, the successful doctor could change his role and become a sorcerer, *ah pul yaah,* and bring disease to the one suspected of causing the malady. He could return the disease and so parlay malevolence into death.

25. Death and Transfiguration

When death approached, the Maya feared it and wailed its coming. And why not? One always feels to excess the bitterness of any departure. After all, what is life but a succession of little deaths? We lose a little bit of everything hourly. The dying Christian should say, "Now I am going to live." Not so the Maya. Despite the fact that much of his waking life had to do with death and the appeasement of the dead, he did everything to stave it off. He was not too sure of a future life, and he believed only in the sensuous here and now. Thus he wailed.

"They have a great and excessive fear of death," said Bishop Landa, who after all was sure he would sit on the right-hand side of God; "all the services performed for their gods were for no other purpose than that they should give them health and life . . . when death occurred they wept the day in silence, and at night they wailed."

A dying man confessed to a priest in the same manner

as the dying Aztec, for confession was necessary to neutral-
ize the evil influences brought about by one's death. Dying
was a form of social defilement; it was an antisocial act.
It was individual, setting one apart from the clan wherein
all acts of life were collective.

Dead, a man was wrapped in a shroud, usually his own
manta. Into his mouth was placed ground maize, *koyem*,
with a few jade beads, "which they also used for money so
that they should not be without means to get something to
eat in the other life. . . ." The lower man was buried in the
hard-mud floor of his house with the things of his life; if
a fisherman, nets and harpoons; if a warrior, shield and
lance. All had pottery filled with drink and food, so "that
they should not be without something in the other life."
Time has caused all of this to disappear except the pottery, and it is on this pottery that the Maya archaeologist
depends in order to formulate a historical stylistic sequence
of Maya history.

Houses were abandoned after a generation of burials,
becoming in effect family shrines. The possessions of the
dead man were usually taboo, and most of them were buried
with him. "If he was a priest they buried with him some of
his witchcraft stones." A *chilan*, soothsayer, was often buried
with his "books" (Kidder found evidence of one so buried
at Kaminal-juyu, in Guatemala), which may account partially for the disappearance of many of these writings.

Very few well-preserved graves have been found. Nobles,
which included priests, were often buried in small stone-
lined vaults; they were laid out full length and surrounded
with pottery vessels. In A.D. 500 a chieftain at Kaminal-juyu
was buried in a sitting position along with two adolescents
and a child "elected" to be killed and sent with him into the
afterworld. Even his dog accompanied him, so as to guide him
to death's abode.

The noble dead were buried in the plazas of the temple
cities. In Chichén Itzá the high priest was found in a
sumptuously appointed stone-lined grave. Around what had
been his neck were baroque pearls brought back from
Venezuela by the seafaring Maya tradesmen. A chieftain's
tomb found recently under a temple at Palenque is as
elaborately splendid as anything found in the Old World.

In Yucatán, nobles were cremated and their ashes placed
in an urn (made of ceramic or wood) that portrayed their
features. Portrait statues were made of deceased "people
of position." The back of the head was left hollow and the
ashes of the dead placed in it. "They preserved these statues
with a great deal of veneration." The Cocoms, the dynasty

that ruled Mayapán toward the end of the "empire," devised
a unique burial; they decapitated their dead "and after
cooking [the heads] they cleaned off the flesh and then
sawed off half the crown at the back, leaving entire the front
part with jaws and teeth. Then they replaced the flesh
. . . with a kind of bitumen [and plaster] which gave them
a natural and lifelike appearance . . . these they kept in the
oratories in their houses and on festive days offered food
to them . . . they believed that their souls reposed within
and that these gifts were useful to them."*

The Greeks made similar burials at their tombs in Myrina,
where archaeologists have found mirrors, spatulas and
strigils, ornaments, diadems, cups, plates, and statuettes of
the lesser gods in baked clay. Both Maya and Greek suffered
from the same pious illusion. The living wanted to surround
the dead with the familiar objects amongst which their
lives had been spent, for finding it disagreeable to go alone
to the afterworld, the dead might wish to carry along the
living to comfort them. The dead had malice toward those
who still had the light of the day—so the living had to
propitiate them with living-comforts.†

The Maya believed in immortality and a form of heaven
and hell. Those who kept the rituals, that is, "the good,"
went to a place shaded by "the first tree of the world,"
and drank their fill of cacao under it. Where the others
went is not clear. The Aztec elaborated gods and places of
the underworld which in their complexity could have drawn
praises from a Greek himself. We do not know how closely
the Maya paralleled these concepts. The name-glyphs of the
nine Maya lords of the night and the underworld have been
identified (the Aztec had thirteen heavens and nine hells),
but remain unnamed. This is evidence that the Maya had,
like the Aztec, a vertical world, layers of heavens and hells
to which the dead souls journeyed. These afterlife dwelling
places had no moral significance. In the Maya mythology one
was not "rewarded," as in the Christian mythology, for
pious or useful acts. Where you went after death depended
more on what you were in life than on what you did. Warriors, fishermen, priests, mothers who died in childbirth,

* Landa was confirmed when archaeologists dragged up from the
sacrificial *cenote* of Chichén Itzá a skull with the crown cut away,
just as he described it, with remains of the plaster and wood that
had given the skull a lifelike appearance.

† This primitiveness of giving the dead the best of everything
is reflected in the advertisements of present-day morticians—those
burying beetles of mankind—who stress the disintegration of wooden
coffins underground and insist on the need for "eternal protection" in
cement sarcophagi: "Don't let this happen to your loved ones."

all went to that departmentalized heaven or hell where their tutelary genii lived. Suicides went to their own heaven; they were sacred. They even had their own goddess, Ixtab. Depicted as hanging from a halter, she can be seen thus illustrated in the Dresden Codex.

As everywhere, the survivors had their taboos. They were socially defiled; by the clan custom they must keep the rituals or the dead would come back and claim something from the living. Privations of various kinds were imposed upon them. Her husband's death made a widow "unclean," and so long as the tie to the dead was unsevered, the uncleanliness persisted. As for the dead, they were occupied with getting out of life into death. Martin Luther remarked that he envied the dead because they rest. He was wrong. The dead have much to do—they prepare life.

Thus went the daily round of life (and death) of the Maya lower man. He was the taxpaper by whose tribute in work service the temple cities were built. Above him were the directing classes: the town councilor, the *batab* who collected the tribute, the governor who "sat-at-the-head-of-the-mat," the *chilan* soothsayer, the war chief; and highest of all, the hereditary leader—both high priest and great lord, functioning like a baroque archbishop—an embodiment of temporal and secular power, the "true man,"* the *halach uinic* who sat at the very pinnacle.

* Who bears no relation to another recent ruler of similar name.

26. The Maya Lords

At the head of the Maya city-state stood the *halach uinic*. He was *the* man, the "real" man, the "true man," endowed with plenary powers and restrained only by a council who were presumably related to him by blood ties. He was absolute and, as in all theocracies, a demigod. When one of these lords met the Spanish conqueror Montejo in 1542, even though his lands were laid waste he was still carried on a litter and surrounded by an imposing retinue.

A Maya *halach uinic* surrounded himself with suffocating ritual. He was, said the Spaniards, trying to define him, "the [state's] father, lord and *halach uinic* . . . which in our language is Great Lord. . . . They were absolute and what they ordered was carried out without fail."

Like other demigods the Maya lords were given an obeisance of humility by their inferiors. This was similar to the Aztec practice; when a chieftain entered Moctezuma's presence, "he had to take off his rich mantle and put on others of little worth . . . to enter barefoot and not look at his face." The Inca lord was of so exalted a position that all who came before him, even rulers of vast provinces, had to put a symbolical cargo on their backs, as if they were the lowest of Indians.

The Maya lord wore the breechclout, and it was superbly embroidered. The wealth of information on this has been minutely analyzed.[51] His skull was flattened so that it reached a narrow peak at the top, and his face was tattooed, actually scarified. He remodeled his nose with putty, making it a hooked beak to "conform with the concept of beauty." The prominent nose is the dominant feature of many stone bas-reliefs.* Hair was allowed to grow long and into it

* At Yaxhilan, Palenque, and Tomb Stela 9 at Oxkintok, Yucatán.

1. Temple I in the Great Plaza at Tikal. Tikal was the largest as well as one of the oldest of Maya cities. Its first recorded date is A.D. 416. These are eight large temple pyramids, but Temple I soars 229 feet. The ruins are now being restored by the University of Pennsylvania.—© *George Holton*

2. Carved, dated lintels of sapota wood, found in Temple III at Tikal. To the left, the face of a god above a Maya glyph: to the right, a part of a woven *pop*-mat, a symbol of authority. Pop was also the first month in the Maya calendar.—© *George Holton*

3. This stela is one of the twenty sculptured time-markers at Tikal; the other sixty-three are plain. It is believed that the first stelae were either painted or stuccoed.—*Victor W. von Hagen*

4. One of the four stairways of the Pyramid of Kukulcan at Chichén Itzá. While restoring the pyramid, archaeologists of the Carnegie Institution found that it was built over an older, inner one. The original pyramid contains a startling life-size jaguar with jade spots.—*Victor W. von Hagen*

5. The Pyramid of Kukulcan at Chichén Itzá in Yucatán. Chichén Itzá was founded by Itzá-Maya emigrants from central Mayadom in the fifth century, and was occupied by the Toltecs between the tenth and thirteenth centuries, during which time this pyramid was built.—*Victor W. von Hagen*

6. The building called the Monjas in the Nunnery Triangle at Chichén Itzá. It is south of the main group, in what is regarded as the older part of the city. The structural features are typical of Puuc architecture. The same motifs appear in Uxmal, Kabah, and other Maya sites far removed from Chichén.—*Silvia von Hagen*

7. The Temple of the Warriors at Chichén Itzá. It is so called because of the hundreds of columns with carved warriors. The temple is a copy, in all of its main features, of the Toltec temple at Tula, Mexico, 800 miles northwest of Yucatán.—*Silvia von Hagen*

8. The Palace of the Governor at Uxmal. It is 320 feet long, 40 feet wide, 26 feet high, and rests on an artificially raised triple terrace that is 50 feet high. It covers five acres of ground, and was probably the administrative center of the city-state of Uxmal, which included many other sites, some known, some lost.—*Victor W. von Hagen*

9. Frederick Catherwood's drawing of the north façade of the Nunnery Quadrangle at Uxmal. It is done with warmth and fidelity. The original is at the Museum of the American Indian, New York. Stephens stated that Catherwood made enough architectural drawings of Uxmal to erect a city just like it. Unfortunately, most of these have been lost.

10. Maya pottery from the Copán area in Honduras. This is cruder and less sophisticated than most Maya pottery.—*Victor W. von Hagen*

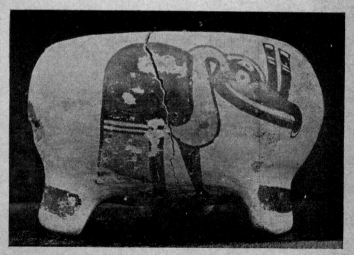

11. The ceramics of Copán, contemporaneous with the building of the Maya city called the "Alexandria of the Maya world," does not reflect its grandiose architecture.—*Victor W. von Hagen*

12. Left, the sculptured profile of the sun god carved in low relief. This was found in the debris about the court of the Hieroglyphic Stairway at the ruins of Copán.—*Victor W. von Hagen*

13. Above, a grotesque head of a serpent god. It is one of the two similar figures which guard the approaches to the Hieroglyphic Stairway at the ruins of Copán.—*Victor W. von Hagen*

14. Copán is famed for the majesty of its stelae. This is Stela P, erected in A.D. 623. — *Victor W. von Hagen*

15. The obverse side of a stela at Copán, showing how hieroglyphics, which give the dates of its erection (and other details that still escape the scholar), are placed inside a curving mass of feathers.—*Victor W. von Hagen*

16. A carved stone figure of a man in Maya headgear and cotton armor, from Ti'ho (now Mérida, the capital of Yucatán). Ti'ho, site of the Spanish capital, was used as a quarry. This is one of the few identified remains of the great Maya city.—*Victor W. von Hagen*

17. Detail of Plate 16, showing the individual character a sculptor could give a figure, even though it was carved in porous and friable material such as Yucatán limestone. The carving was done with stone celts. — *Victor W. von Hagen*

18. The gateway and the building presumed to be the priestly residence, at Labná. This impressive site lies ten miles beyond Sayil. The architecture is Puuc in character. The fret above the doorways is also found at Kabah, Uxmal, and Chichén Itzá.—*Victor W. von Hagen*

19. On the Maya road between Sayil and Labná are the ruins of Xlah-pak. The long-nosed rain god adorns the sides of the building. —*Silvia von Hagen*

20. The corbeled arch at Kabah, first found and described by John Lloyd Stephens in 1842. Now restored by Mexican archaeologists, it stands isolated on an elevated stone terrace. The road from Uxmal to Kabah passed through the arch.—*Victor W. von Hagen*

21. Chac, the long-nosed rain god (the nose is broken here), as seen on a façade of the ruins of Sayil in the Puuc of Yucatán.—*Victor W. von Hagen*

22. Sayil (circa A.D. 850) is five miles north-east of Kabah. It has one imposing building, Casa Cerrada, with Doric-like pillars. In the hills beyond Sayil are other structures, as yet unexplored.—*Victor W. von Hagen*

23. Maya sculpture, from a slab found at the ruins of Jonuta, state of Campeche, Mexico. The purity of line, done in low relief, shows the sureness of the fine Maya hand. The head of the kneeling figure has been artificially flattened, the eyes reveal the epicanthic fold, and the scraggly beard suggests an old man. The figure of the parrot is very lifelike (an unusual Maya feature). —*José Limón*

24. A Jicaque Indian of Honduras. The Jicaque lived adjacent to the Maya and had commerce with them. They are the only people, with the exception of the Maya-speaking Lacandones, who continue to live in their traditional way in Central America.— *Victor W. von Hagen*

were braided various ornaments. Ears were perforated and gradually enlarged, and enormous ornaments were passed through the lobe. (This custom recalls that of the Inca nobles, the "Big Ears" whom the Spaniards called *Orejones*.) The nose septum was pierced and a jade ornament passed through the perforation. The left side of the nostril was perforated and kept open by wooden plugs, replaced on festive occasions with a topaz that the Spaniards called "amber."

Fig. 27. The ruling chieftain of the Maya was the *halach uinic*, the "true man," as pictured on the Bonampak murals. He is dressed in full costume with the symbols of office. From the murals of Bonampak.

The Maya's horror of empty space caused their art to be confusingly luxuriant; every part had to be covered with ornament. Their bodies were similarly treated; heads flattened, earlobes widened until they would admit a turkey egg, the nose perforated and artificially deformed, the eyes purposely made crossed, facial hair pulled out, teeth filed and inlaid with jade, face and body tattooed. Finally, even the penis was transmogrified; this was often so cut that the glans looked as beribboned as a tassel.

The Maya sported jade rings on their fingers and toes; wrists and ankles were cuffed with ornaments. Sandals were often as gaudy as their loincloths. The Maya lord put over his breechclout a long skirt, often ankle-length; sometimes the skin of a jaguar was attached to it. Belts had rows of small human heads, symbolical of course, but suspiciously like those *tsantsa* made by the headhunting Jivaros of the Upper Amazon.

The headgear of the Maya lord was monumental. Often it was as large as himself. The headpiece was a mask, symbolical of the rain god or the sun god, and carved of wood or made of wickerwork. On this framework there was elaborated a superb feather ensemble topped with swirling masses of iridescent green quetzal feathers.

He dressed differently for each of his various offices, religious, military, or civil; for each he carried a symbol of authority. As statesman he carried a scepter; and often he is depicted as carrying a shield (a symbol of the sun god). In his religious role he held a double-headed ceremonial bar of snake heads resting in hallowed arms. As war leader he wore a sort of body armor and carried lance and shield; sometimes he is shown standing on the body of a squatting Indian, a symbol of victory.

The glorious headdress of the Maya lord, the focus of his attire, was in contrast to the simple cloth "crown" worn by Moctezuma and a far cry from the "crown" of the Inca, which was a mere *llautu,* a sling worn about the head to which was added "royal fringe." The headdress worn by the Maya "true man" and his cohorts was often so elaborate that it is difficult to think of their moving through the jungle while wearing it. A scene in which headdresses are being made ready appears in the mural at Bonampak. Detachable feather ornaments, mounted on winglike wooden elements shaped like inverted *U's,* are attached to the belt of the Maya lord. The headdress is again as tall as he is and it certainly restricted normal movement.

Color was the outstanding feature of Maya costume. In fact, everything in their life, including themselves, was painted. Stucco ornaments were a riot of color. Even the great stone sculptures were colored (traces of the color still remain). They made no point of being drab. It was quite the same with the Greeks, who painted their sculptures in garish colors, a fact which came as a great shock to many modern scholars.

The *halach uinic* had one legitimate wife. Her title

is not known. He also had his concubines, although there are no figures as to their number. (Moctezuma had "many women as mistresses," and the Inca rulers had a ménage of royal concubines *(pallas)*; one of the last of the Incas had, in the male line alone, 500 descendants!) Whatever her title, the wife of the Maya lord was herself "lordly." She was held in high respect, as can be seen from the superb modelings in clay of women of the upper classes. In the Bonampak murals the wife of the *halach uinic* can be seen with head flattened and ears pierced, and wearing earrings and a necklace. Her hair is tied up and made into a swirling coiffure. A white *huipil* hangs off the shoulder, and a red stole is draped carelessly around her arms. Her hand holds a folding fan. So "modern" is her appearance—except for the flattened head—that she could walk right out of the murals, which were painted in A.D. 800, and take her place in modern society. There is a queenly aura about her.

The office of the Maya *halach uinic* was neither elective like the Aztec, nor selective like the Inca, but hereditary. The office descended from father to son. "If the lord died . . . it was the eldest son who succeeded him." However, if the sons were not fit to rule, a brother of the ruler became head of state; and if none were available for succession, a capable person was chosen by the council, probably a relative of the late lord, with the same patronymic. Such methods of succession were also employed in the valley of Mexico.

Of the precise functions of this "man of the greatest importance" we have no more than a philologist can ferret out of the scant factual material that exists. For the period from 2000 B.C. to A.D. 928 we have nothing other than the interpretation that each scholar wishes to make of what he *feels* that he sees on the sculptured monuments. From A.D. 1000 until the first appearance of the Spaniards in 1502 we have records of a sort, that is, verbal recitative history with Maya glyphs used as mnemonics—and later an interpretation by the men of conquest and the men of God of what they believed to be the order of things. The personal equation is never missing. There is no such thing here as impartial history, for each orders and interprets events according to his own idiosyncracy.

What seems to be fairly clear, however, is this: the functions of the "true man" were as a leader, spiritual and temporal, of a given territory within a Maya city-state. There were many such in Mayadom before A.D. 1000. "They were ruled not by one head, but by men," wrote Diego de Landa. It was not until Mayapán functioned, after A.D. 1200, as "kingdom of the Maya" that one *halach uinic* controlled a great number of cities and geography. "The Kingdom of Yucatán which extends for a length of three hundred leagues [approximately 1,000 miles] was not only filled with people but was ruled by individual lords . . . they were governed by laws and good customs . . . which is a proof of good government. This was aided a great deal by the fact that they were all of one tongue. And this is a cause of not a little wondering that such a large race and so widely extended, stretching for so many leagues, should be understood with one single language."

Fig. 28. Detail of Maya *batabob* conversing over a fill-dish. Highland Maya from the Nebaj vase, Chixoy Valley, Alta Vera Paz, Guatemala.

First this *halach uinic* was executive of his own city-state. The head chiefs of other towns allied to his were *ahau*, or, since the word is more dominant, *batabob*. They were local governors of territorial divisions. The lord laid down his extratribal relationship or "foreign policy" through them. They were more than likely related to him by blood ties.

Batabob were "they-of-the-axes." One might almost find the title equivalent to the modern slang term "hatchet-men." They carried out the upper-man's orders with force, if need be. A *batab* was responsible first for the well-being of his own resident city. He had a staff of bailiffs or deputies to aid him. However, there was a town council composed of chiefs from the various subdivisions of the town, who though nominally under him had a veto power on his actions. These councilors were called *ah cuch cabob*. To explain the power and the functions of the council, a Spaniard wrote: "Next in

order were the town councilors . . . of whom there was said
to be two or three; each had his vote like an official voting
in a municipal government in Spain and without his vote
nothing could be done. . . ." The council then had direct
contact through the clan heads with the lower man. The
arbitrary powers of the governor were held in check by these
means.

A *batab* had much discretionary power. He was held in
awe much as a viceroy would have been. The office was hereditary and the functions were judicial and military. Manpower

Fig. 29. *Batabob*, the functional officials in the hierarchy, concerned themselves with administration and the
collection of tax tribute. From the Bonampak murals.

was raised on a selective proportional basis to build temples,
roads, or residences for the nobles. The *batab* settled disputes in judicial matters, usually contract violations and
land disputes, if the disputants belonged to his own administration, otherwise it went up to the "true man." When the
priests made known their oracles as to when the people should
sow, reap, or make merry, the *batab* saw to it that the
functions were carried out. In time of war, although he was
de facto head of the province, actual command was in the
hands of a war captain (*nacom*) elected for three years,
but when there was an all-out war, such as that against the
Spaniards, the *batab* was expected to—and did—appear at
the head of his army. When he traveled he was carried on a
litter and attended by a large retinue. The people were scattered to allow him passage, and cloaks were spread on the

roads for him to pass over. Women served him. He was attended by fan bearers who waved beautiful feather fans and beat the air to drive away the blood-sucking flies and exudate-loving bees. In short, he was treated as a demigod. When Captain Montejo visited the *batab* of Loche in Yucatán, during a lull in the battle, the Maya received him reclining à la Récamier, fanned and fawned upon by his flunkies. He spoke to the Spaniard through a cotton cloth curtain suspended between them.

There was enough bureaucracy to satisfy the most exacting—governors, bailiffs, war captains, and so down to the very lowest, the *tupil*, a kind of constable.

All these were of the upper classes and nontaxable.

The state's, or rather the *halach uinic's* income to maintain all this was derived from the food tax, produce tax, and work service performed by the lower man. Each inhabitant of village, town, or city-state, collectively or singly, contributed maize, beans, chili, poultry, deer, honey, wood, wax, copal, cloth, salt, fish, jade, or whatever he produced. There are no records of Maya contributions such as are available for Aztec history. However, one known record tribute is enough for example. One small village, Tahdziu, of twenty households, paid an annual direct tax to their lord of twenty loads of maize (approximately 1,200 pounds) and twenty turkeys. If one then considers a city-state of 50,000 people, the amount of tribute tax is considerable. The chieftain then traded this in the gross through merchants for cacao or slaves, which in turn were retraded in the local markets for feathers, jade, and later in Maya history, gold and silver.

There are no details of the court that surrounded the *halach uinic*. The Spaniards have left word pictures of Moctezuma attended by a concourse of lords, wives, and concubines; of a table where he ate like some grand vizier; of retinues of servants who attended chieftains from other lands and how these chiefs and their wives and concubines "filled two or three courtyards and overflowed into the street"; of how the royal aviary had ten large pools of water and was attended by 150 people. Of the Inca who lorded it over Peru we have exquisite details—of his life, concubines, royal will; of the thousands who attended him; of his clothes, woven of the finest vicuña, which were never donned more than once.

If the Maya *halach uinic* led a similar existence and was similarly attended, we must be content to surmise it. The stone monuments and painted murals suggest it, but that is all. The Maya glyph-writing, which was intricate enough to count the steps to the moon, is silent on the details of their lives.

27. Government: City-State and Village

How did such a theocracy function? Diego de Landa thought it functioned very well. "Before the Spaniards had conquered that country, the natives lived together in towns in a very civilized fashion. They kept the land well cleared of weeds, and planted very good trees. The manner and order of their towns were as follows—in the middle of the town were their temples with beautiful plazas; all around the temples stood the houses of the lords and the priests, and then came the houses of the most important officials. Next were the homes of the rich men, and then those who were held in the highest estimation of the merchants. At the outskirts of the town were the houses of the lower classes."

The theory of most archaeologists is that the Maya city "was not a city at all in our sense of the word because it was a ceremonial, not an urban center." There is indeed little archaeological evidence of Maya cities; most of the buildings found are temples, pyramids, and ceremonial structures. Dwellings were built on clay platforms and made of perishable materials, wattle and daub and thatched with straw. These were obliterated by the centuries of cultivation about them. However, among those towns of the highland Maya recently studied—[52] which have been subject to less destruction than those in the humid areas—there are those that do show an urban Maya pattern. Of the hundreds of sites that were surveyed (dates range between A.D. 300 and 1200), these reveal the essentials of town planning. Whether the town conformed to the terrain or to the caprice of the builder, it contained certain common features: the central ceremonial court, surrounded by a large plaza where markets were held, and in the following echelon were the houses of chiefs, priests, and the other functionaries—and after them the houses of the common people. A ball court, if not part of the sacred precincts, was close by. A. Ledyard Smith, in his survey, found these sites "with buildings arranged in orderly fashion and orientated with each other." So that archaeology agrees in general with Diego de Landa's description of the form and function of a Maya city. In their theocratic spirit the Maya were similar to the absolute monarchs of the European baroque, who were aware of the emotional interplay between a monument of enormous dimensions and a

parade street. Absolutism and enormous plazas belong together.

The immense city-states built by the Maya presuppose a
high degree of social organization. A city structure must be
planned. Manpower has to be organized and close at hand
if the buildings are elaborate, as most Maya temples were.
Artisans had to be trained and available. The earliest and
the greatest of Maya cities was Tikal. It is so immense that
its full size has not yet been determined. At present it is
calculated to cover over 25 square acres of jungle. The great
court, lying roughly in its center, is 400 by 250 feet in size.
About it are its tallest pyramids, the largest of which towers
259 feet above the plaza. There are many other such and
hundreds of structures, from small plazas to enormous
reservoirs, broad causeways, ball courts, and a still undetermined number of lesser monuments. Each of these large
pyramids contains something like 200,000 cubic meters of
filling. It would require something like 100,000 man-hours
merely to place the core. The number of skilled artisans
needed to cut and lay the stone, to plaster, carve, and cast,
is not readily calculated. Tikal consists of 40 large structures
and 200 lesser ones. How much manpower was needed to
raise these immense piles in a hostile jungle is incalculable,
especially when it is remembered that the Maya had neither
metal instruments nor dray animals. Moreover, there was
presumably no professional labor force, since every man was
a craftsman of lesser or higher degree.

The Maya temple city was a civil as well as religious center.
It was *le fait urban,* a townscape with buildings.[53] The
reason one finds no evidence of "city" at such sites as
Copán, Tikal, and Palenque is that the dwellings were made
of very perishable materials and have vanished, leaving
nothing behind except the remains of postholes. To find and
to outline such a city is a laborious and often unrewarding
archaeological labor, but to argue that such a city as
Tikal could have been built by a people whose houses were
scattered at random throughout the jungle, miles from the
center, provides no idea of how the cities were erected or
how such a society functioned.

Mayapán was the only known organized Maya capital.
The evidence of its existence is authentic—a written glyph
history, a long tradition, and the proof offered by archaeological excavation. As it is the only Maya site that has all
these, it is the site that one must examine to form some idea
of the structure and function of the Maya city. Founded by
Kukulcan in A.D. 987 after the Maya-speaking Itzás had
taken possession of Chichén Itzá and the surrounding

areas, Mayapán gave its name, which means "standard of the Maya," to the league of city-states in which it was, according to tradition, associated with Chichén Itzá and Uxmal. The league probably controlled much more than this. A Spanish report states that Mayapán "conquered all these provinces," and time and exploration in this area will reveal through the roads that lead to Mayapán that it was specifically erected for the purpose of controlling most of the north of Yucatán. The towns, villages, and city-states controlled by the league were so many, said Diego de Landa, "that the whole land appeared to be one town." In 1194, as victor in a war with Chichén Itzá, Mayapán became the major power in northern Yucatán.

There had been a previous settlement at Mayapán, but its name is not known. Since the "natural Maya lords" had warred with one another for a thousand years over slave-raiding expeditions, it must have been difficult to determine where among the three cities the League of Mayapán should place its capital; presumably the old site was chosen to avoid squabbling. The availability of water must have been inviting; within the walled enclosure have been found at least nineteen usable *cenotes*. Around the city was built a wall of dry-laid stone over 12 feet in height, from 9 to 12 feet in thickness, and 5½ miles long. It had 9 formal entrances; the gates measured between 3 and 6 feet in width and so were easy to defend. The area within the city has been calculated to have been 2½ square miles. "In the center of Mayapán they built a pyramid, which is like that of Chichén Itzá (except that it was smaller)." Archaeology has confirmed Landa's statement. The four stairways of the pyramid were oriented in the four cardinal directions.

The houses of the principal nobles were located close to the central plaza. In fact, all of the "natural lords" of the country were obliged to build a house within Mayapán and dwell therein for certain seasons of the year. This was similar to a custom of the Inca; when they conquered new territory the chieftains were required to reside in Cuzco to ensure their loyalty.

Mayapán was divided for administrative purposes into four quarters, corresponding to the cardinal directions. It had its markets, its officials, and even a system to care for the socially unfit. "It was the custom to seek in the towns for the maimed and blind and there they supplied their needs." An early Spanish report said that Mayapán, "walled in like those cities of Spain, had within sixty thousand dwellings." A modern survey by Mr. Morris Jones reveals more than 3,500 houses, but to account somewhat for the discrepancy between the two estimates, there have been 400 years of tree growth and destruction. Moreover, the modern calculation was made from an air survey. Take then the 3,500 houses; this would presuppose a population of over 20,000 inhabitants. As it was, there was overcrowding. The Maya informants of Diego de Landa told him—since the city had been destroyed and abandoned only in 1441, the information was still unclouded—that the governing lords "ordered that houses should be constructed outside of the walls."

In each house a Maya kept his *caluac*, a sort of major-domo, who made himself known by a wand of office which he sported when he went to the center of the city "for what was needed . . . birds, maize, honey, salt, fish, game, cloth and other things because each of these houses outside of the walls was, as it were, the office of his lord." The merchants, a rising new class within the Maya realm (the class was unknown to the Incas), also had their houses there. As in all urban societies, the dollar patricians tended to move into the orbit of the upper classes.

The "lords of Mayapán held the entire country in subjection and the natives of it were tributary to them. All the citizens and inhabitants who lived within the walled enclosure of Mayapán were exempt from tribute tax and in it dwelt all the nobles of the land . . . . the lands were held in common so that between the towns there were no boundaries or landmarks . . . salt beds were also held in common [which bears out the author's contention that the League of Mayapán extended beyond the three cities] in those provinces on the northern seacoast which supplied all the inhabitants of the land."

During the two and a half centuries that Mayapán functioned as a capital, its administrators were appointed by the *halach uinic*. Selection of qualified men was based on some sort of examination. It was called "the interrogation of the chiefs" and occurred every katun, that is, every twenty years. A candidate had to offer proof of his legitimacy, his nobility, and that he knew the traditions and the occult knowledge known as the "language of Zuyua." In this way there was a weeding out of misfits. However, most offices were hereditary. "The lords appointed the governors and if they were acceptable they confirmed their sons in office," so that the office of *batab* became in time like the Italian *podestà;* it was *de facto* hereditary.

Mayapán then, had all the elements, geographical and political, of an urban organization. Moreover, it is not even unique. Tulum is a walled city which lies on the open sea; it was Mayapán on a smaller scale and dates from the "Old

Empire." Another walled city, Xelha, lies a few miles farther north on the same coast. It also antedates Mayapán and was connected with the interior city of Cobá by one of the longest and best-known causeways. Cobá itself dates from the "Old Empire." However modified in some ways by the Toltecs, the idea of the city as shown by Mayapán is doubtlessly Maya.

Mayapán did not have the ordered beauty of Chichén Itzá. It is considered to be "sad degeneration" of the latter; the stones are roughly dressed and the masons covered up the casual construction with stucco. The Castillo is almost a replica of the one at Chichén Itzá, except that the former is smaller. The citizens of Mayapán built four rounded structures therein, fashioned somewhat like the famed Caracol at Chichén Itzá (which is presumed to have been a form of astronomical observatory), and there are remains of a long colonnaded hall as at the Temple of the Warriors in the more famous city. However, it is not worked stone but plaster. The word "decadent" has been applied to it by some archaeologists. The fine Puuc architecture—which includes Uxmal, Kabah, and Sayil—is also sometimes referred to as "decadent." They are different, not decadent. There is nothing in the records that allows so moralistic an appraisal of Mayapán as has stirred the otherwise judiciously calm Dr. Eric Thompson.

Though founded very late in Maya history, Mayapán is as "early" as the capitals of the other theocratic Sun Kingdoms of America. Cuzco, the celebrated capital of the Incas, was not such before 1100, and the island capital of the Aztecs, Tenochtitlán, was not even founded until 1325.

In about 1450 there was a revolt that destroyed Mayapán. A chieftain named Ah Xupan, who was of the important Tutul Xiu family (the rivalry between the two families contending for Mayapán, Cocom and Tutul Xiu, is reminiscent of the struggles between the Guelphs and the Ghibellines that was occurring about the same time in Italy), raised the revolt on the pretense that the rulers were not "natural lords" and that they were selling Yucatec Maya as slaves to the Aztecs. The revolt was planned when all of the ruling family was present in the confines of the walled city. There is a record of the fall of Mayapán that tells of the "fighting with stones within the walled fortress-city." It was a live and throbbing tradition when the Spaniards arrived fifty or more years later, and there is a murky echo of it in deep and powerful poetry.

This is the pronouncement of 7 Ahau.
This was when there occurred the death of Mayapán.

Evil is the pronouncement of the Katun in its great power. . . .

Thus it reoccurred when the great priest Chilam Balam painted the aspect of the Katun 8 Ahau.*

Collective hatred is an easy thing to drum up. As Aldous Huxley says, "Hate is like lust in its irresistible urgency; it is, however, more dangerous than lust, because it is passion less closely dependent on the body . . . hate . . . has what lust lacks entirely . . . persistence and continuity."

The attack on Mayapán had just that sort of "persistence and continuity"; the walls of buildings were pulled down, and the statuary, principally of the god Quetzalcoatl, which most of the inhabitants seemed to have kept in individual shrines, was smashed. It showed the violence of the onslaught.†

It was the end of the only known capital of the Maya.⁵⁴

28. War and Weapons

Man has a double nature. There is scarcely any situation where man will not display, "simultaneously or alternatively," thinks Aldous Huxley, "repulsive characteristics combined with heroism." This dichotomy is nowhere more clearly shown than in the character of the Maya. They were master builders, and architects, carvers of wood and jade, potters of some of the finest and most sensitive ceramics in America, if not in the world. They were artists working in fresco and water colors; they were sculptors fashioning little clay portraits of extraordinary mastery in realistic handling of form and movement. They were aesthetes. They were astronomers

---

* Ahau is a period in the Maya calendar, 7,200 days (20 years). 8 Ahau ran from 1441 to 1460; within that time it is certain that the destruction of Mayapán occurred.

† John L. Stephens and Catherwood first observed Mayapán in 1841. No archaeologist thought much of Mayapán until Morley in 1938 made the first investigation. This was followed by Carnegie's "first team" under the direction of H. W. S. Pollock in 1952. A. Ledyard Smith and Karl Ruppert were assigned to study the houses and burials; Edwin Shook, now superintending Tikal, worked on and investigated pottery styles; Gustav Stromvik had charge of some restoration; Robert Smith worked on pottery sequences. Tatiana Proskouriakoff worked on mapping and architectural restorations. The data still await publication.

of no mean sort, who charted the course of the planets and formed a calendar which in precision was better than that of either Greek or Egyptian. They were builders of roads, the finest form of communications the Americas knew (outside of Peru) until 1800. And they were seafarers of unusual courage, trader merchants with far-flung interests.

They were also warriors; "for any little cause they fought." "They never knew peace," said a chronicler, "especially when the corn harvest was over." The old myth of a peace-loving people passionately dedicated only to erecting dated monuments, tracing the planets in their flight, and preoccupied with writing complex glyphs, has been fully exploded. At every turn the scholar is confronted with sculptures showing Maya lords sitting on the necks of slaves, of battle captives being seized by the hair. The murals of Bonampak bristle with the sound and fury of battle. Yet one reads again and again about the peace-loving Maya. This has the odor of exquisite archaism.

Fig. 30. The farmer was both agriculturist and warrior. There were no professional soldiers as war was of short duration. War dress was magnificent. From the Bonampak murals.

War was continuous. It could not be otherwise. There were contending city-states with no set boundaries. Farmers by the very nature of their agriculture moved back and forth in trespass. Commerce was carried on, then as now, at friend or enemy's expense. Slaves were important, and the only way to get them was in battle. Victims were needed for sacrifice, since an individual was not expected to immolate himself for the gods if someone else was available.

The war chief, *nacom*, was a professional. There were two.

The office of one was hereditary and dealt with sacrifices. The other was a military leader elected or chosen for three years, and held in "high honor." During this time he could neither drink nor have traffic with women. The *nacom* had to conduct the war festival during the month of Pax (beginning the 12th of May). At this time "they bore the *nacom* about on a litter in great pomp, perfuming him with copal smoke

Fig. 31. The *nacom* (*right*) holding judgment over prisoners of war. There were two such war chiefs—one was permanent, the other was elected for a three-year period. From the Bonampak murals.

as if he were an idol." Armies were gathered in the villages and towns. Every able man who knew how to use bow and arrow and lance was liable for service. The *ah holpop*, a town official, raised the troops. There was also a trained group, called *holkans*, who acted as mercenaries; they were led into battle by their own captains and "guided by a tall banner they went out in great silence . . . and when upon those marked for attack . . . with loud cries and great cruelties fell upon the unprepared enemy."

In present-day military terms, the Maya, especially the

"Old Empire" Maya, were lightly armed. Their primary weapons were the spear, the obsidian-edged war club (called *macuahuitl* by the Aztecs), and the spear-throwing *atl-atl,* the last a very effective weapon as Bernal Díaz confirms ("our captain was wounded in no less than twelve places by these arrows"). For close-quarter fighting they used a broad-bladed flint knife and a three-pronged claw knife, made out of a large shell, that could work havoc. Slings (*yuntun*) were used; there is extant a sculpture showing a warrior carrying into battle a basket of stones the size of hen eggs.

The *nacom* died gloriously. No knight went into battle more panoplied than he. His wooden headgear had a magnificent stream of quetzal and parrot feathers cascading over his shoulders, his face was gaudily painted and his jade bracelets and necklaces flashed like emeralds under the Maya sun. A marked man in battle, he was its primary object. When he was captured, his warriors usually fled—and he was sacrificed.

War, although continuous, was waged in relatively short battles. The Maya were at the mercy of their logistics. Women prepared the food (corncakes, maize gruel), and porters carried it on their backs "for want of beasts of burden." Wars often occurred in October when the farmer-soldier did not have to work his cornfield and the granaries were full. Surprise was the desired tactic. Where it could not be effected, as in the wide grass savannahs of Campeche, there were elaborate ritualistic promenades to overawe the enemy. If the land was high bush or jungle, tactical surprise was used. An attacking force sent out scouts—"road weasels," the Maya called them—to feel out a town's defenses. These might be barricades, wooden palisades, and pits dug on trails with spikes to impale the unwary. Barriers were erected in a semi-circular fashion and camouflaged. Larger cities were sometimes surrounded by a deep ditch as at Champotón or walled as were Mayapán, Tulum, Xelha, and others. The argument that the old Maya were not warlike because their cities were not walled lacks historical perspective. Very few Inca towns were walled; people retired to a *pucara* fortress in case of attack. The Aztec cities were rarely fortified or walled. Many of the Maya towns were, however. Hernando Cortes in his wonderful march across Yucatán and El Petén found a Cehache village encircled by a wooden rampart raised back of a dry moat in early American frontier fashion. At another Cortes found the Indians waiting for him behind a veritable *cheval-de-frise* of cactus.

When defenses were plumbed, the Maya warriors attacked en masse. If the defenders were too firmly entrenched, the

Maya hurled entire hornets' nests into the enemy and set
thatch roofs afire. Then in a chaos of sound, drums beating,
conch shells and whistles blowing, they fell to. Slaughter was
not the primary aim of warfare. Like the Aztecs, the Maya
wanted prisoners—the distinguished ones for sacrifice, the
less worthy as slaves. After a victory the dead were decapitated and their jaws cleaned of flesh "and worn on the
arm." Captains were sacrificed immediately; they did not
wish "to leave anyone alive who might injure them afterwards."

Fig. 32. Techniques of war: Mexican-Toltec invaders
swing the spear-throwing *atl* and shields. They are
raiding a Maya village. From the murals at Chichén
Itzá.

The Mexican intrusion in the ninth century gave these
wars even more ferocity. The motives for war remained the
same—commercial aggrandizement, slaves, tribal insults—
but the Toltecs reintroduced the bow (*chulul*) and arrow
(*halal*), which "they shot with great skill and force." The
spear was better made, and the lance (*nabte*) was fitted
with sharpened flint. The *atl-atl* spear-thrower made this

weapon deadlier. All this is well illustrated on the walls of the ball court at Chichén Itzá.

Defense also improved; shields (*chimas*) were heavier and warriors now wore a quilted cotton jacket (*euyub*) that was soaked in salt brine to toughen it.* It covered the chest and the entire left arm, which held the bow. The spearmen were armored with the *euyub* from neck to ankle.

When the Spaniards met the Maya in 1517 for their first formal battle, they encountered a well-organized foe. Even though the whole of Yucatán had been torn by internecine wars for a hundred years, the Maya united against the foreign invaders, and neither the shock of hearing and being torn apart by firearms nor the surprise of seeing horses deterred them in the defense of their land. Bernal Díaz, who was twenty-three at the time, recalls that day in 1517. The battle had begun at dawn, with "troops moving towards us with flying colours." Maya battle techniques were similar to the Spaniards': divide, surround, outflank. They "divided themselves into different groups; arrows were released by the bowmen, some 300 feet in the rear, and acted as a barrage for the advancing spearmen and rock-throwers; when close they used the two-handled obsidian-bladed swords." Díaz concedes the effectiveness of the Maya assault: "eighty of our men were wounded at the first onset." Even when fighting white men the battle objective of the Indians remained the same—to capture their captain alive. Over the din of battle could be heard "*halach uinic*," and the warriors pointed to Captain Valdivia. In their practice, battle was usually broken off when the *nacom* was killed, and warriors slung their shields on their backs, dropping their lances. This was called *cuch chimal*, a figure of speech for anyone cowardly. This battle technique, which the Maya never altered, worked to their disadvantage.

In the field the Maya were supplied with food, drink, and fresh supplies of stones, lances, and arrows. They showed, said the Spaniards, good military discipline and sound tactics.

The defects of Maya warfare were in its ceremonial and ritual characteristics. When the chieftain died, war ended; they did not fight at night; the farming instinct was stronger than the warring. The Inca revolt against the Spaniards in Cuzco in 1536 might have been won had not the soldiers melted away as the planting season came upon them. The Maya had the same obsession; as late as 1848 during the

---

* This was the Aztec *ichcau-ipilli*. It has often been described. The Spaniards later adopted it as better for tropical warfare than their own steel armor.

"war of the castes" the revolting, badly used Indians had Mérida, the capital, surrounded, until there came the time to plant maize and . . .

Was war bad? One might put it paradoxically thus: Is evil necessarily evil? Could not that which began as bad not end in becoming good? The Maya thought so. If evil did

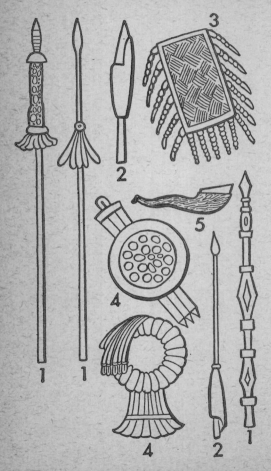

Fig. 33. Types of Maya weapons: (1) Throwing spears. (2) Types of obsidian-tipped arrows. (3) Shield made of mat. (4) Other types of shields. (5) Wooden club set with flint or obsidian.

not exist, neither could good. War was evil insofar as things that Maya man made were destroyed, but it was "good" insofar as it brought new ideas in art, weapons, commerce, government; it helped in its way to develop the great Maya achievements.

29. Religion

Religion pervaded everything. The whole of Maya life was religiously oriented—birth, death, agriculture, time-count, astronomy, and architecture. Life itself was bound up with religion and its rituals.

The Maya cosmos was much like that of the highland Mexicans. They had thirteen heavens and nine hells. The heavens were a number of horizontal layers, one above the other, where the gods dwelled, and they were sustained by four gods who stood at the four cardinal directions and held up the heavens and the world. Each of these four gods had a symbolical color; this was important to the Maya mind (and also now to the archaeologist who is trying to understand this complex cosmology), since elements in their calendar are connected with gods, direction, color.

The Chinese believed the world rested on a tortoise; the Maya thought it rested on the back of a crocodile. The Greeks pictured the Pleiades as birds, while the Maya thought them rattles of a snake and called the constellation *Tzab*.

The World of the Maya, according to them, had suffered cataclysmic destructions four times. When the veil lifts on Maya history they are living in its fifth re-creation. They even had traditions of a flood, and on one of the fascinating pages (74) of the Dresden Codex is a symbolical destruction of the world by a universal deluge, *haiyococab*, "water-over-the-earth."* The earth-upholding gods "escaped," the Indians told Diego de Landa, "when the world was destroyed by the deluge."

Gods pervaded the underworld, walked the earth, and animated the sky. Itzamna—the word meant "lizard"—is

* In Greek mythology there was a similar flood, caused by Zeus's anger against the impious sons of Lycaon. The myth, brought from Asia, has the same origin as the Biblical legend of Noah.

symbolized as an old cross-eyed man with a lizard's body. He headed the Maya pantheon. He had various attributes, as food-giver, patron of medicine, inventor of writing. There followed all forms and fashions of gods, in all walks of life, all crafts, all professions; each had its patron. The beekeeper, the corn grower, the fisherman, the warrior, the traveler, the merchant, even the comedians and the dancers had their own deities. Ixtab, "the lady of the rope," was the goddess of suicides; and Ix Chel, whom we met earlier, was patroness of weaving and childbirth. Her shrine on Cozumel Island was visited by women who were in labor or expected to be. All women were expected to visit this mecca once in their lifetime. "Those two wicked sanctuaries of Cozumel where they sent an infinite number of poor wretches to sacrifice," bemoans one of the friars.

Because each had so many different aspects, the Maya gods were considered multitudinous by the Spanish prelates who were trying to suppress them. "They have such a great quantity of idols, that as if their own personal gods were not enough there was not an animal or an insect of which they did not make a statue." A Spanish mayor ordered in 1565 to put down idolatry in his city, was aghast at what his harvest of gods yielded: "In my presence, upwards of a million were brought."

The idea of gods was an excitant. It also had mystery, and all mankind suffers from the same great uneasiness in the presence of the unknown. The Maya thought of the gods as do all primitives. Life is subject to external powers; man cannot control the weather, even though he can count the steps to the moon. The best, the Maya thought, is to keep on good terms with the gods and cajole them. Images of the rain god Chac—an old man with an elongated nose and *T*-shaped eyes that symbolize tears and, therefore, water—are found as a decorative motif on almost every building in the Puuc. He was a quadruple god, with four directions or beings just as the Christian deity has three. Chac was indiscriminate. The rain he caused fell equally on the just and the unjust. Still, he had to be propitiated. In Mexico the same rain god was fed human hearts; in Yucatán, where drought was not so severe, human sacrifice occurred less frequently. In Peru, where agriculture was highly developed—with terracing, aqueducts, and so on—the rain gods were given short shrift.

Yum Kaax, thought to be the corn god, was youthful and depicted as holding a flowering plant. His portrait found at Copán is as moving as anything in Old World sculpture. Death was called Ah Puch and represented as a skeleton; he was the patron deity of the Maya day Cimi. The war god was painted red and black just as warriors were painted when going into battle. Wind, war, death, all had their individual traits and symbolical glyphs. All these were the unseen partners allied with man in the problem of survival. All gods had to be treated with scrupulous respect. Sacrifice had to be offered to them in a prescribed form and at the right time. Since the gods were so numerous and complex, the priests had to observe the rituals with almost legalistic exactitude based on long-observed formulas.

Fig. 34. Itzamná (*left*) was always drawn as old and therefore wise. He was the sky god and also the god of learning. Yum Kaax (*right*), god of corn, is always pictured as being youthful.

Religion is a system of ceremonies. The most primitive myths, ours included, attest the fatal chain of causation. The Maya lower man, who was told when to sow, reap, weep, and rejoice, must have found that ignorance had immeasurable consolations. Still he feared. And he gave eager ear to the god-man who provided the oracles, the *chilan*, "he who had the duty of giving the answers of the gods."

*Ahkin** was the title of the Maya high priest. At the time of Mayapán there were twelve. In the Bonampak murals, which provide so interesting a picture of Maya

* *Kinyah* meant "to divine."

social organization, the high priest is flanked by eight others no less resplendent than himself. This suggests that priestly power was not concentrated in the hands of one individual. Yet in plural or singular form the priests had a social power almost as great as the Maya lord. Their functions were to train the *chilanes,* examine them in the sciences, ceremonies, and duties of teaching, and send them, when trained, to villages and towns in the necessary numbers. "They taught the sons of other priests and the second sons of the Lord Maya." The Aztecs, it will be remembered, had a similar school, a *calmecac* for teaching the occult. Montezuma was so trained; when chosen as Chief Speaker, that is, "king," he was found sweeping down the 113 steps of the great temple at Tenochtitlán.

Fig. 35. The Maya high priest (ahkin) taught the ruling classes and others "the letters and reckoning of months and years."

"In the high priest," states Diego de Landa, "was the key of their learning and it was to these matters that they dedicated themselves." What they taught was "the computation of the years, months, days, the festivals and ceremonies, the administration of the sacraments, the fateful days and seasons, their methods of divination and their prophecies, their events and the cures for disease [disease was magical], and their antiquities and how to read and write with the letters and characters . . . along with the drawings which illustrate the meaning of the writings."

Beyond what we can infer, we have no idea of education among the Maya. It is presumed that they had analogous institutions to those of the Aztecs, wherein sons of the lower man attended a clan-house school and sons of the directing classes went to a *calmecac* school. What is certain is that the lower men could not read the glyphs; they did not know how to calculate time nor interpret the almanacs. This was reserved for the nobles and priests who taught the sons of other priests "and provided them with books."

In contrast to the Aztec, who had rank without class, the Maya found it was not easy to escape the confines of caste. But, while we do not know enough to analyze the Maya social system, it can be said that a slave might obtain rank through his own efforts. One of the two Spaniards captured by the Maya and held in slavery was Gonzalo Guerrero. He lived as a slave for eight years and, when Cortes arrived, refused to return to the Spaniards.* Instead he went to Chetumal near the Honduras border and when the Spaniards began their conquest, he was elected war lord by the Indians and led attacks on the conquistadors until he was killed in Honduras on August 14, 1536. He had married a woman of rank and reached one of the highest positions in the land. It gives the idea that rank and class were not fixed and that a man could obtain rank through tribal service.

Generally, however, all culture was in the hands of the directing classes, since they alone had the time and energy to create it. "All cultures," as Oswald Spengler developed the theme, "are town cultures." This is especially true among the Maya. The lower man's roots are in the soil that he cultivates, "earth becomes the earth-mother . . . the town

* Bernal Díaz gives this version of Gonzalo Guerrero's apostasy: to his companion Aguilar, who went to Cortes, he said: "Brother Aguilar, I am married and have three children and the Indians look upon me as a cacique and a capitán in wartime—you go and God be with you but me, with my face tattooed and ears pierced, what would the Spaniards say if they saw me in this guise? . . ."

is *not* his habitat and so all great cultures developed in towns."

History, as Spengler envisioned it—and this is confirmed by what we know of the Maya—is the history of civic man, and all effectual history begins with the primary classes, the nobility and priesthood. The lower man is history-less; he is the eternal man and independent of every culture, which he precedes and outlives. Writing and written history belong to the nobleman. Priests of the Maya were, as Diego de Landa said, the key to their learning, and it was to these matters that they dedicated themselves. In all high cultures the script was in the keeping of the priesthood and knowledge, technical knowledge, in the hands of the few. It is not otherwise in our modern world. "A selective massacre of three or four thousand technicians . . . would bring the whole economic life of England to a standstill." [55]

Under the *ah kin* were various priestly officeholders; *chilan, chac,* and *nacom* (to be distinguished from the war chief of the same name), and the cure-doctors. The classification was almost the same as that found in Mexico. The *chilan,* an interpreter of the gods, was carried on a litter. When about to make a prognostication, he retired to a darkened room and fell into a trance; later he delivered it in "measured words." He read the *tzolkin,* "book of days." The *chacs* were four old, honored men "to aid the priest." The *nacom* was the one who cut open the chests of the sacrificial victims and jerked out the beating hearts.

The *ah kin's* office was hereditary; his sons or nearest relative succeeded him; they were nontaxpaying and lived mostly on contributions. The dress of the priest was of monastic simplicity. In a sense it was symbolical, being a long, white, sleeveless robe of bark cloth, beaten from the fiber of the wild ficus tree. Around its edge it was sometimes ornamented with shells. His mitre was a bark-cloth "crown." The hair, left long, was unkempt, unwashed, and "stinky" from the blood of sacrifice.

Sacrifice had the magic virtue of a charm. It has been common to all cultures, our own included, even though it is often represented as something else. It was practiced by the Maya, one supposes, from their very beginnings. The fact of human sacrifice has been sicklied over with a pale cast of thought by those archaeological historians who, having made of the Maya the "Intellectuals of the New World," believe that it is not compatible with their calendrics and glyph-writing. But then the Greeks too were bloodthirsty and had human sacrifices, and this has not marred our interest in them. Besides, most civilizations have their private horrors and it has been said "to understand is not necessarily to pardon, but there is no harm in trying to understand."

The gods had to be nourished, like any other living beings, and as the gods proceeded necessarily from the Maya brain they were human and imperfect. If rain was withheld or disease appeared, it was because the gods were not properly propitiated. Blood and, most of all, throbbing human hearts were cherished by the gods. War yielded prisoners for sacrifice; in addition women and children were immolated, "and were made much of before sacrifice and feasted up to the day; they were well guarded so that they would not run away or pollute themselves by any act of carnal sin."

A victim marked for sacrifice was painted blue, that famous Maya blue which is found on murals and stone carvings. If he was to be sacrificed by the arrow ceremony (we do not know the Maya word) he was tied in crucifix fashion to a wooden frame high off the ground, and they "danced a solemn dance about him." The priest wounded the victim in the place of shame (that is, the penis), and the blood that dripped from the wound was smeared on an idol nearby. Then at a given signal the dancers one by one, as they came in front of him, released their arrows: "in this way they made his whole chest look like a hedgehog of arrows." There are those who would like to believe that this sacrifice is un-Maya (the Plains Indians, such as the Pawnees, did it the same way), yet an illustration of the ceremony is found scratched on the walls of a temple at Tikal.

The most spectacular sacrifice was, literally, heartrending. The blue-painted sacrificial figure was spread-eagled over a sacrificial stone so shaped that it arched the chest. The arms and legs were held by four priestly *chacs,* and the *nacom* ripped a flint knife across the victim's chest, exposing the heart. Then, says Landa, "the Arm of God plunged into it and seized the heart like a raging tiger and snatched it out alive." This was a common ceremony among the Maya and shown in murals and sculpture—though, to be sure, they were not so demoniacally devoted to it as the Aztecs, who in the year 1486 sacrificed 20,000 persons.

Another form of sacrifice was to throw the "selected one" into wells. The great *cenot*e at Chichén Itzá was the best known depository, and Landa described it. Four hundred years later Thompson proved him correct when he dredged that sacred well and found the skeletal remains of men, women, and children, as well as the artifacts that had been thrown with them into this clouded water.

To primitives blood had a mystical significance. The

folklore connected with it lies so deep in the human consciousness that it has slipped over into most religions; "washed by
the blood of Jesus" is only a passing reference. Smearing the
body with blood, or with a blood surrogate, increased the
vital principle. The Maya, however, "offered sacrifices of
their own blood." They pierced their cheeks, their lower lips,
"and their tongues in a slanting direction."* Blood so ob-

Fig. 36. Sacrifice was made at the *cenote* at Chichén Itzá.
This occurred only on unusual occasions of drought, epidemic,
or invasion. The remains of bodies and ornaments have been
found at the bottom of the well.

tained was smeared on an image of the god that was being
propitiated, or onto their hair and bodies. Like other primitives, they did not consider blood as we do. Blood to them
expressed vital principles even when outside the body. Its
magic arrested witchcraft; it made the gods beholden. So
obsessed with blood and its magical qualities were the Maya
that "they even," wrote Diego de Landa, "split the super-
fluous part of the virile member, cutting it and fraying it as
they did their ears to obtain blood on account of which some
were deceived into saying that they practiced circumcision."
Blood from the penis was considered especially efficacious.
Another friar witnessed the ritual: "I saw the sacrifice.
They took a chisel and a wooden mallet, placed the one

* There is a sculpture done in low relief, in the province of Yaxchilan, Chiapas (dated A.D. 750), that shows a kneeling Maya passing a spine-decked cord through his tongue while a fan bearer waves
away the agony of his hurt with a feather fan.

who had to sacrifice himself on a smooth stone slab, took out the penis and made three cuts into it an inch long in the center; all the time they murmured incantations." Landa says, ". . . it is a horrible thing to see how inclined they were to this ceremony. A group of Indians who initiated this form of sacrifice had holes drilled completely through their virile member . . . obliquely from side to side and through this hole . . . they passed a thin cord." Thus fastened together, "they danced and the flowing blood was caught and then the idol anointed with it. . . ."

All this was so that the gods would be properly propitiated and that they should not withhold the proffered gifts of life. A nineteenth-century philosopher summed up man's religious history with an ironical apothegm: "Blood and cruelty are the foundation of all *good* things."

30. Architecture

The Maya have left behind a mass of structures that forever will remain a monument to their aesthetic sensibilities and their muscular energy.[56] Cities and ceremonial centers are found geographically everywhere throughout Mayadom, and in every conceivable landscape—on the edge of the sea, in the flat, dry interior, along the sides of rivers, beside lakes and in the jungles. The cities varied in size and purpose. There were those, such as Tulum and Mayapán, where the whole seemed to be a city in miniature. There were others such as Tikal where pyramids soared 229 feet high so as to dwarf the jungle. Others stretched along the rivers. Most structures were built of stone, since limestone was usually available. When it was not, they used baked brick, and stucco for ornamentation.

This architecture differed from that of the other Sun Kingdom civilizations because of the use the Maya made of lime mortar. Their buildings, said one writer, "are essentially monoliths of rubble and lime with an exterior veneer of cut stone."

Just as the use of the arch and a superior, almost imperishable, mortar were the distinguishing characteristics of Roman architecture, lime mortar and the corbeled arch distinguished that of the Maya. Pulverized limestone makes a cement that forms so tight a bond with the cut stone that the whole structure appears to be monolithic. When the cement had hardened the building was polished and glazed. Bark was stripped off the *chocom* tree and soaked in vats of water. The resulting solution was applied to the walls, which when dry took a superb polish, becoming impervious to rain and in time turning a bright brick-red.

Stone was quarried, shaped, and sculptured with stone; metals such as gold and soft copper came very late to the Maya. Danish neolithic peoples used thin-butted, polished-stone blades, and a reconstruction of such axes shows them to be empirically effective; a large tree can be felled within one hour. The cutting edges of stone axes are almost as sharp as steel, and they can be sharpened by rechipping. Similar stone hammers and chisels were the tools of the Maya builder.

Plans for Maya buildings were made on either paper or wood, all perishable. There must have been a unit of measurement, although no one has attempted to discover it. They undoubtedly had, like the Inca, professional builders or architects, that is, nontaxpaying specialists. Yet as great as is Tikal, not one architect's name has come down to us.

The *nā*, the simple fascine house daubed with wood and thatched with palm leaf, was the humble origin of Maya architecture. The Maya acknowledged this on one façade of the finest building in the Puuc, the Quadrangle at Uxmal, where a sculptor depicted a series of these houses as decorative motifs.

Inca architecture also evolved from the simple native house, in their case the *kancha*, built of fieldstone and adobe-cement. The Vitruvian theory, which holds that features of stone temple construction derive from wooden-house prototypes, can apply to many cultures. In Greek temples the architrave derived from the frame of a peasant's roof, and the triglyph from the ends of the beams.

Out of this house of the "eternal peasant," the Maya shaped the most distinctive feature of their architecture, the corbeled arch. In this, the stones are placed so that each projects beyond the one below it; eventually the walls meet and a vault is formed. To support this type of arch, a weight-mass was necessary. This developed into the roof-comb, an overhang to act as cantilever to the vaulting, that became for Maya sculpture a façade on which to lavish intricate and swirling design. The Maya have been known to raise a massive pyramid with an estimated 250,000 cubic feet of fill, only to place at its pinnacle a building of less than 150 feet square. Aware of the self-limiting aspect of the corbeled arch, the Maya later used massive wooden beams and wooden lintels as well; these were made of sapodilla, a metal-hard wood. They counted on everything but the termites.

The sheer number of Maya remains is staggering. No one has yet tried to give them a precise figure. Those ruins which have been surveyed and photographed number in the hundreds. Those which have been merely noted total even more. It can only be surmised that the scrub jungles and the rain forests yet hold hundreds more from man's sight.

Fig. 37. Stages of quarrying: Rock-mass was broken out from rock-outcrop.

Fig. 38. Rock-mass was rolled on hard wood rollers and pulled with thick ropes.

Fig. 39. Roughed-out stela was set up in this fashion into a previously prepared foundation. Note the protruding nubbins, which were left on for leverage and pulling.

Fig. 40. The carving of Stela E at Quirigua, close to Copán. The intricate design and complicated calendric computations were first worked out on paper and painted boards. The base material here was a coarse red sandstone, the tool was the basalt stone celt.

Aside from cities and ceremonial centers, there is in the Maya architectural vocabulary a variety of other specialized constructions—ball courts, gateways, sweat baths, vaulted bridges, and raised platforms where plays were performed. Much of this the early Spaniards saw while it was still in its pristine form. When Grijalva sailed along the coast he saw "three towns separated from each other by about two miles. . . . There were many houses of stone, very tall towers . . . and then a city or town so large that Seville would not have seemed more considerable." Uxmal had been seen and described as looking "like a painting of Flanders" by Antonio de Ciudad Real, a priest of facile intelligence who wrote *Of the Very Renowned Edifices of Uxmal.* He described the façades, "carved with wonderful delicacy," and remarked on the glyphs that appeared on the sides of the buildings, "carved with so great a dexterity as surely to excite admiration." Diego de Landa said that "there are in Yucatán many beautiful buildings, which is the most remarkable thing

that has been found in the Indies. . . ." In Izamal there was,
for example, "a building of such height and beauty that it
astonishes one. . . . And Chichén Itzá, a very fine site
where there are many magnificent buildings . . . and around
the sacrificial *cenote* can be found . . . buildings of the
country almost like the Pantheon at Rome."

So many were there of these stone cities that Landa said
"the whole land appeared to be one town." And so many are
the remains of these cities today that neither this nor any
one book could hope to cover all in full detail. Besides, to
say everything is to say nothing. Here then is a selection of
Maya cities with brief accounts of their form and function.

Uaxactun (A.D. 328) is located where one might believe
that men with a wide choice would never have found a city, in the
low, humid jungle-bound El Petén. It is (at this moment of
writing) the oldest known Maya city. Here are found, too,
the finest examples of polychromic pottery; and until Bonampak was discovered, it had the finest murals extant, very
spirited figures painted in red, orange, yellow, gray, and
black on a whitened background.

There are eight principal groups of buildings. The low-
lying hills were artificially leveled and then built up into a
series of large and small plazas. These lie close together and
are connected by wide causeways. The principal temple
pyramid, although only 27 feet high, is interesting since it
shows the evolution of the pyramid form, which in nearby
Tikal was to soar over 200 feet in height. The wide stairway
is ornamented by grotesque stucco masks 8 feet high. An
interesting study has been made of the evolution of the
temple complex from the original palm-thatched native house.
In a series of isometric drawings it can be seen that the first
structure was a raised stone-adobe platform on which rested
a wooden house (the postholes of this have been found). In
the next stage of development, three identical temples were
built with similar stairways and decorated roof-crests facing
each other. A high priest, having died, was buried in the
plaza; the floor level was raised to contain his tomb and a
similar temple, presumably above the grave, was added.
Slowly, with the accretion of years and techniques, the temple
evolved into a complex of buildings.

Tikal (A.D. 416) was the largest of Maya cities. Although it
is only thirty-five miles from Uaxactun (they were connected
by a causeway), its format is different. Tikal rests on a gigantic limestone outcrop. The surrounding forest is as thickly
treed as the Amazon. Cedars, mahogany, palms, and strangler
ficus are dominant. Jaguars, tapirs, and snakes prowl the
jungle floor, while monkeys and a variety of birds rule the

treetops. It is here that these machine-less men built their greatest city.

On an artificially leveled tongue of limerock, between two ravines, the center of Tikal, civil and ceremonial, was built. Since there was a lack of dependable water supply, even with a high incidence of rainfall, the two ravines were converted into reservoirs and spanned by a raised causeway that is also a dam. There are five separate groups of buildings all connected by wide causeways, covering a square mile. Beyond this in every direction Tikal stretches out for several miles. So immense is the site that no one has yet even attempted a definitive calculation. Since 1956 the long-held dream of archaeologists has been in the process of realization: the University of Pennsylvania is now at this moment of writing excavating and restoring the ruins.

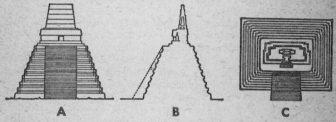

Fig. 41. Architectural form and structure of Temple V, Tikal. This temple, south of the great plaza, faced the south ravine, which was a water reservoir. (A) The elevation, showing handling of mass. (B) A profile that exhibits the manner of crowning the truncated pyramid. (C) The structure; note the narrowness of the room caused by corbeled arching. Taken from the drawings of Maler, Tozzer, and J. A. Gomez.

Tikal is best known for the number of its monuments; thus far eighty-three stelae and fifty-four altars have been found. The city has the finest wood carvings known in the entire Maya area, twelve doorways and lintels carved on sapodilla wood, of which the first and the finest was carried off to a Swiss museum.

The pyramids of Tikal, which push their verdure-covered heads above the jungle, arrogantly towering above all else, were, one may well assume, its pride. Interior space was sacrificed to height and grandeur. In the great court, in the center of Tikal, two of these massive pyramid-temples face each other. In the plaza, which measures 400 by 250 feet, stands a structure not unlike a Mesopotamian ziggurat; it rises to 229 feet. A stone staircase follows the setback structure to its apex. There, with decorated roof-crest, is the temple—three dimly lit rooms with a gross space of less than 150 square feet. It is for this that Maya laborers worked incredibly long years to carry on their backs enough limestone rubble to fill 250,000 cubic feet. It is estimated that 25,000 man-hours were required merely to build up the core of one of these pyramids. The labor required to cut, set, and finish the stone of the surface and rear the temple, with its florid and decorated roof-crest, cannot be easily calculated. This must have cost the skilled masons twice as many man-hours as were required to build the inner core.

Next, lime mortar had to be made. It has been estimated that one-sixteenth of most Maya structures are lime mortar. To reduce limestone to cement, which was done by burning, required four times as much wood, by volume, as limestone.

For every sixteen cubic meters of lime cement, a cord of wood was consumed. The immense labor service needed merely to fell trees with stone axes, then carry the wood to the lime kilns, can be grasped if not precisely calculated.

At Tikal there are eight such immense temple pyramids. Lesser structures—palaces or habitations—total ten times this number. There were acres of stucco surface to cover, and many of these structures are covered with glyphs. The mind reels at the thought of the organization required merely to supply labor to a city such as Tikal.

According to its own records, Tikal survived from A.D. 416 until 869, though it is possible that it was reoccupied briefly in the fourteenth century by the Itzás. Its existence was made known to the outside world in 1696, when a Franciscan monk, Antonio de Avendaño, on his way to "reduce" the remaining Maya about Lake Petén, stumbled upon "a number of ancient buildings which although they were very high and my strength very little, I climbed them. . . ."

San José (A.D. 435), minuscule when compared to the other Maya centers, is situated in British Honduras, less than fifty miles from Tikal, with which it was, in all probability, bound by a causeway. No one knows what its Maya name was. San José lies in the ancient Maya area called Chetumal Province, where cacao was raised and canoes manufactured. Here Gonzalo Guerrero, Spanish castaway-slave turned Maya war chief, repelled the Spanish conquistadors.

San José is small; still, it conveys an idea of what smaller ceremonial centers were like. There are four building groups set on artificially leveled hills. The largest is composed of temples and a habitation complex; another has a modest pyramid fifty feet high. There is also a water reservoir and the inevitable ball court. The decoration shows sophistication.

The head of the maize god is a lively piece of imagery, and the polychromic pottery found there is similar to that of Uaxactun, where the best in Mayadom has been found. This pottery shows a continuous occupation from A.D. 435 up to the Toltec period (987) and perhaps beyond. A thousand or more families lived about the center or within reach of it. Although small, its tastes were cosmopolitan; trade pieces found within the graves show that it imported shells from the Pacific, obsidian from Zacapa, copper from Mexico, marble drinking vessels from Ulua in Honduras, spindle whorls from faraway Huasteca (which, as the *zopolote* flies, is a good thousand miles north). San José is listed here not because of anything spectacular, but because Eric Thompson, its excavator, thought it to be a "small-scale ceremonial center of which there must be literally scores" still buried in the jungles.

Copán (A.D. 460), the most southern of the great Maya cities, lies at an altitude of 2,000 feet in what is now Honduras. It was bound to those cities already mentioned by sea road and land road. Copán was built at the edge of the Copán River, which flows into the Motogua River, which in turn debouches into the Gulf of Honduras near Omaa, in ancient times a large Yucatán Maya trading post. The region was known for its cacao and obsidian, its fine Ulua marble vases. In the high rain forests was the habitat of the red-green *guacamayo* and the quetzal. It was the only Maya city to be known, at least in the literature, outside of the Yucatán area. Diego García de Palacio, a judge of the Audiencia Real de Guatemala, was led to Copán in 1576. He wrote in a speculative letter to Philip II, ". . . They say that in olden times a great lord of the Province of Yucatán came here, built these buildings . . . returned home and left them empty. . . . According to this book, which I have . . . it seems that in ancient times people from Yucatán did conquer these provinces." It was the same Copán that was purchased for fifty dollars by John Lloyd Stephens more than two and a half centuries later.

Copán covers seventy-five acres; beyond this lived the people. It is the second largest of Maya cities and composed of five main plazas and sixteen subgroups. The enormous main plaza, surrounded by tiers of stone seats, has been likened to a Roman *circus maximus*. The compact acropolis, overlooking the Copán River, is an amazingly wonderful complex of temples. In the eastern courtyard are tiers of stone seats and, at one end, the Jaguar Stairway, flanked by the stone jaguars from which its name is derived. The animals are rampant, one forepaw outstretched, the other akimbo. Their coats were

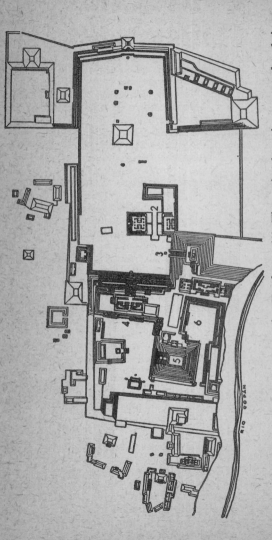

Fig. 42. Plan of the Maya acropolis at Copán, Honduras. (1) The main plaza; its extreme length is over 800 feet. Scattered about the plaza are the dated stelae for which Copán is famed. (2) The ceremonial ball court. (3) Temple 26, crowning the Hieroglyphic Stairway finished 756 A.D.). (4) The eastern courtyard, dominated by the feline heads with snakes issuing from the mouths. (5) The pyramid with adjoining structures. (6) The western court-yard with the Jaguar Stairway. Taken from S. G. Morley, *The Ancient Maya*, Stanford University Press, 1946, Plate 34, with additions.

spotted with rounded pieces of inlaid obsidian. The architects of the temple that dominates the courtyard made use of a squatting stone Maya figure to support a panel that is obviously allegorical—a cacoplastic mélange of arms, gnomelike figures, dragonlike heads; a design that is mobile, moving out into space, formless yet form-consuming.

In the western court is the Reviewing Stand, which is dominated by a god entwined by a snake, in the fashion of Laocoön. From the same courtyard rises the famed Hieroglyphic Stairway; thirty feet in width and sixty-three treads in height. Each tread is decorated with a running commentary of glyphs. The dates, which alone have been deciphered, show that it was dedicated in A.D. 756. It is calculated that there must be 2,500 glyphs in the stairway.[57] Stephens hoped that when read they would reveal the "entire history of the city," but as only ten treads were found in their original positions, the restoration, completed in 1942, is at best tentative and conjectural.

Beyond this is the great plaza, at one end of which is a small temple. Carved and dated stelae, the most beautiful in Mayadom, are scattered throughout this area.

Copán was no isolated city. Nearby is Quirigua, which is believed to have been intimately connected with its history.[58] Northeast of it are several other known Maya sites.

Palenque (A.D. 642) is 280 miles north of Copán. No direct trade contact between the two cities has been established, but their art, sculpture, calendrics, and glyph-writing are similar. The two cities are separated by rivers, high mountains, deep ravines, thick jungles, and almost 300 miles. Geography did not prevent the interchange of intellectual ideas between independent Maya city-states. Despite political disunity, there was a cultural unity.

Palenque is the Spanish for "palisade." The Maya name for the city has not been revealed by its multitude of glyphs. Palenque is unique in that modern Maya history began there. What it has lately revealed and is expected to reveal has changed our concept of Maya history.

The city is barely visible in a sea of jungle. Set at a 1,000-foot altitude in the Chiapas forests, near a small river (the Otolum, a tributary of the Usumacinta), Palenque by river travel is less than eighty miles from Xicalanco, the great trading center, with which it had trade connections. The city became known in 1773, when an Indian brought it to the attention of a priest who, amazed by all he saw, drew up a report. It was later visited by a Spanish captain of engineers, who wrought havoc there with his ramming-battery techniques. He was accompanied by an Italian architect, Antonio

Bernaconi, in the Spanish service. When these reports were brought to the personal attention of Carlos III of Spain, a ruler of the Enlightenment, he ordered that all antiquities found at Palenque be well preserved so that they could illustrate an *Historia antigua de América*.

The history of the exploration of Palenque covers two centuries. Many of the explorers of Palenque were later persons of distinction, such as Count Waldeck, a wonderfully baroque character.[59] He showed up at Palenque in 1832, at the age of sixty-four. The places of his birth are given variously as Paris, Prague, and Vienna. Waldeck was characterized by an observer as "a racy and on the whole, despite dubious foibles, attractive personality." Of himself he modestly said, "I am the first competent person who occupied himself with the ruins of Central America." However, his facile drawings were deliberately falsified so as to give the impression that Maya ruins had been built by Phoenicians or Romans. "He talks so big," said William Prescott, "moreover his drawings do not have the true weathertints of antiquity. . . . I have a *soupçon* that he is a bit of a charlatan."

Stephens arrived at Palenque in the spring of 1840 with his long-suffering companion Frederick Catherwood. Since their publications, the history of the city has been set on a firm archaeological basis.

That part of the site thus far uncovered consists of two groups of eight structures divided by a small ravine with river water that has been canalized to flow through a corbeled arch sewer (an unusual Maya engineering feature). On the west bank is the Palace, an irregular rectangular structure 340 by 240 feet and 60 feet high. This is where Stephens lived. It is thick-walled and many-chambered, and has an interior court from which rises—unique in Maya architecture—a tower four stories in height with an interior stairway. At the entrance to the Palace are archaically carved stone figures, and the sides of the edifice are decorated with stucco figures in high relief, regarded by all as the finest anywhere. Within, there are carved stone panels with a remarkable series of well-preserved Maya texts. Four of the other structures, the temples of the Cross, the Sun, the Inscriptions, and the Foliated Cross, are outwardly similar—an artificially raised pyramid, with a single structure atop that is crested by an immense, decorated roof-comb. The engineering purpose of the latter is to act as a counter-level to the corbeled arching beneath. All are decorated on the exterior with figures and ornaments in stucco, which were once brilliantly painted. Each of the large rooms has an altar and a carved wall panel. In one, the Foliated Cross,

Fig. 43. Stucco figures in relief from the façade of House D at Palenque. The art of stucco-sculpture reached its height at Palenque during the ninth century A.D.

are two life-sized figures (Maya dimensions) holding a man-
nequin up to the gaze of a bird, which despite embellish-
ments is the sacred quetzal. There are many inscriptions on
the tablet. On the altar of another, the Sun Temple, the two
figures stand upon the bodies of prostrate men. In the center is the symbol of the sun, the face of which some have

Fig. 44. A cross-section of the Temple of the Inscriptions at Palenque showing the long-lost stairway
that led down to the grave of the high priest. It was
found in 1951 by Antonio Ruz Lhullier, a Mexican
archaeologist.

likened to a Gorgon's head. Once again mannequins are
held up in reverence. The Temple of the Inscriptions, which
lies near the Palace, has lost its roof-comb. It retains its
decorations. The date that has been deciphered is A.D. 692.
   In 1951 the Mexican archaeologist Alberto Ruz Lhullier
was assigned to restore some of the structures at Palenque.
When his investigations brought him to the Temple of the
Inscriptions, he noticed in the inner room a large slab set
neatly into the floor, with finger holes in it so it could be

raised. He raised it, and following a narrow corbeled stairway downward, first in one direction and then another, he
reached another large slab poised horizontally, sixty feet below the surface. In front of the door were the skeletons of
six Maya who had "elected" to remain as guardians of the
tomb. Beyond the stone door, a few steps down, was the
tomb. When discovered it was a veritable fairy palace.
Through the centuries the dripping water, lime-saturated,
had formed many stalactites.[60]

Over the tomb was a beautifully carved slab in relief. A
portrait with hieroglyphics, it weighed five tons. Within was
the skeleton of the "true man," bejeweled with enormous jade
earrings, a jade necklace, and a pear-shaped baroque pearl.
It had been long held that the Maya pyramids were built
solely to support temples and did not contain the tombs of
important personages, as pyramids do in other lands. The
findings at Palenque changed this attitude.

Piedras Negras (A.D. 534), one of the great cities of the
Maya, is sixty bird-flight miles from Palenque. On the south
bank of the Usumacinta River, it is set in the jungle. The
city begins at the river's edge, and the structures go from the
simple to the complex, the latter occupying the undulating
hills. The palaces, even though in advanced decay, give the
effect of one huge monument. The sculpture of the stelae and
lintels in low relief is of the finest, sharply delineated and
sensual. War motifs dominate many of such sculptures; often
Maya overlords appear looking down on massed prisoners.
There are over seventy-five dated stelae (between the dates of
A.D. 534 and 800), altars, lintels, thrones, and even sculptures
chipped out of the *piedras negras,* the black stones that lie
above the river. One of the features is the *zumpulche,* a
building which housed the sweat bath. It had two large rooms,
one hot and one cold, reminiscent of the Roman baths, if not
as magnificent. In the steam room were two stone benches,
and the steam was made by throwing water onto hot stones.
This description might seem contrived were it not supported
by a combination of good archaeology and good reconstruction.

Yaxchilan (A.D. 514) lies higher up on the Usumacinta,
twenty miles from Piedras Negras. Yaxchilan (called thus
from a rivulet that flows through it) lies on the north bank,
where the river makes a large curve. The structures of this
city are spread along the river for almost a mile. Eight undulating hills overlook the esplanade, and on each is a temple
structure. Its sculpture, chipped out of finely textured limestone, is dramatic. In one lintel a priest is seen passing a
thorn-studded cord through the center of his tongue, drip-

ping blood onto a piece of *huun* paper, while a servant fans
him to ease away the pain. The surface of Yaxchilan has
only been touched by archaeologists.

Bonampak (A.D. 540) was an architectural satellite of
Yaxchilan, some eighteen miles from the other city. Because
it was recessed in the jungles away from the river, no one
ever heard of Bonampak before 1946. In Maya the word
means "painted walls." When the city was discovered the interest created by the paintings found there was second only
to that caused by the earlier discoveries of John Lloyd Stephens. Bonampak lies in the area where the Maya-speaking
"wild" Lacandones live, they who carry on many traditions
of the old Maya. It is also a region much penetrated by the
chicle gatherers, who search for new stands of gum-yielding
sapodillas.

Giles G. Healy, a photographer pursuing a Maya chase
under the aegis of the United Fruit Company, pressed the

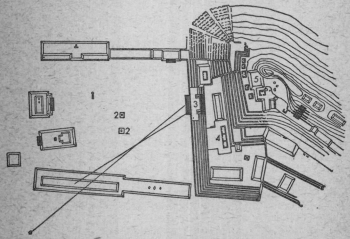

Fig. 45. Plan of the ceremonial center of Bonampak (eighteen
miles southeast of the well-known ruins of Yaxchilan on the
Usumacinto River), where the famous murals were discovered
during May, 1946, by Mr. Giles G. Healy. Bonampak is small
but carefully laid out. Its plaza (1) measures 270 by 370 feet.
Two dated stelae (2) stand in the center of the plaza. Approached
by a series of steps (3) is the principal structure (4) of Bonampak. This is the building that houses the famous murals. Other
smaller buildings decorated with stucco (5) dominate the rise
of ground called the Acropolis. From K. Ruppert, J. E. S. Thompson and T. Proskouriakoff, *Bonampak* . . ., Washington, D. C.,
1955. Surveyed by Ruppert and Stromsvik.

search for Bonampak when he heard the Indians say "painted walls." He was led to the city on May 21, 1946. Hidden in the innermost recesses of the Lacandon jungles, Bonampak proved to be one of a constellation of unrecorded sites. There Healy found a local ceremonial center, with eleven buildings and part of a carefully laid compact plaza 270 by 370 feet. Here were several dated stelae and decorated, carved, and dated altars. On a slight rise were several structures; one had three doorways. Its façade revealed marvelously molded figures in stucco. (All of the sculpture found here is superb; it much resembles that of Yaxchilan.) Within this building Healy found the murals. Painted in A.D. 800, these rank as art with anything of similar antiquity, be it in Crete, India, China. As history they are one of the best sources of information of Maya life patterns, showing warfare, dress, musical instruments, religious ceremonies, sacrifice, and, above all, the attitudes and expressions which make a new analysis of Maya social organization possible.[61] (For a more detailed discussion of the Bonampak murals, see the section on Maya paintings.)

Uxmal (A.D. 900) lies in the Puuc of Yucatán, a range of low hills, rolling limestone ridges, with alternate pockets of soil. It is not only the most uniform of Maya cities; it is also the most beautiful. Moreover, it is quite probable that "Uxmal" is what it was called by the Maya themselves. It has history, written, recitative, and traditional. Uxmal was part of the League of Mayapán. It even has a date in the literature: "In Katun 2 Ahau [A.D. 987] the Maya Lord Ah Suytok Tutul Xiu was established in Uxmal."

There was a time when archaeologists cast Maya culture into two chronological categories: "Old Empire" (the cities of older date described as such) and "New Empire," those which were concentrated in Yucatán. It is now known that those of the New have dates almost as old as the Old, so these terms have been discarded. It is not known with certainty whether the Maya cities in the humid interior were abandoned after A.D. 890 with a precipitous mass migration of people toward Yucatán. Still, Maya tradition and history speak of descents great and small, to account for the fact of the abandonment of the interior for the dry, coastal Yucatán.

Uxmal was a city of the Maya Renaissance. The Maya-speaking Toltecs had already invaded Yucatán and permeated the land with a renewed vitality in religion, trade, and warfare. Ritual was dominated by the mystical Quetzalcoatl cult. All this found a reflection in Maya architecture. Uxmal is fifty miles from the sea and a hundred from

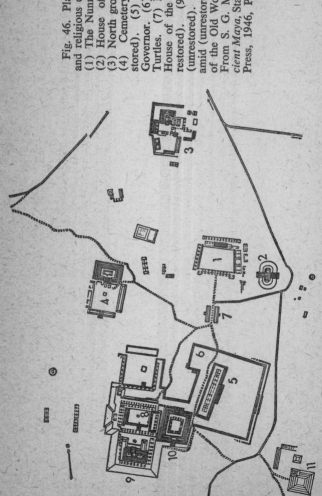

Fig. 46. Plan of the civic and religious center of Uxmal. (1) The Nunnery Quadrangle. (2) House of the Magician. (3) North group (unrestored). (4) Cemetery group (unrestored). (5) House of the Governor. (6) House of the Turtles. (7) Ball court. (8) House of the Pigeons (partly restored). (9) South group (unrestored). (10) Great pyramid (unrestored). (11) House of the Old Woman (in ruins). From S. G. Morley, *The Ancient Maya*, Stanford University Press, 1946, Plate 49.

Chichén Itzá. It is the main city of the Puuc. About it are scores of cities, small and large, all of a similar style. The site of Uxmal is unusual because it was built near a *cenote*. The region has rich soil and plenty of rainfall, but no wells. So, as the Romans did at Capri, the builders of Uxmal relied on underground cisterns that collected the runoff of rain from roofs. It has been calculated that the plaza of Uxmal if used efficiently as a cistern could have kept 6,000 people in drinking water throughout the year. All the Puuc cities provided themselves with underground cisterns, an engineering feat which would have brought encomiums from the Romans themselves.

There are eight groups of buildings at Uxmal, covering an immense area. The House of the Governor and its related structures stand at what is considered to have been the secular administrative center of the city. Mounted on an artificially constructed mound, fifty feet high and reached on all sides by stone steps, it covers five acres of ground. The palace itself is 320 feet long, 40 feet wide, 26 feet high, and it is the single most magnificent building ever erected in the Americas. The whole is covered with a veneer of ornamented stone, the joints fitting as perfectly as a mosaic. Each stone is an element in this immensely beautiful façade, which is a masterpiece of precision and craftsmanship. On an altar in front of it rests a double-headed jaguar, heads fore and aft. In front of the main flight of steps was an enormous stone phallus, which is broken in half and for "moral reasons" has never been restored. It stood ten feet high when in its pristine state.

About the House of the Governor are pyramids, other palaces, and the House of the Pigeons, so termed by someone because the roof-comb resembles a dovecote. Close upon the palace, on the same raised plaza, is the House of the Turtles (the decorative motif on the façade is a parade of realistically carved box tortoises). South of this, where went the great *sacbe* causeway (it ran directly in front of the House of the Governor and led to Kabah), there are other buildings, now mostly amorphous except for the Temple of the Phalli, where there are enough reminders of the worship of the ithyphallic to make even Aldous Huxley change his assertion that "there was no sex in the art of the Maya."

Stephens lived in the Governor's Palace during November and December 1841; Frederick Catherwood sketched that monument for two months, making so many detailed drawings that he had "materials for erecting a building exactly like it." It was here too that Count Waldeck lived in 1836 (his drawings of Uxmal are still extant).

The ball court is north of the palace, and beyond it is the second group of buildings: the Nunnery Quadrangle and the temple Pyramid of the Dwarf. The latter is an oval-shaped pyramid. On one side a broad flight of stairs mounts at an almost perpendicular angle 125 feet high to the temple, which had as its motif Chac, the open-mouthed god, patron of rain. Immediately below the pyramid, so close that in the late afternoon it shadows it, is the Nunnery.

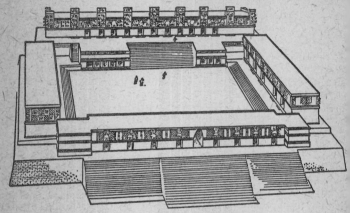

Fig. 47. The Nunnery at Uxmal. The finest of late Maya Puuc architectural planning.

This is a slightly irregular-shaped quadrangle, enclosed by a low range of buildings, each with different motif. Like the Governor's Palace, the whole is faced with a veneer of cut stone set into designs which "project"—the white stones are set so as to create a chiaroscuro of light and shade. One of these buildings is multi-storied, a temple dramatically set back with intricate ornamentation. On another the corners have the long snout of the rain god as decoration. The third has as its motif the simple *nā* house of the common Indian, immortalized in stone. The fourth shows another variation of the fret design, over which stone snakes coil, twist and entwine. At intervals there are figures of men with abnormally large penes, fortunately not in an erected state, which would have brought about their destruction by the self-appointed administrators of public morals.

Although still little explored beyond its immediate confines, Uxmal has been partially restored. There is much contradiction here. Mentioned in the Maya chronicles as having been built by the Maya-speaking Toltecs, it possesses the least of Mexican architectural traits. Uxmal is supposed to have been one of the triumvirate of the League of Mayapán, but archaeologists suggest that it was abandoned before the league was in operation. It has been called "decadent," whereas it has a style wholly its own. Sixteen dated stelae have been found in and about Uxmal. When read, the dates are within the tenth century. The style of the sculpture, ornate and flamboyant, is "decadent," says one writer, in comparison with that of Tikal.

Kabah (A.D. 879) lies nine miles southeast of Uxmal. The ancient Maya *sacbe*, which leads to it, leaves Uxmal in front of the Governor's Palace and goes past the Hacienda San Simón (which belonged to Simón Peón, host to Stephens and at that time owner of Uxmal). Nearby is a stone arch similar to the one at Kabah. It stands in isolation and is not related to any other structure. Six miles further, following the *sacbe*, one comes to Kabah. The main road continues southeast, but a branch of it makes a sharp left turn and comes up and passes under the Great Arch of Kabah. Stephens discovered it and Catherwood made a drawing of it, but latter-day archaeologists, who could not find it, politely smirked at this "triumphal arch." Today it stands restored, and is the formal entrance to Kabah.

As Kabah now stands, there are three groups of buildings visible to the eye, and uncovered mounds and temples abound. About Kabah, in the eleventh and twelfth centuries, was one of the densest populations in Yucatán. The Palace of the Masks—for once rightly named—is Maya baroque; the long-snouted masks of the god Chac are repeated over and over again along the whole range of the 151-foot-long building. The effect of this lavish use of the motif is simply overwhelming, and if Aldous Huxley found Maya art "often incommeasurably alien" it is because he did not see Kabah. In front of it there is an altar filled with a running commentary of glyphs. Before it and underground is a huge cistern, a *chultun*, which was the depository for water collected from the roofs. Kabah had two dated wooden doorjambs (A.D. 879) showing warriors with spear-throwers—an indication of Toltec presence in the Puuc.

Labná (A.D. 869), which was one of the constellation of cities about Uxmal, is only six miles from Kabah. Its architecture is characteristic of the Puuc. Labná lacks architectural continuity. One feels that the project was larger than the labor supply and that buildings grew by accretion; many structures were left unfinished. There are only two known dates from Labná. One of these, A.D. 869, is carved on the elongated proboscis of the god Chac.

The palace, imposingly set on an artificial hill, has two immense cisterns, one within the building itself and another that takes up the whole front of the palace (the very one into which John Lloyd Stephens lowered himself, despite all warnings, to make sure that it was a cistern). This palace, presumably an administration center, was joined to the other group by a raised causeway, a ceremonial road 450 yards in length, 10 feet wide, and varying between 2 and 8 feet in height. There is here, as at Uxmal and Kabah, a gateway; it is part of a building. As at Uxmal, the native house, the common dwelling of adobe and thatch, is immortalized in stone. Here it is used on either side of the gateway as a decorative motif.

Sayil (A.D. 800) is the oldest of the group. The dating is based more on its style than upon any dated stelae. Its center of interest (although there are many other ruined structures about it) is its palace of a hundred rooms arranged in three stories. The second and third are set back, leaving terraces as rest areas for the occupants. A great stone staircase beginning at the bottom leads to all three terraces. It is 210 feet long and 75 feet wide; it has magnitude, proportion, order, and sensibleness. The style is massive and simple and has the classic qualities of Green Dorian architecture. About its façades is the ubiquitous mask motif. It has, wrote Tatiana Proskouriakoff, "a freedom from the oppressively monotonous intricacy of ornament that mars many *Puuc* structures." *

Chichén Itzá, thrice founded (A.D. 432, 964, and 1185), was the greatest of the coastal Maya cities. On a plain so flat that its great pyramid can be seen for miles around, Chichén Itzá was joined by road to Izamal, thence to the seacoast at Polé, in direct line with Cozumel Island. Important in the history of the city are its two enormous natural wells, one of which was used for human sacrifice and the other as a source of water.

The first founding of the city (A.D. 432) was by immigrants from the "Old Empire" during the "Little Descent." They formed their city around the salubrious Xtoloc well, where they built two masonry stairways descending precipitously sixty feet to the water's edge. The architecture of old Chichén is reminiscent of the Puuc style. Many of the buildings have almost identical motifs, masks, colonnettes, and frets, especially the building named the *Abab dzib.*

* There are so many late Maya cities within the Puuc, each with something individual about it, that it would take more space than we have at our disposal to do more than list the names of the more important: Xcalumkin; Chacmultun, with its interesting murals; Holactun; Almuchil; Kickmool; Keuic, visited by Stephens, who spelled it "Kewick"; Huntichmool; Sabacche; Yache; Xkalumpococh.

Traditions and dates give this further proof. The rounded "astronomical tower," certainly one of the most interesting in the area, is dated A.D. 900.

Chichén the "new" was founded at the north end about the sacrificial *cenote*. This well is 190 feet in diameter and now contains 36 feet of water, green with algae, and 40 feet of detritus. Its water level stands 65 feet below the surface. The "new" part of Chichén Itzá was reoccupied by the Itzás between the years 987 and 1185.

Fig. 48. The Pyramid of Kukulcan at Chichén Itzá. Although a great part of the city is late Maya, Chichén Itzá was occupied as early as the fifth century A.D.

There were two distinct invasions of Mexican Toltecs into Chichén. The first were Maya-speaking although of Mexican highland origin. They had lived about Tabasco for several generations, close to Xicalanco. There were profound population shifts during the years before A.D. 900; in Mexico, Teotihuacán, the capital of the Toltecs, which had controlled so much of the central highlands, collapsed; some say it was attacked and burned and whole masses of its people were in movement. This was about the same time that the Maya inland cities—Tikal, Palenque, Piedras Negras, and hundreds of others—ceased to erect time markers, and it is believed this was the time of the populational dispersal of the "Great Descent." It is recorded in Maya traditions.

Chichén Itzá was then unoccupied. These Itzás took it over and amalgamated with the Yucatec Maya. Some time after A.D. 900 they built the first pyramid at "new" Chichén. This was discovered in 1937 when archaeologists of the Carnegie Institution, while restoring the Pyramid Temple of Kukulcan, found a smaller one underneath it that served as core to the larger. It was Maya in style, but with Toltec

motifs, that is, marching jaguars such as are found at Tula.
A secret stairway led to the Red Jaguar throne room. Here
a life-sized effigy of an open-mouthed jaguar, painted a man-
darin red, stood guard. Its spots are seventy-three round
disks of polished jade.

The Maya were now tied up with the destinies of the
highland Mexicans. Teotihuacán disintegrated, and the Toltecs moved northward to build another capital called Tula.
The ruined site now lies sixty miles north of Mexico City.
In the eleventh century it was again the center of Toltec
culture. The great Temple of Tula has as motif the plumed-
serpent, immense snakes rampant, formed into fifteen-foot-
high caryatids. Inside the temple were immense warrior
figures as colonnades. About the lower portions of the temple
were motifs of marching jaguars and rampant eagles. Above
all else there appeared the terrible figure of the Chac Mool,
a prone stone figure with a vacant expressionless face. Its
hands held a stone dish, and into this freshly torn human
hearts were flung during sacrifices. Quetzalcoatl was the
culture-hero of Tula. Before he became divine, he was a

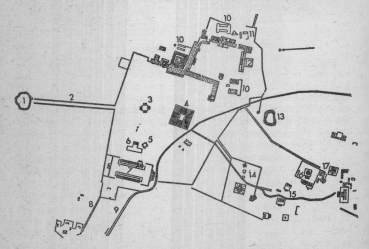

Fig. 49. Plan of Chichén Itzá. (1) The sacrificial *cenote*. (2)
The *sacbe*-causeway. (3) Temple of Venus. (4) Pyramid of Kukulcan. (5) Platform of the Eagles. (6) Tzompantli, or Place
of the Skulls. (7) Ball court. (8) The modern road to Mérida.
(9) Temple of the Warriors. (10) Ball courts. (11) Sweat baths.
(12) The market. (13) Fresh-water *cenote*. (14) High priest's
grave. (15) House of the Deer. (16) Caracol, the observatory.
(17) Sweat baths.

man. He was priest, ruler, demiurge, then god; he lorded it over Tula for twenty-two years, lost a civil war, and was forced into exile with a sizable body of warriors. The time given to this hisorical fact is A.D. 116. He moved south to Cholula, the land of the Mixtec, and there acquired fame as a builder and "bringer of laws."

The next time Quetzalcoatl appears, he is in Yucatán. Was this the same Quetzalcoatl or was it another who bore the same name as a title? If we are confused, so were the Maya. "They do not agree upon the point as to whether he [Quetzalcoatl] arrived before or after the Itzás."

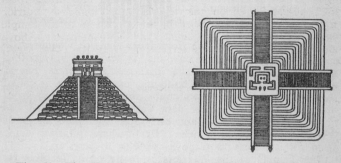

Fig. 50. The Temple of Kukulcan, Chichén Itzá. When the city was reoccupied, this temple was set over an older one that had Tula-Toltec characteristics. The new temple is notable for the use of wooden beams, making larger rooms possible. The figure of the Plumed Serpent is a direct architectural borrowing from the Toltec temple at Tula. The temple also served as a fortress during the brief occupation of the Spaniards under Francisco de Montejo.

This much is certain: that some time in the eleventh century Chichén Itzá was reoccupied for the third time and that the people were of Toltec-Mexican origin. Archaeology, history, and tradition, except for precise dates, are for once in full agreement; "it is believed," wrote Landa, "that with the Itzás who [re] occupied Chichén Itzá there reigned a great lord named *Kuk* (quetzal) *ul* (feather) *can* (serpent) and that the principal building is called the Temple of Kukulcan." This temple was erected over the first, at the top of the truncated pyramid. The Toltec builders introduced carved wooden beams to provide larger space, since Maya rooms were severely restricted by the use of corbeled arching. The walls were muraled and still survive to show many aspects of Maya-Toltec life. An open-mouthed plumed serpent is on the balustrade on each of the four stairways ascending the pyramid. On top, at the temple, the serpents appear again, this time as sculptured columns—precisely like those at Tula. To make doubly certain that people knew it was the Temple of Kukulcan, the top of the building is decorated with the symbol of the sky god, Quetzalcoatl.

The square where the temple rests is a huge, roughly trapezoidal walled square, 1,600 feet by 1,400 feet. Within this is a gigantic ball court (its tribunes carry architectural motifs derived from Tula). There are low platforms, "theater," reached by stone stairways (Landa refers to "two small stages of hewn stone where they gave farces . . . and comedies for the pleasure of the public"). Nearby is a 30-foot-wide ceremonial causeway, leading 900 feet to the sacrificial *cenote*.

The Temple of the Warriors faces the great square. Its corridor of the "thousand columns" is below, within another walled enclosure. This, smaller than the great plaza, has at one end another group of buildings, one of which is called the "Market." There is no doubt about this feature; from indisputable archaeological data Tatiana Proskouriakoff has made a restoration of it, and early Spanish reports speak of the great market at Chichén Itzá "where pilgrims came from foreign parts to trade as well as to worship."

The Temple of the Warriors in many of its features resembles the Toltec temple at Tula: the plumed-serpent columns, fanged mouths open and tails rampant; the motifs of marching jaguars and pumas and eagles, symbolizing the military orders of highland Mexico; the dwarfed figures at the temple's edge that held feather banners; and that Tula fixture, the reclining figure of Chac Mool. Finally, the "thousand columns," which once supported carved wooden roof beams, bear the same martial motifs as those of Tula: armed spearmen with helmet and body armor of Mexican origin.

Tula, near Mexico City, lies more than 800 miles from Chichén Itzá. This is not mere distance. Between the two cities are swamps, jungles, rivers, high mountains, and if mere physical barriers are not enough, there were numerous hostile tribes. "The extraordinary fact," as Eric Thompson has said, "is that nowhere between central Mexico and Yucatán have buildings or sculptures [such as the Temple of the Warriors and the Temple of Tula] in this distinctive style been found." Another archaeologist says flatly that "the draftsmen and architects must have been Toltec . . . the craftsmen, Maya." There is no other instance in pre-America history where two tribes, so distant from one another, erected identical temples in so widely separated places. How did the Toltecs remember the details, for Tula was built between A.D. 900 and 1000, the Temple of the Warriors in Chichén Itzá about 1200? The *Popol Vuh* of the high-land Quiché Maya, which though written in European characters is a literal translation from a Maya painted book, confirms that "Quetzalcoatl . . . after his departure from Tula . . . left . . . with those Toltecs who escaped . . . went to the region of Xicalanco . . . later at Chichén Itzá . . . and the priests as they journeyed . . . toward Yucatán took all their paintings in which they had all things of ancient times and of their arts and crafts . . . and other things that were what they called *u tzibal tulan* . . . the paintings which they put in their chronicles."

This, then, supported by tradition, written record, and archaeology, is the history of Chichén Itzá; and with it, the architectural history of the Maya-Toltecs.

Tulum (A.D. 564) is a walled city lying on the open Caribbean Sea coast opposite (and twenty-five miles from) the extreme southern tip of Cozumel Island.[62] The present-day Maya have in their folklore a tale that in ancient times Tulum was connected to Cobá, Chichén Itzá, and Uxmal by *cuxan san,* a road suspended in the sky. This *cuxan* (living) *san* (rope) is based on considerable archaeological fact; stone-laid causeways at one time did connect all these.

The beginnings of Tulum, anciently called Zama, stretch back into the earliest time. It was being added to during the late Toltec period in Yucatán, and it was populated when the Spaniards in four ships under command of Juan de Grijalva sailed along the coast in May, 1518. The chaplain reported seeing "three large towns separated from each other by two miles. There were many houses of stone . . . we perceived a city or town so large that Seville would not have seemed more considerable . . . there was a very large tower; on the shore was a great throng of Indians, who bore two standards which they raised and lowered to signal us to approach." There were really four towns—Xelha, Soliman, Tulum, and Tancah—situated so close to one another as to give the impression of one continuous city. At that time the chieftain of Tulum was the captor and master of the Spaniards Aguilar and Guerrero.

Tulum is the largest and most impressive Maya city on the east coast of Yucatán. Although, as we have seen, the city had been sighted in the sixteenth century, John Lloyd Stephens and Frederick Catherwood, who journeyed to Tulum during the ides of March, 1842, may be considered as its discoverers.

Tulum is mounted on the summit of a limestone cliff forty feet high, lashed by waves of the open sea.

The cliff is covered with a cheval-de-frise of cactus and thorned plants, a veritable barbed wire. On its other three sides the city is protected by a great wall, 3,600 feet in length and averaging 15 to 20 feet in height. It is pierced by five narrow gateways, each of which will admit only one person at a time. Guardhouses are placed at the western end. Beyond is a solid mass of vegetation growing out of swamps that stretch for many miles inland. The northeast gate was the sallyport to the causeway that led to Xelha, six miles distant, and somewhere near it was the turnoff for Cobá and thence to Chichén Itzá. A three-roomed

Fig. 51. The diving god. A stucco decoration from the Temple of the Diving God at Tulum.

structure was built inside this gateway; it stood over the only water supply, a *cenote* into whose deep hollow there is an underground drainage from the land thereabout.

The Castillo, the largest structure at Tulum, stands close to the cliff that faces the open sea. It is twenty-five feet high. On the top is a squat temple that had a wooden-beam roof and was ornamented on the exterior with stucco figures. The frescoes inside still reflect something of their original beauty.

Within the walled enclosure dominated by the Castillo are ten other structures, exhibiting various periods of construction. The largest, at the southwest end, is the Temple of the Diving God. Twenty-seven feet wide by 20 in depth and 9 feet in height, it is not only the most picturesque building at Tulum, but one of the few that have been preserved. The interior, the outside walls, and both sides of the doorway are painted with frescoes. Over the door, in a niche, is a winged deity plunging earthward. This particular god also appears on the multistoried palace at Sayil; it has been identified as Ah Muzen Cab, the bee god.

On the coastal causeway, north and south of Tulum, were a number of Maya centers, large and small. In the sixteenth century, Maya villages and cities were almost continuous along the east coast—from the large city of Ecab at Cape Cotoche, the most northern point of Yucatán, 150 miles southward to the Bay of Zambac (now called Bahía de la Ascención). Some of these were settlements that dated back to early Maya times; others were erected during the suzerainty of the League of Mayapán—Tulum in particular was expanded then—but most found final flower when the Maya earth took on new vigor, during the Mexican Toltec political absorption, from the twelfth century far into the fifteenth.

31. Sculpture

The function of sculpture was twofold. It was first architectural. In most Maya buildings sculpture wss an integral part of the structure. Secondly, it stands on its own as an art form; sculpture had various voices and various mediums —stone, stucco, wood, and clay.[63]

Most conspicuous, since they are massive and impressive,

are the carved stone monoliths called stelae. These large, shaftlike obelisks appear scattered throughout the Maya cities that existed between the dates A.D. 328 and 889. They represent portraits of priests or rulers, and are carved in relief or in the round, with rows of glyphs that record their dates. As they served a hierarchic purpose, the figures are formal, austere, overpowering. Only the backgrounds have freedom, and some are vehemently alive, the sculptor having been allowed to carve animals, birds, and men that flow about the religious format. One such stela is thirty-five feet high and weighs fifty tons.

Maya sculpture is of wide variety, gods in various forms, doorways, busts, masks, tablets, panels. The material for study is enormous. There are over 400 examples of monumental sculpture that fall within the extreme dates given above, enough for Miss Tatiana Proskouriakoff to have made a minute analysis of styles, traits, and mannerisms. Six broad phases can be distinguished in the evolution of Maya sculptural art.[64]

The sculptor's tool was the stone celt made from either basalt or diorite. His usual medium was limestone, which often had the texture of marble. Inexhaustible patience had taught him to transcend the limitations of neolithic technics. Despite what we would regard as inadequate tools, he was able to simulate in stone the delicate shimmering swirl of quetzal plumes and the texture of a drapery, to represent elaborate bead necklaces and even tattooing, so cleanly carved that the sculpture provides important data on the customs of the ancient Maya. Hieroglyphics are so delicately carved that they have survived the awesome centuries of tropical destruction and can still be read. So complete was the mastery of the Maya sculptor over his material that he seems to have handled large rock masses as dexterously as a Chinese craftsman handles ivory.

Stylistic changes in Maya sculpture make it possible to follow the shift from static to dynamic, from the simple to the ornate. Overemphasis in design, a baroque trait, seems to appear just when Maya society itself becomes ornate. There is a shift from religious to secular themes, from communal emotions to particular ones, that coincides, as Maya history is now read, with a breakup of the older cities, a shift from the purely theocratic to the secular.

Some aesthetes have thought Maya sculpture to be "incommeasurably alien." The Maya, like other peoples of the Americas, had developed an ideal of beauty untouched by historical influences of the kind that figured in the development of European art. It is florid and austere, and yet at its best ranks without question with the best of the art of other world civilizations. At least Roger Fry believed so: "In the finest works of Maya culture . . . we find . . . a plastic sensibility of the rarest kind. I do not know whether even in the greatest sculpture of Europe one could find anything exactly like this in its equilibrium between system and sensibility, in its power to suggest all the complexity of nature."

Stucco allowed the Maya artist greater freedom than stone, and one feels this in the swirling movement of designs modeled in stucco. This form of sculpture is found at widely separated areas, from Tulum on the coast, to newly excavated Dzibilchultun, and up to Palenque in the humid jungles. Stucco is a natural outgrowth of hand-modeled clay. As sculpture, it also was closely allied with architecture, since it appeared usually on the façades of buildings. It is at Palenque, however, that "stucco came into its supreme expression . . . whether frugal or abstract it speaks one idiom . . . it is highly articulate and technically pre-eminent." There are in Palenque whole galleries of stucco figures that are almost Oriental in feeling.

Stucco as an art form is very old. The immense eight-foot-high masks that decorate the temple in Uaxactun, the oldest in Mayadom, were of stucco, as was the heroic-sized head, found at Izamal, that a French explorer sketched in the late nineteenth century. Wherever the Maya went, stucco was sure to go.

Clay sculpture preceded stone sculpture and modeling in stucco. The small clay heads made to propitiate the gods were among the earliest artifacts to be found. While Maya modeling does not have the force of the Aztec, it has great merit. The life-sized funeral urns seen by Diego de Landa and dug up in fragments show how large a clay mass the Maya artists could handle with elaborate appliqué decorations.

Figures in sculptured clay have been discovered throughout the Maya area, but the finest are those found in a cemetery on the island of Jaina, off the Campeche shore; these are the jewels of any Maya collection. The Jaina figures are portrait statuettes. Although small, ranging from six to twelve inches in height, they are majestic in concept. Little else in the whole range of Maya art is more sensitively wrought. Of the Jaina pottery the late Miguel Covarrubias, one of the few creative artists who weighed these as art, said: "It shows an extraordinary mastery in handling, a realistic knowledge of form and movement." The statuettes reflect the Maya ideal; there are figures of warriors and actors with arms outstretched in dramatic movement, chieftains sitting cross-legged and festooned with elaborate headgear; in a sort of Susanna and the Elders theme, an elderly man caresses a young woman. This is the kind of detail for which a historian searches when trying to construct what the Maya looked like behind the luxuriant façades of surface decoration. In these the faces are so exquisitely modeled that every nuance of expression can be seen. Calm, defiance, lust, all can be discerned. More than half of the Jaina statuettes found are of women. These meet Huxley's complaint ("the most conspicuous absence from Maya sculpture is that of the female form—*et tout ce qui s'ensuit . . .*"), for here women as subject matter are treated with concern and feeling.

Wood carving was for the Maya only another form of sculpture, except that wood is a more obedient medium than stone. A considerable number of wood carvings have been found in Yucatán, but the finest are those discovered at Tikal.

Before the Maya carved their calendars on stone, they carved on wooden stelae. When they used wooden beams for ceilings, instead of stone corbeled arching, the beams were carved. Landa referred to some he had seen as "great beams standing erect and ornamented with carvings." At Tikal several of the temple pyramids yielded, even after a thousand years, wooden panels carved of sapodilla wood. One, with a spread-winged quetzal and a fantastically conceived god, is seven by seven feet; a carbon 14 dating confirms the date given on its own glyphs, A.D. 741. Several such have been found at Tikal; they are now all in European museums. Wood carving was practiced extensively by the Maya. They made idols, helmets, ceremonial masks (which were adorned with feathers), masks for actors, intricately adorned wands of office, and carved boards that served as bindings to their "folded books." Landa admitted even in his time that the Maya earned "a great deal making idols and carvings . . . of wood."

Yucatán produced neither gold nor copper. It was just as well. The lack of them delayed their conquest while the Spaniards followed the golden scent to the Aztec realms. Metallurgy developed in South America—all of the very ancient cultures there had it—with its greatest fluorescence in Colombia. On this point there are no dissenting voices. The art of goldsmithery was centuries old in Panama and Costa Rica when Columbus set up a colony at Veragua in 1502 and found the natives gold-spangled. He called the place "Golden Castile" and the king of Spain conferred on him the Duchy of Veragua. Today his descendant still carries it as one of his titles. Veragua (its precise location has not been determined) was a center for casting gold ornaments, and through trade many of these traveled north to the Maya.

By the early eighth century gold began to filter into Mayadom. After 900, when the Maya were concentrated in the Yucatán peninsula and trade was extended, gold and copper began to appear with some frequency. It was further quickened by the coming of the Itzás. Copper brought from Oaxaca to trade at Xicalanco was made into bells; gold plate and leaf brought from Panama were fashioned into ornamental disks and crowns. All that is now known of Maya gold concerns the objects dredged from the *cenote* at Chichén Itzá by Edward H. Thompson. Reposing in the Peabody Museum at Harvard for many years, they have recently been the subject of a splendid brochure.[65] Many of those objects found are in the style of Veragua, suggesting that they were cast there. The gold disks a foot in diameter are interesting for the history of the Maya, for despite the Maya glyphs that rim the disks, they are decorated in Toltec themes—the ritual of tearing the heart from a sacrificial victim, the scenes of naval battle between Itzá and Maya—evidence of how late goldwork came to the Maya.

The Spaniards never found much concentration of gold among the Maya. At Potonchon in 1524 Cortes found various gold objects: crowns, headbands, necklaces, earplugs, little cast figures of gods, lizards, and ducks. The forms show that these were imported from Panama. The only gold cache, which was enough to whet a conquistador's metallic appetite, was seized in Chetumal Province in the early days of the conquest. Chetumal, the center of seagoing-canoe construction, was also a large trade area. The Spaniards seized gold bullion and objects to the value of 2,000 pesos in weight.

The Maya were not given time in which to develop a metallic complex.

32. Painting

Maya painting, as revealed in the frescoes, shows a realistic perception and a more advanced realistic style than that of any of those civilizations numbered among the Sun Kingdoms of the Americas. Art was not for the masses. Despite this, the Maya approach to art form is realistic. Art was not meant to be educational and rarely designed to commemorate historical events. Art was religious, symbolic. It never completely lost its symbolism so as to become purely decorative. Like all symbolic art—including the present-day avalanche of non-representationalism—it was antisocial. Colors, arrangements, signs, symbols meant nothing to the viewer unless he was of the *cognoscenti*.

Because art was religious it concerned itself little with the secular. Despite this the Maya artist limned real people in naturalistic poses. There is an emphasis on movement and an attempt at perspective. People are differentiated by headdress, costume, action. The earliest-known mural—that found at the ruins of Uaxactun—depicts what is easily seen to be a conversation between Maya lords (precisely what they are talking over the glyphs do not reveal). It has gesture, color, movement. Those found at Chacmultun, in the Puuc region of Yucatán, removed by a distance of 210 miles and 600 years from the one at Uaxactun, reveal a continuity of the same spirit.

Murals have been found elsewhere in Mayadom, unfortunately in fragments. The narrative quality of the murals at Chichén Itzá, created during the Toltec period, is almost wholly secular. Those within the Temple of the Warriors, which covered a wall space 9 feet high by 12½ feet wide, belie the name of the temple, for they show scenes of everyday life in a coastal village in Yucatán, a type of picture seldom found among the Maya. Here are realistic and representative drawings of Maya dugout canoes, trees, houses, and even the tall feather-and-wood markers that were used to signal the landfall for sea traffic. Here the artist does not depict temples and priests, but as a sort of Maya Pieter Breughel he shows the simple native house, women at work and rest, and men "who were the oxen of the land," carrying their trade goods to market. On the walls of other structures at Chichén Itzá—the ball court, the Temple of the Jaguars—there are animating scenes of battle. Instructive as to Maya armor and weapons and military technique, they are also revealing tableaux of dress and postures.

Bonampak as place and architecture has already been discussed. The murals of Bonampak, discovered in 1946, have so revolutionized our earlier concept of Maya society that the literature has yet to come fully to terms with the change.

There are three rooms of murals at Bonampak. Taken together they form a continuous narrative: a raid on enemy territory, a consultation among the chiefs, a judgment of prisoners, and a festival to commemorate the victory. The figures are almost life-size and give a sense of arrested

Fig. 52. Mural painting is related to book illustration. It is quite possible that both were directed by the priests. Here artists paint the murals of Bonampak. The room is precisely drawn. Adapted by Alberto Beltran.

movement as if they had been caught by a daguerreotype plate. It is a dynamic composition with a superb handling of masses of color.

The technique was done in classic fresco. Cement was applied to the walls, and while it was still wet the artist drew his cartoon on it. Then his assistants—and there must have been many—applied the colors. As analyzed by the Mexican muralist Villagra, who aided in the copying of the Bonampak pictures, the whole of the three rooms must have been painted in forty-eight hours. Plasterer and artist have to work together in this medium, and since Villagra could not detect where the plaster was laid, the making of a fresco must have been a continuous process. The palette of the Bonampak

artists was rich. The famous Maya blue dominates, and there
are yellows and browns and a lustrous black. The colors
were mostly mineral. The reds and yellows were ioxides;
Maya blue came from a blue chromiferous clay; and black
was carbon. One authority believes that the ground colors
were mixed with the resin of the *pom* tree, from which var-
nish is now produced commercially. The murals of Bonampak
show us the Maya artists' mastery of line and color, and a
passionate movement of figure, a limitless freedom of pos-
ture, that has never before appeared in primitive American
art.

Although the Bonampak murals have disintegrated they
were superbly copied, and the small temple containing the
murals has been duplicated at the Archaeological Museum in
Mexico City.

The decoration of polychromic pottery can also be considered painting, and there are many superb examples of it.
The Maya "book" itself was only a continuation of the
mural. And in turn, many murals, especially those found at
the ruins of Tulum and Santa Rita (in British Honduras),
would appear to be copies of pictures in the "books."

33. The Calendar

The thoughts of Hans Castorp as he contemplates the flight
of time on top of the Magic Mountain, in Thomas Mann's
novel, would have found a sympathetic response among the
Maya, for no other people in history made of time so great
a fetish. "What is time?"

The whole of Mayadom with its hundreds of stone cities
and thousands of sculptured stones may be said to be one vast
monument to their extraordinary preoccupation with time
and its consequences. On ball courts and temples, on lintels,
sculptured panels, shells, jade, polychromic dishes, on wood,
on stone and modeled stucco, the Maya over a period of a
thousand years carved the date when each particular piece
was finished or begun, or a date that marked some important
event of the past or present. At Copán the famed Hieroglyphic Stairway—composed of 62 flights, 33 feet wide—has
more than 2,000 individual glyphs carved on its risers. The
dates of completion can be read from these, but little else.

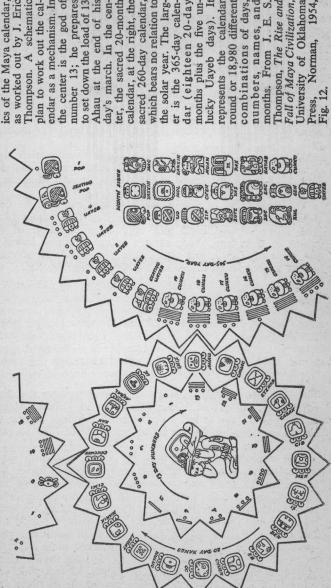

Fig. 53. The mechanics of the Maya calendar, as worked out by J. Eric Thompson. A schematic plan to work out the calendar as a mechanism. In the center is the god of number 13; he prepares to set down the load of 13 Ahau at the end of his day's march. In the center, the sacred 20-month calendar, at the right, the sacred 260-day calendar, which bears no relation to the solar year. The larger is the 365-day calendar (eighteen 20-day months plus the five unlucky Uayeb days). It represents the calendar round or 18,980 different combinations of days, numbers, names, and months. From J. E. S. Thompson, *The Rise and Fall of Maya Civilization*, University of Oklahoma Press, Norman, 1954, Fig. 12.

People of other civilizations were beset by time. What is a calendar when all is said and done but a method of classifying time into periods—days, weeks, months, years, centuries—for the convenience of civil life and, in the realm of religion, for fixing the precise moment for rituals. The Greeks bewailed, with a rare eloquence, the transience of youth and the flight of time. Other peoples have felt the pressure of endless continuity so depressing that in order to make it reasonably bearable they organized it into cycles— hence our calendar. Almost everyone, at one time or another, is made aware of time's flux, and one often feels to excess the bitterness of departure; but the Maya . . . One scholar found a Maya inscription that probed ninety million years into the past. Time, the Maya concluded rightly, has no beginning and eternity was an everlasting moment. Still, why this obsessive preoccupation with time?

There have been attempts ever since the dawn of man to work out a satisfactory calendar. Man began to observe and record the positions of planets, the phases of the moon, and the eclipses of the sun to organize this celestial phenomena into calends, months.[66]

Greek chronology before the appearance of the philosopher Erastosthenes was absurdly inadequate. A Greek lunar calendar was calculated on the appearance of the first crescent moon, yet the city-states differed among themselves on when to insert the intercalary month, so that there was great confusion as to the correct date. Aristophanes made great sport of this confusion in his *Clouds*, where he makes the moon complain that days were not being correctly kept according to her reckoning.

The Egyptians after 3000 B.C. used a lunar calendar and divided their seasons into three: flood, seed, and harvest time. Like the Maya, they had both a religious and civil calendar. The Jewish calender was also lunar; it featured the seven-day week and the Sabbath. The Roman lunar calendar was hopelessly confused until Julius Caesar called in Sosigenes, who suggested that the Romans use the uneven month and the leap year.

The Mayas believed that time was cyclical, that the same influence and thus the same consequences would be repeated in history. Why did they not then use the lunar month?

The Maya had not one calendar but three. The *haab* year was made up of eighteen periods, or months, of twenty days each, plus a terminal period of five days called *Uayeb* (the empty or unlucky days). The second was the *tzolkin*, a sacred calendar of 260 days. The Aztecs and Toltecs also had the *tzolkin*. No one knows why they settled on this precise number of days, unless it comes out of some "crystallized pantheon," for it has no astronomical significance. The third calendar was the "long count," which reckoned the number of days since the mythical beginning of the Maya era, which was dated 4 Ahau 8 Cumhu for reasons unknown (equivalent to B.C. 3111). What occurred at this date? We do not know. There is no clue, for archaeology reveals that at this time the Maya as such did not even exist. Still, all of the known calendars of the world hark back to a date which represents the beginning of time.[67]

Twenty *kins* or days, made up the Maya month (*uinal*). Eighteen *uinals* plus the five-day Uayeb brought the total of the Maya year (*tun*) to 365 days. Next came the *katun*, a period of 7,200 days or twenty years. Then there was the period of 52 years now called the "Calendar Round." Each day of the *haab* year had a name and number, as did each day of the sacred *tzolkin*. The coincidence of any given *haab* day with any given *tzolkin* day occurred every 18,980 (*haab*)

KIN   UINAL   TUN

KATUN   BAKTUN   PICTUN

CALABTUN   KINCHILTUN   ALAUTUN

Fig. 54. The nine known Maya time periods with the corresponding glyphs. *Kin* was a day; *uinal*, twenty days or a month; *tun*, 360 days; *katun*, twenty *tuns* (7,200 days). Time proceeded in this manner until *alautun*, which was 23,040,000,000 days in length.

days, or 52 years. The Aztecs had a similar obsession with the 52-year cycle.

Maya calendrics were not mere intellectual gymnastics. The farmer had to know when to plant and when to sow. He depended on the priest-astronomer to tell him when rain could be expected. The seafarer had to know when to expect a full moon, an eclipse, or a hurricane. The Maya were dominated by fear and superstition, and used astronomy as a handmaiden of astrology, but they were sometimes remarkably accurate observers of the heavens. Maya astronomers calculated that the synodical revolution of Venus took an average of 584 days. The count made by modern astronomers, using precise instruments, is 583.92. The famed Dresden Codex is apparently a table of eclipse syzygies showing the revolutions of the planet Venus over a period of more than three centuries.

They had names for Venus (*chac noh ek*), the North Star (*xamann ek*), Ursa Minor (the Maya name meant "guards of the north," the Pleiades (*tzab*: "rattles of the rattlesnake"), the Gemini (*ak ek*: "turtle stars"), and Scorpio (*zinaan ek,* which curiously enough meant the same as the Greek, "scorpion stars"). They believed that eclipses—they could predict the lunar eclipse every 173.31 days—were caused by ants eating at the planets.

Every moment of their lives was involved in the position of the planets. They feared that if the gods were not propitiated they would put an end to the world, and that is perhaps the reason for their obsession with having an almost exact calendar, so that each god at the right moment might have his prayers or the sacrifices meant for him.

Many scholars seem in agreement that the Maya, no matter how widely dispersed, exchanged astronomical data to perfect their calendar and that there was a "congress" at Copán in A.D. 765 to adjust the calendar and the accumulated errors of the past 52 years. The month of Pop began their year, and they gathered at Copán to put Pop in order. The presence of the same date on Maya monuments as distant from one another as 300 miles suggests intimate contacts for exchange of this data.

Diego de Landa was the first to call attention to their calendar. "They have their year as perfect as ours, consisting of 365 days and six hours. They divided it into two kinds of months, the one kind of thirty days . . . and the other kind of twenty days. . . . The whole year had eighteen of these months plus five days and six hours . . . for these . . . they have twenty days or characters by which they name them." Landa fortunately had the good sense to copy down the glyphs of the day-signs, with their Maya names in Spanish script, and upon these sketches all subsequent study by epigraphers has been grounded.

Of the *katuns,* Landa said: "By them they kept an account of their ages marvelously well . . . and thus it was easy for an old man to whom I spoke . . . to remember traditions going back three hundred years. . . . Whoever put in order this computation of *katuns,* if it was the devil, he did it, as he usually does, ordaining it for his own glory." The *katuns* set down in books were the mnemonic device by which past events were remembered. Here were records of eclipses of the moon, and of unlucky days (floods, hurricanes, pestilence). If a pestilence had occurred on the date 13 Ahau, the Maya were certain that pestilence would occur again on the same day. Typical is this prophecy in the Maya books: "13 Ahau. There is no luck for us on this day." Another entry: "5 Ahau . . . harsh is the face of this day-god and harsh are the things he brings."

Thus Maya religion made use of every possible device to exert control over the people, for, as in all theocracies, astronomy, religion, ritual, and science were interlinked.

34. Land Communications

Apart from the famous Inca road system which they somewhat resemble, the Maya communications were the best in the hemisphere until the Lancaster Turnpike was opened in North America in 1792. Those Maya *sacbeob* which are best known are ceremonial, for roads everywhere played a part in religion. Those who took part in sacred voyages were sacrosanct, and the curious trait of "right of asylum" extended to roads; wayfarers were under the protection of the gods. Anyone who dared attack Aztec merchants moving on roadways underwent swift retribution, and travelers walked the Inca royal road in perfect safety even though it went through hostile territory.

Early Spanish settlers in Yucatán noted the remains of Maya roads. "There are signs even today," says Diego de Landa, writing in the sixteenth century, "that there was once a handsome causeway from T'ho [now Mérida] to the other city, Izamal." This Izamal, another Spaniard noted, was a center of great pilgrimages: "for which reason there had been made *four roads* running out to the four cardinal points which reached to all ends of the land, Tabasco, Guatemala, Chiapas, so that today [1633] in many parts may be seen vestiges of those roads." In 1883 there were still, as reported by a traveler, remains of it; "a road from this Izamal ran to Polé, facing the sea and island of Cozumel." Polé was in a direct line with Cozumel Island and the road from Izamal was "used by pilgrims going to Cozumel to visit the shrine."

Fig. 55. Inland communications. Raised causeways connected many of the Maya centers.

And there were other *sacbeob* connecting various ancient cities. "There are remains of paved highways which traverse all this kingdom and they say they ended in the east on the seashore . . . these highways were like the Spanish *caminos reales,* which guided them with no fear of going astray." Roads were also seen in the jungles. A Spaniard reported that on his journey in 1560 from Chiapas to Champotón one league from Mazalan (near Lake Tacab in the Petén) they came upon a fine road, broad and level, which led to the city. Other *sacbeob* moved through the jungle from Campeche to Lake Bacalar, one of the centers of Maya canoe building. A padre in 1695 states that he "followed roads through the swamps which had been built in ancient times and still were well preserved." Aerial photographs recently taken by oil geologists confirm the existence of these roads.

Hernando Cortes, in his celebrated march through the heartlands of the Maya in 1524, proved the reality of these roads. He was given by some Xicalanco merchants a detailed map, painted on cotton cloth, which showed the route. At various places he followed causeways which went through mangrove swamps. He took the river route, up the Usumacinta; it was the interior route followed by Maya merchants going from Tabasco to Honduras. They made the first portion of the journey by canoes, but Cortes was impeded by his cavalry and was forced to build bridges. Above Iztapan "a fine large town on the back of the magnificent river [Usumacinta] he ordered a bridge to be built . . . it was done in four days . . . and horses and men passed over it . . . it contained more than a thousand logs the smallest of which was the thickness of a man's body. . . . I do not know what plan these Indians used to build this bridge; all that one can say is that it is the most extraordinary thing one has ever seen."

Once into the interior of Acalan Province, Cortes found his map listed seventy-two towns all connected by road; again he followed the route used by the Tabasco merchants. Itzamkanac was the Acalan capital. It had temples and 900 houses; and beyond it Cortes had found rest houses. Since Cortes' route lay near the ancient cities of Tikal and Uaxactun, he crossed remains of roads that once connected these to all of the other Maya cities. At Tayasal, the Itzá Maya capital of El Petén, Cortes found many merchants, their produce carried by slaves, on their way to the fairs of Nito and Naco; he shaped his way there. South of the river Polochic, which feeds into Lake Izabal, in turn flowing into the Gulf of Honduras, Cortes entered the city of Chacujal (it remains unexplored). There he found a city with several roads leading into and out of it. The Spaniards followed one to Nito (now named Livingston), which is on the left, or north, bank of Lake Izabal; this was an important trading center frequented by Maya and Nahuatl-speaking traders. From Nito travelers were transported by canoe to the other bank, where the road began. It wound for fifty miles through the rugged mountains of the Sierra de Espíritu Santo, down into the lower Motagua River valley and across the Sierra Mico. It was the same route taken by Stephens and Catherwood in their memorable journey. Stephens remembered those five hours, "dragged through mud-holes, squeezed in gulleys, knocked against trees and tumbled over roots; every step required care and physical exertion. . . ." When Catherwood was thrown clear off his mule and struck his head on an outsize tree, Stephens felt that their inglorious epitaph might be: "tossed over the head of a mule, brained by the trunk of a mahogany tree and buried in the mud of Mico Mountains." Yet 300 years before there had been a fine road, and Bernal Díaz, that honest conquistador, mentions the wide, "direct" road he followed from Nito to Naco; others with him commented on the wide roads "bordered with fruit trees."

Maya roads constructed during the "classical period" (A.D. 300–900) seem to have connected most of the inland cities with those of the coast. A recent aerial oil survey in El Petén has revealed the scars of roads comparable to the known Maya road-axis at Cobá. Tikal was bound with a causeway to Uaxactun and thence onward toward rivers which by canoe connected them with the sea in the Province of Chetumal. Although there has been one very limited study of a Maya causeway, it may be presumed that many of the Maya centers in classical times were bound together by roads; trade routes have everywhere been reported by the early padre-explorers. Typical was that of Las Casas, who was poled up rivers and followed roads from the Rio Tacotalpa to Chiapas by way of Teapa and Solosuchiapa, thence took the old trade route over which came the yellow topaz beads that the Spaniards called "amber."

Maya cities in the Puuc, of which Uxmal was the center, were connected by roads, as Stephens first noted in November, 1841. The writer of this book has explored those roads during his various periods in Yucatán. A causeway fifteen feet wide, varying in height from two to four feet, runs from Uxmal to Kabah (where it still can be seen). One part there makes a 180-degree turn to enter the gateway of Kabah; another leads on to Sayil, Labná, and other cities of the Puuc. Northwest Uxmal was connected with Mayapán and from there to Chichén Itzá. The latter has eight *sacbeob* within the city, and at least two of the roads lead out of its environs toward other Maya centers. Best known at Chichén Itzá is the ceremonial causeway that leads from the Temple of Kukulcan. Nine hundred feet in length and 33 feet in width, it goes to the edge of the sacrificial *cenote*. Not so well known are the *sacbeob* that led out from Chichén Itzá. These have been traced by the writer from an air survey. Photographs reveal that a road went from Chichén Itzá toward Chabalam, where it undoubtedly connected with the well-known (and only really surveyed) road that leads from Yaxuná sixty-two miles toward Cobá.

Ceremonial roads within some of the greater Maya city centers are, of course, well known. As was mentioned earlier, those of Tikal, built between A.D. 400 and 900, were economic as well as ceremonial. A causeway in the south ravine of the city acts as a dike; the ravine itself, its porous limestone cemented, served as a reservoir. The wide surface of the dike was a ceremonial road which passed from one center to another. All of Tikal is bound by wide stone causeways.

Many other Maya sites have causeways. The one at Labná, 600 feet long and 25 feet wide, is well known; it went from the principal temple to a smaller one famed for its gateway. The newly uncovered ceremonial road at Dzibilichaltún, twice the width of the one at Labná and possibly a thousand years older, reveals the form and function of a Maya ceremonial road.

And at the shrine on Cozumel Island the first Spanish expedition there in 1517 reported that "this town was well paved . . . the roads raised on the sides . . . and paved with large stones."

The only *sacbe* which has been formally explored is the so-called Cobá–Yaxuná axis. The study took twenty days, and is described in a small brochure.[68] The known length of the road is 62.3 miles. It begins at the site of Yaxuná, 13

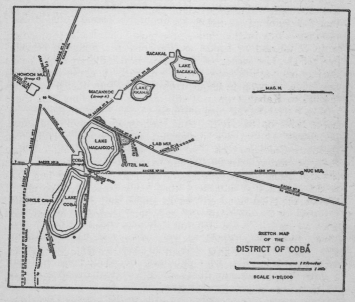

Fig. 56. The *sacbe*-road complex about the Cobá lakes. Cobá lies inland twenty-five miles from the coast, in a direct line with the walled city of Xelha, to which it was connected by road. The complex of roads about Cobá was explored by J. Eric Thompson as part of his study of the ruins. From Cobá, the road runs for sixty-two miles toward Yaxuná. Redrawn from the plans accompanying *A Preliminary Study of the Ruins of Cobá*, J. E. S. Thompson, H. E. D. Pollock, and J. Charlot, Washington, D. C., 1932.

miles southwest of Chichén Itzá. Like most *sacbeob*, it is a causeway, raised above the surface of the land, and despite the depressions it keeps an even level. It varies in height from 2 to 8 feet, and is 32 feet wide. Maya *sacbeob* have various widths, so that we do not yet have a standard. The Inca coastal road, 2,520 miles long, had as its standard a width of 24 feet. One asks rhetorically, Why so wide a road when the people did not have the wheel? The Inca, of course, used llamas for transport. With the Maya "the people were the oxen themselves." Although Maya architecture has been minutely studied as yet no one has suggested what was the Maya standard of measurement.

The *sacbe* was dry-laid. The Maya engineer first laid down a roughly dressed limestone bed; the stones in this varied in weight from twenty-five to three hundred pounds. On top of this went a limestone gravel which when wetted and tramped down made a hard, smooth surface. The result was the *sacbe*, the white road which the early Spaniards found "fine, broad and level."

In its 62.3 miles the Cobá–Yaxuná road makes six changes in direction. There is no topographical reason for this, but the remains of a Maya city lying in the direction of every shift suggest that the road was built to reach towns already in existence.

At stated intervals ramparts cross the *sacbe* transversely; it may well be that these held "stations of the road," as was first suggested by Teobert Maler. The Inca maintained rest stations (*tampus*) along the entire length of their royal road, every twelve to eighteen miles. We know from the literature that the Maya had a similar system, but we have neither its name nor precise function. We know much of the Inca *tampu* system, but nothing of the Maya other than a post-conquest reference to an *alcalde meson* who in each village was designated to keep up the traveler's house and see that wood, maize, and other provisions were always at hand. Markers have been found along the road every eight kilometers. Señor Alfonso Villa, who explored the road, believes them to have been boundary markers rather than distance markers. It would be strange, however, if the Maya did not mark distance, since most peoples did this on their roads. The Inca marked theirs by a *topo;* the Persians set up "pillars to indicate distances," the Greeks, as bad as their roads were, marked them at intervals with piles of rocks, onto which travelers were expected to toss an "absolution stone." Roman roads were marked; when Ptolemy built the African desert road, distance markers were placed every four miles. There must have been some sort of markers on the Maya *sacbeob*, for

Landa stated it as a fact that travelers on the roads were expected to burn copal to honor the Ek Chuah, the god of traders and merchants.

Cobá was a large city.[69] Built between two lakes, it contained clusters of interrelated buildings. The city was a hub of a series of roads. More than sixteen have been found within the environs. One of them even crosses the arm of one of the lakes. On some roads there were nearby gateways with rectangular pillars and buildings, which suggest that tolls were collected or at least passage was controlled. The main road (*Sacbe* 1) continues in a southeastern direction from the junction point, goes through Nohogh-mul, and is then lost. No known exploration has been undertaken from this point eastward. The author, first by ground then from a low-flying plane, saw the unmistakable welts of a road running toward Kelha, which lies directly adjacent to the Caribbean Sea facing the southern end of Cozumel Island. Xelha lay on a road, fragments of which remain, that followed the coast twelve miles southward toward Tulum; north of Xelha the *sacbe* led to Polé and Mochi.

This road complex unmistakably exhibits that the *sacbeob* were not only ceremonial; they were trade arteries as well.

Having no dray animals, the Maya carried all produce on their backs. The chieftains were carried in litters. Though none of these survive, there is an illustration of a very elaborate one scratched on the walls of a temple at Tikal; a chieftain being carried in a wickerwork palanquin is pictured on a vase from Guatemala; and there are several eyewitness accounts of Maya chieftains being carried "in large litters decorated with plumes."

All people who possessed roads had a developed messen-

Fig. 57. (Pp. 186-87.) A schematic plan of the Maya *sacbe*-road complex, based on the scattered observations of 400 years, some excavations and explorations, and one specific, although limited, study of a road. The map is based on that of S. G. Morley, *The Ancient Maya*, Stanford University Press, 1946, Plate 19, with additions.

The authorities used for this first compilation of Maya roads are: Hernando Cortes (1524); Bernal Díaz del Castillo (1568; pub. 1904 and 1908); Diego de Landa (written 1556; pub., Tozzer edition, 1941); Antonio Ciudad de Real (written 1588; pub. 1872); Joseph Delgado (1677; unpub.); the map of Melchior de Alfaro Santa Cruz (made in 1579; pub. 1938); John L. Stephens (1841-1843); Desiré Charnay (1863); Bernardo de Lizana (1633); Teobert Maler (1932); M. H. Saville (1930); R. R. Bennett (1930); Ralph Roys (1943); Thompson (1928, 1932); Alfonso Villa (1934); Victor von Hagen (1931, 1937, 1958, 1959).

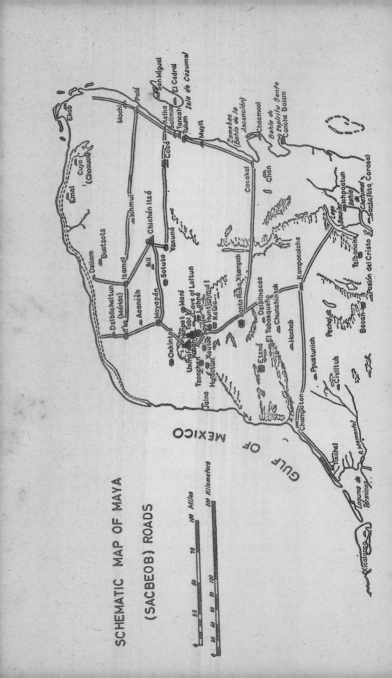

SCHEMATIC MAP OF MAYA

(SACBEOB) ROADS

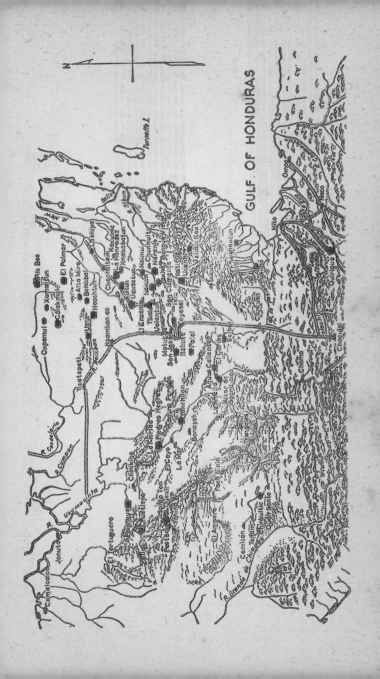

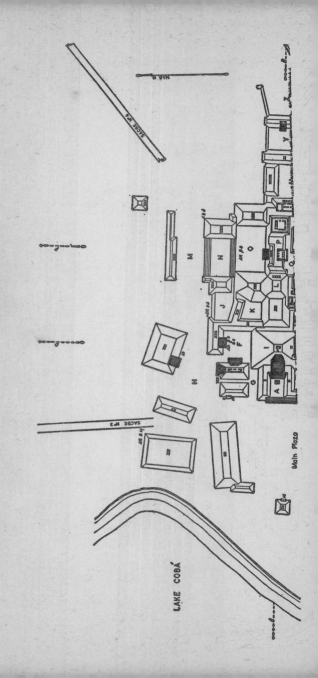

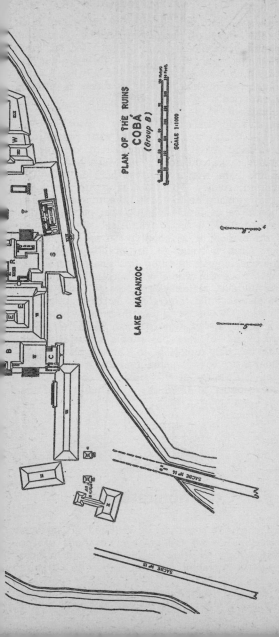

Fig. 58. Maya roads and Maya city planning: This plan illustrates how the causeways enter Cobá, the city of the lakes. The precise terminus of the roads has not been found. Note that *Sacbe 14* is directed through the edge of the lake. Redrawn from the plans accompanying *A Preliminary Study of the Ruins of Cobá*, J. E. S. Thompson, H. E. D. Pollock, and J. Charlot, Washington, D. C., 1932.

ger service. The Inca had the *chasqui,* which system continued down to the nineteenth century in Peru as an integral part of the Spanish post-office system.[70] The Aztec had runners who carried ideograph messages in a forked stick. Of the Maya system nothing is known except that when Cortes sent a letter to the two Spaniards living as slaves among the Maya, an Indian carried it "wrapped up in his hair."

On the methods of Maya road building again there is nothing. Presumably, it was carried out by a *corvée* levied on the Maya villages through which the road passed and each particular village or city was required to keep up its share. Maintenance makes the road. The Maya had to fight constantly with the plant life; a tree seed here needs only a handful of earth to fructify. The Cobá road has now been destroyed by trees growing on top of it, spreading their roots through the interstices of lime rock. On top of the Cobá–Yaxuná road, near Ekal, a large cylindrical stone thirteen feet long was discovered; it weighed five tons. It was first thought to have been a roller to flatten down the road, but now most archaeologists question this interpretation for technical reasons. Since the whole of Yucatán is a mass of lime rubble and building material lies close at hand, it was not a herculean task to build these roads. It did réquire considerable engineering knowledge to pass through swamps and to lay down a straight, undeviating roadbed. Since an Indian can move 1,500 pounds of lime-rock rubble on his back per day, a road could be fairly rapidly built. There is one record: when the Spaniards in 1564 wanted to open a road from Mérida to Maní, a distance of fifty miles, it took 300 Indians only three months to open the forest and build the *sacbe.*

35. Communications

The Maya also used the sea road. It required no upkeep. They and they alone of all the great civilizations of the ancient Americas were a maritime people, going out in large ocean-going dugouts, traveling over thousands of miles of coastal sea.

The first things that Columbus met when he landed at Guanaja in 1502 were Maya boats. At one of the islands he saw and examined one "as long as a galley, eight feet in breadth, rowed by twenty-five Indian paddlers," and laden with commodities—cacao, copper, bells, flint-edged swords, cotton cloth—brought from the mainland, twenty miles distant.

As Spanish voyages began to multiply, others reported seeing immense dugout canoes that held as "many as forty Indians." In 1542, at the siege of Omoa, a trading colony in

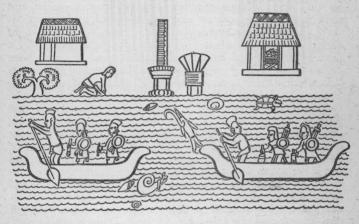

Fig. 59. Immense sea-going canoes "with as many as forty passengers" sailed the Gulf Coast, said Bernal Díaz (1517). A Maya drawing of canoes with houses along the coast, from the Temple of the Warriors, Chichén Itzá.

Honduras, fifty war canoes were sent at one time all the way from Chetumal, a distance of over 200 sea miles, to aid in resisting the conquistadors. Many of the early Spanish accounts mention the tremendous number of canoes and the amount of canoe traffic along the entire coast from Tabasco to Panama.

The Maya canoe *(chem)* was usually made from cedar, and carved out of a single tree trunk often as long as eighty feet. It was built with a high bow and stern more or less as the Maya have themselves pictured it in the murals of Chichén Itzá. There were several well-known canoe-building areas. The fallen cedars were dragged from the woods over log rollers by means of rope cable and manpower. At the town of Buct-zotz, a little west of Cape Cotoche, there was a special enterprise for cutting cedar and making it into canoes; these were largely used for the salt trade at Ekab.

In the province of Uyamil, near the inland lake of Bacalar, there is an immense area of cedar. The Maya at Mazanho made a specialty of dugout building destined for the coastal sea traffic. Small rivers flowed out of the lake (the ruins of Ichpaatun, which date from the sixth century, are close by) into the large Chetumal Bay. Between A.D. 400 and 800 Tikal and other interior cities had contact with the sea, using the river roads that emptied into Chetumal Bay. Further north, at the Bay of Ascención—anciently, Zamabac—was a place for the embarking of "maritime traffic destined for Honduras and other regions south." [71] Later, at the Spanish arrival, circa 1511, trade had shifted further north to Tulum. This city was connected by road to Xelha, thence to Cobá and the interior cities such as Chichén Itzá. So complete was their dominance of the coastal sea that the Maya of Chikin Chel were known as "lords of the sea," while those seafarers about Chetumal were called "guardians of the sands," presumably because they protected the coast from the incursions of the Mosquito Indians from Nicaragua (who were still attacking up to the eighteenth century) and perhaps from stray Carib raiders who followed the spoor of trading canoes.

The whole coast about the Laguna de Términos—where Xicalanco was located—was a network of rivers, bayous, and creeks. A Spanish map of the seventeenth century shows inland waterways and describes in detail routes by narrow channels, such as appear on the Florida coast where craft of small draft can move without actually going out into the open sea. This coast was difficult for European ships, which had to stand out to sea, but not for the Maya dugouts.

Inland waterways led to the Usumacinta River, which (by portage and prayer) the Indians managed to navigate upstream two hundred miles. The rivers of Honduras were navigable for canoe traffic many miles inland, and salt, for example, was carried in sacks direct from the Yucatán salt ponds to the interior of Honduras. There they were filled with cacao and obsidian for the return voyage. The whole coast was a Maya economic block, with some concessions to the Nahuatl-speaking traders from Xicalanco. Seafaring was coastal. Signs were erected, feather banners, to help sailors navigate the flat shore. The murals of Chichén Itzá, which illustrate Maya canoes, also show signs that could be so interpreted. One writer with lively imagination says they had a "lighthouse service"—perhaps there was an occasional fire, but scarcely a "service." The Romans, who hated the sea and called it "the pasture of fools," hugged the coast with their ships. So did the Maya. Only in dire emergency, one gathers, did they navigate at night, at which time they used the North

Star to guide them. The large canoes used a lateen sail—
Bernal Díaz saw it—but mostly it was manpower; the trading canoes were "paddled by slaves just like the galley slaves
of Venice."

There were limits to Maya seafaring. There is no evidence
that the Maya had contact with Cuba, even though it is
only 125 miles away, perhaps because a bewildering and
dangerous current runs between Cuba and Yucatán. Yet there
was an occasional accidental, if not purposeful, contact with
the Antilles. Bernal Díaz met at Cozumel Island "a good-
looking woman who . . . spoke the language of Jamaica. As I
. . . knew the language . . . we were very much astonished
and asked her how she happened here . . . two years earlier
she had started from Jamaica with ten Indians in a large
canoe intending to fish . . . the currents had carried them to
Cozumel where they had been driven ashore; her husband
and all other males had been killed and sacrificed to the
idols. . . ."

One wonders how far Maya sea traffic extended. There is
evidence, archaeological and historical, that these voyages
carried them from Tampico down to Panama. Following the
coast line, this is over 2,400 sea miles, and it reaches an impressive 3,000 miles if they went as far south as Margarita
Island, which lies 15 miles off Venezuela opposite Araya
Peninsula. It was the pre-Columbian source of pearls. A
baroque pear-shaped pearl was found in the tomb at Palenque
under the Temple of Inscriptions (dated A.D. 700) and another
was found in the tomb of the high priest at Chichén Itzá.

The Maya maintained trading stations along the Caribbean
coast in Yucatán and Quintana Roo; at Nito, where Lago
Izabal debouches into the sea; inland at Naco; and along the
Honduran coast at Omoa and Trujillo. This last was seen by
Cortes in 1524: "There was a mighty and haughty lord who
commanded 10,000 people or more . . . the Maya traded for
birds, feathers, salt, and achiote."

From here the Maya skirted the treacherous Mosquito
coast, full of shoals and cays—where Columbus floundered
on his last voyage in 1502—down to the San Juan River in
Nicaragua (the same river for which William Walker and
Commodore Vanderbilt contended in 1846, seeking for control of the Nicaragua Interoceanic Canal). There a trading
station was maintained. Their canoes, we know from historical evidence, were poled up the San Juan River well
over a hundred miles to Lake Nicaragua. "Other nations,"
stated a Spanish historian, "traded in the province of Nicaragua . . . especially those [Maya] of Yucatán who came
by the sea in canoes." The Spaniards immediately went there,

guided by Maya traders, "because gold was carried from there."

After A.D. 900 the Maya seemed to have extended their commerce to Panama, for from that time on gold frequently appears. Emeralds, if the Maya had them—and the writer has seen none which are really emeralds—would have come from the same Panamanian source. The gold-working Indians about Coclé, in Panama, traded with the Chibchas of highland Colombia who exploited the emerald-producing lands about Muzo and Chimor, then the only source of emeralds in the New World.

There is no evidence of any direct Maya penetration into South America. No pottery has been found in South America which is unquestionably Maya. Finally, there is no hint in the traditions of any southern cultures that they were even dimly aware of the existence of the Maya.

The Maya navigated to islands only if those islands could be seen from land. Cozumel—its real name was *Ah-cuzumil peten* (Swallow Island)—lies close to the mainland. Yet as an arm of the Gulf Stream runs between it and the mainland, sailing is treacherous. When Captain Montejo tried on one occasion to force the Indians to make the run when the sea was high, they refused. The water was *homoc-nac kaknab,* it boiled yellow. It is just this *homoc-nac kaknab* that kept Carib and Maya from any certain contact. Nothing Antillean has yet been found in Maya graves. However, as evidenced by the instance of the Jamaica woman and the famous castaway Aguilar, there must have been enough casual contacts to make the Maya aware of "something out there." It is even possible that Carib canoes occasionally came purposely into Maya territorial waters; many of the coastal cities were walled for some reason.

Archaeological evidence shows that trading voyages went as far north as Tampico, to the Huasteca, who spoke a Maya dialect. Bitumen, which was widely used for boat caulking, at that time could be obtained only from oil seepages, and the latter were in Mexico. The Maya also used bitumen in the preparation of effigy masks. Huasteca-made spindle whorls for making cotton thread are found in Maya graves. Even Tikal, which seems so hemmed in by jungle, yields sting-ray barbs, seaweed, and shells from the Pacific; Palenque, pearls from Margarita; the well of Chichén Itzá, gold from Panama; and other sites, pottery from Veracruz.

Evidence of their use of the sea roads considerably changes the tribal portrait of the Maya, who are so often pictured as cloistered in their green mansions and occupied only with the metaphysics of time.

36. Glyph-Writing

"The Maya," said a sixteenth-century writer, "are commended . . . among all other Indians in that they have characters and letters with which they write their histories and ceremonies." And Diego de Landa agreed: "These people made use of certain characters . . . which they wrote on their books." Maya glyph-writing was, in all of its aspects, the most advanced in the Americas, even though it was not unique. Many tribes of Mexico had a form of writing although not in so advanced a form. It is fully possible that the Olmeca, who were the northern neighbors of the Maya, were the originators of glyph-writing.

What Maya writing really *is*, is disputatious. For long it remained an utter enigma until Bishop Landa's manuscript *On the Things of Yucatán* was uncovered in 1864. He thought that there was an alphabet in Maya writing. What the Maya informants gave the bishop was no ordinary alphabet at all. When he asked for a letter, his informant drew "a glyphic element resembling the sound." For example, *E* (pronounced "ay" in Spanish) was in Maya *be*, which means "road"; so the artist-informant drew the ideograph for "road," a pair of parallel lines representing the *sacbe*. When the outline of a human footprint was drawn between the parallels, it was the glyph for "travel." The discoverer of the Landa manuscript was the diligent though erratic scholar Charles Etienne Brasseur (the title "de Bourbourg" he had discarded with the fall of Napoleon III), who had held an administrative post under the ill-fated Maximilian of Mexico. He rushed into print with Landa's book and tried with fervid imagination to use it in reading the Troano Maya Codex which lay in Paris. The result was catastrophic. A sentence read: "The master is he of the upheaved earth, the master of the calabash, the earth upheaved of the tawny beast; it is he, the master of the upheaved earth of the swollen earth, beyond measure, the master of the basin of water . . ." All attempts to read Maya glyphs with this "alphabet" have been dismal failures; still, Eric Thompson believes that what Landa recorded still is as close to a Maya Rosetta Stone as will ever be found.

Maya writing was ideographic, thought William Gates, a

Fig. 60. Glyphs of the Maya days: Each of the twenty days of the month had a name.

very lucid writer-scholar. It had system; there are main elements, names of things, words of action (which imply verbs). There are a number of adjectival glyphs, such as those representing colors, and a set of minor glyphic elements wholly undefined, which could be "very necessary parts of a written language." Gates set out to make a tabulation of Maya glyph forms, a sort of Maya dictionary (which is not too highly approved by scholars now because casting the glyphs into type, it is felt, reduces their value for students); the work was left unfinished at his death in 1940 and his materials were dispersed.[72]

Maya writing is ideographic, since the characters stand for abstract ideas. It also has rebus-writing elements. It is pictorial and symbolic but not syllabic, yet there is a considerable amount of phonetics in the writing. Aztec writing was simpler in form, and was capable of iconomatic punning: a grasshopper, *chapul*, is drawn on top of a mountain, *tepec*, resulting in the word "Chapultepec" which can be easily read. The system was exact enough so that the names of every Aztec city, village, province, and chieftain are known, whereas among the Maya not a single glyph has been identified that is associated with any person or place. It is known that the Maya had their own names painted or tattooed on their arms or hands. If in the future glyphs that "identify" are recognized, then one may have the material to read a Maya sentence.[73]

The Maya glyph was self-contained. It filled its appointed place. There are glyph-compounds. The main element has various affixes which modify it and extend it. A prefix could be placed to the left or below a postfix, to its right or below; where it was placed depended on the space that was being allowed for it. William Gates, when redrawing all the known glyphs that occur in the three surviving codices, found that there were many different types of affixes, subfixes, prefixes, and postfixes. Some were pictographic, others symbolical. He found numerous minor elements which in their way are the traffic of Maya speech.

Of this extensive corpus of Maya texts, 60 per cent remains undeciphered. Those glyphs which deal with dates and calculations can be read; those that deal with ritualistic matters and history cannot.

Since much of the preoccupation of the Maya was with calendrics, calculation was well developed. Our counting system is decimal. Theirs was vigesimal; twenty, the number of toes and fingers, became the base. As numerical symbols the bar (——) had a value of five and the dot (●), a value of one. They counted in groups of twenty. Twenty was represented by a shell (the symbol of zero) with a dot over it. In-

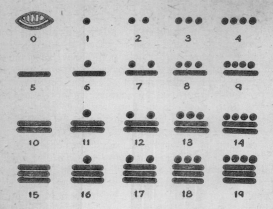

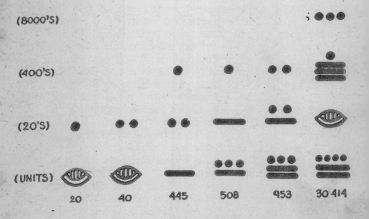

Fig. 61. Maya numeration: The mollusk shell is the symbol for zero; the dot is one; the bar, five. By combining forms, large totals could be calculated. From J. E. S. Thompson, *The Rise and Fall of Maya Civilization*, University of Oklahoma Press, Norman, 1954.

dependent discovery of the abstract zero gave the Maya a system of place notation, and with it they were able to calculate immense sums. As a system it was far better than the Greek, Egyptian, or the cumbersome Roman method. The early Spaniards were most impressed with the facility the Indians had for counting cacao beans, which were not sold in dry measure or weight but counted bean by bean and sold in lots of from 400 to 8,000 beans, which could be calculated very quickly.

Maya scholars, having worked out a method of determining the dates from the glyphs, have had many of their deductions confirmed by the carbon-14 system of dating. Of the greater mass of glyphs, beyond those of calendric significance, little else has been deciphered; and the best minds admit that they have reached a stalemate. We are all in the dark together. The only difference is that while the scholar keeps loudly knocking at the door, the ignoramus sits quietly in the center of the room.

Yuri Knorosow, a member of the Russian Academy, has announced that he possesses a "key" to the Maya glyphs. While those who have long worked on the subject state that "it is hazardous to estimate the number of glyphs because most of them are compound, and mostly undecipherable since there is no alphabet," Knorosow [74] has no such qualms. He seems to have carefully studied all the literature, and the most famed of Maya codices, the Dresden, is in Russian hands. He states that the number of Maya glyphs amounts to 270, of which 170 are generally used. He places them in three categories: the ideographic, which are mostly self-explanatory; the phonetic, which appear most often; and the determinative, which are rare and not meant to be read. Knorosow asserts that he is now ready to "read" all of the existing codices. Those who have given much of their lives to the study remain rightly skeptical about the Russian Maya experts. But the Russians have been the first to see the other face of the moon. Can it be that they will show us the other face of the Maya?

It is a historical fact that almost all of the pioneering in the deciphering of the texts of "lost civilizations" has been done by nonprofessionals, that is, those who were not primarily trained in archaeology and did not gain their livelihood by it.

Jean-François Champollion was only nineteen and certainly not an archaeologist when he used the Rosetta Stone to decipher Egyptian texts. Georg Grotefend, a simple German schoolteacher, unraveled the Babylonian cuneiform writing that looked "like bird tracks on wet sand." Diego de Landa, who gave us the clue to the Maya glyphs, was of course a friar; Juan Pío Perez, who worked out the Maya numerical system, was a local administrative official in Peto, Yucatán.

"I have discovered the secret of the shua and Katun count ... I determined the character of the great cycles"—in this manner J. T. Goodman announced his discovery of the reduction of Maya dates. A newspaperman, he was the editor of the *Virginia City Enterprise* who gave Mark Twain his start as a journalist. Goodman had never seen a Maya. Nor had Dr. Ernst Förstemann, the librarian at Dresden where the famed Codex lay. Developing late in life an interest in Maya hieroglyphs, he worked for fourteen years until he "had wrest the secret of the Maya calendar from codex and stela." Benajamin Whorf, professionally an insurance actuary in Connecticut, was an authority on American linguistics. And to shift the archaeological scene but not the theme, it was only recently that Michael Ventris, a young English architect, succeeded where all other scholars had failed in unraveling the Cretan linear script, which he long insisted was really primitive Greek. The talented nonprofessional is an important figure in archaeology because, of all the art-sciences, it is the one that he can enter without an academic gown.

37. Literature

The Maya had books. Mentioned earlier was the chronicler who thought that they were to be commended for three things: absence of cannibalism, lack of interest in sodomy, and the writing of books. These were naturally not our kind of books; they were in effect illustrated glyph-texts. But the fact that they had books astonished the Spaniards most. When young Bernal Díaz thumbed through them in a Totonac temple at Veracruz he saw "many books doubled together in folds . . . it gave me much to think over. . . . I do not know precisely how to describe it." And among the things sent back to Carlos V along with gold and feather ornaments were "two books such as the Indians use." Many of the scholars in Spain were "wrapped in astonishment" at this proof of high culture. For not only the Maya but the Totonac, Aztec, Mixtec, and almost all other Indians of high culture had books. The Maya, however, carried their books over the longest period of time—perhaps as long as 800 years.

At the time of the Spanish conquest, almost every large center in Yucatán had its depository of books. As late as 1697 a Spaniard reported seeing records still being kept in hieroglyphic writing at Tayasal in El Petén.

There cannot be any doubt of the extent to which books were used; the comments left by Spaniards are unusually fulsome on the subject. "The natives had [written] characters and understood one another by means of them." Said a report to the king of Spain: "These *Ah Kines* had books of figures . . . and they knew what happened many years before." Diego de Landa confirms all this. The Maya "knew how to read and write with letters and characters with which they wrote and drawings which illustrated the meaning of the writings . . . their books were written on large sheets of paper doubled in folds, which were enclosed entirely between boards which they decorated, and they wrote on both sides in columns following the order of the folds. And they made this paper from the roots of a tree."

Maya paper was made of bark pounded from the inner bast fibers of ficus trees. The bark was pulled from the tree two palms wide and as long as twenty feet. It was soaked first in water to soften it and to extract the heavy white sap, then beaten with a ribbed beater. This action stretched the fibers so that a piece of bark twelve inches wide was extended to paper forty inches in width. It was beaten until it was, as a Spaniard said, a "leaf the thickness of a Mexican real of eight," that is, two millimeters in thickness. This form of papermaking is widespread; the methods, instruments for beating, and species of plant involved are almost identical in widely separated areas—the Amazon, Africa, Polynesia, and Easter Island. The author, who wrote the first book on Maya papermaking,[75] thought then that the Maya were the earliest American papermakers. He is now not so sure. The craft, like so much else, was practiced by most of the tribes of Middle America.

The Maya used bark paper as clothing before they learned to weave cotton cloth. Their priests continued to wear bark paper clothes even after they had weaving. Making clothing out of paper has an old cultural history.*

* Fiber sources were not available for European paper until men began to wear linen underwear. The cast-off garments were eagerly sought by thirteenth-century papermakers. The Abbot of Cluny on a visit to Italian paper mills was shocked: "God reads the book in Heaven . . . but what kind of a book? Is it the kind we have in daily use, a parchment made from the skins of goats, or is it the rags of all cast-off undergarments . . . and some other vile material?"

This Maya paper (*huun*) had wide usage; plans for building were made on it; it was used in puzzling out the intricacies of glyphs; designs on stelae were worked out on it before carving. We know the Maya had maps. Their contemporaries, the Aztecs, used *amatl* paper for land charts, tribute charges, histories, and genealogies; paper itself was an item of tribute.

A Spaniard who saw the Itzás' books in 1697 gave a fully accurate account of their size and appearance: "Books of a quarter of a yard high [i.e., nine inches] and about five fingers in width, made of the bark of trees, they are folded from side to side to another like screens. These are painted on both sides." [76] The physical appearance of the three surviving Maya "books," in particular the Dresden Codex, fits this description. It is made from a single piece of bark paper beaten from the fibers of the *copo* (*Ficus padiofolia*). It is 8 inches high, 126 inches in length, and folded like a screen. It was sized by means of warm stone-irons (such as the Mexican *xicaltetl*), which would have given it surface (the Renaissance papermakers polished their handmade paper with an agate stone), or it may have been given a sizing with a mixture of lime and the starch yielded by a plant similar to manioc. Diego de Landa remarks about their giving it "a white gloss upon which it was easy to write." The paper was folded into a book by doubling the paper screen-wise; each leaf or page measured 3 inches wide by 8 in height. The ends were glued to wooden boards presumably carved with glyph titles. A Mexican codex that survives is similarly bound and is ornamented with inlaid jade on the order of the jeweled bindings of Europe's Renaissance. The Dresden Codex has thirty-nine leaves painted on both sides, or seventy-eight pages. These pages are the "folds of the katun," of which the codices speak. The Maya priest-scribes worked with brushes made from bristles of the wild pig. The colors used were dark red, light red, black, blue, yellow, brown, green, and a lustrous black.

There is no precise date on the beginnings of the Maya book. The Maya after A.D. 889, for reasons unknown, abandoned the practice of erecting dated carved-stone stelae. After this, it is deduced, they kept similar records on a more obedient medium such as paper. Sometime around 889, then, it is conjectured that the first Maya book came into being.

The Dresden Codex is the finest of the three surviving Maya books, and gets its name from the Royal Library at Dresden, where it was brought from Vienna in 1739. The precise provenance of the book is unknown, but since its latest date corresponds to A.D. 1178, Dr. Thompson believes it was a new edition made about the twelfth century from an original executed in the classic (A.D. 323–889) period. The contents (admittedly only half of the glyphs can be deciphered) are in the form of a divinatory almanac, dealing with women, childbirth, and weaving. There are multiplication tables for the synodical revolutions of the planet Venus and prognostications. The book ends with the sky god Itzamna, as a celestial monster, pouring water out of his mouth and destroying the Maya world by flood. Of the three codices, the Dresden is astronomical; the Tro-Cortesianus, astrological; the Peresianus, ritualistic. They present almost nothing that can be regarded as history.*

The Spaniards said the Maya books treated "of the lives of their lords and the common people" and spoke of "the history they contained." Seventy years after the conquest and the burning of the books, a Spaniard still spoke of seeing "books" painted in color, "giving the count of their years, the wars, epidemics, hurricanes, inundations, famines, and other events." And as late as 1697 an isolated Itzá chieftain knew all about the history of Yucatán because "he had read it in his books." It has been stated that "their hieroglyphic literature seems to have covered nearly every branch of Maya science," but there are no examples of it. That they regarded their books as most sacred is shown by Landa's remark: "The most important possession that the nobles who abandoned Mayapán [on its destruction] took to their own province was the books of their sciences."

Learning was aristocratic and belonged only to the ruling classes, for "priests were the key of their learning . . . they employed themselves in the duties of the temples and in teaching their sciences as well as in writing books about them." Although their interest in their own genealogy was intense, no personal names or names of cities have been identified in the old Maya glyphs. Yet we know that there were painted chart-maps, and it is stated as a historical fact in the *Popol Vuh* that when the Toltecs journeyed toward Yucatán they "took of their paintings, in which were recorded all the

---

* The other two surviving Maya codices, the Codex Peresianus and the Codex Tro-Cortesianus, are respectively in Paris and Madrid. The Peresianus is so called because the name "Perez" appeared on its wrappings when it was found in a chimney corner of the Bibliothèque Nationale, with a basketful of other old papers, in 1860. The Tro-Cortesianus, discovered in the 1860's, was found in two pieces (the Troano and the Cortesianus), each in a different place in Spain. It is composed of 56 leaves of 112 pages, and when extended is 23½ feet long. A late Maya product (c. 1400), it is crudely done and concerned with divinatory ceremonies. The codex has many illustrations of Maya crafts—weaving, pottery, deer snaring—all instructive to the ethnographer.

things of ancient times," and that the highland Maya received *u tizbal tulan,* the paintings of ancient Tula, last capital of the Toltecs, "in which they wrote their histories." In fact, the similarity between some of the buildings at Chichén Itzá and Tula, 800 miles apart, is so exact that the architectural data could have been transmitted in no other way than by drawings painted on paper. They had, in addition, books on medicine, eighteenth-century copies in European script, undoubtedly first translated from the glyphs into written Maya. José de Acosta, who traveled widely in Peru and Mexico (1568), wrote: "There used to exist some books in which the learned Indians kept . . . a knowledge of plants, animals and other things." However, they did not use their glyph-writing for contracts—"in sales and contracts there was no written agreements"—and this was a source of confusion and friction, which often led to war.

The Aztecs, whose writing was less developed than that of the Maya, kept precise accounts of tribute and income, maps of property, and a detailed map of Tenochtitlán. We know the correct succession of their leaders and the names of all the ancient Aztec towns and provinces. (The Aztecs also left behind an impressive literature, which was set down by Aztec-Spanish scribes in the sixteenth century.[77]) As for the Maya, it is not until very late (after A.D. 1250), that we even know the names of their "kings." Even the Incas, who had no writing, had a *quipu* string recorder; this acted as a mnemonic device which gave them and now us a chronology of their history. It could be possible that Maya glyph-writing is not really a written language at all, but rather a mnemonic device by which with dates, glyph pictures of gods, and symbols the reader had his memory jogged. The fact that they had songs in meter raises this question. The early Greeks, guided by mnemosyne, sang in meter the history of things past; the *Iliad* was long chanted before Homer set it down. The druids employed bards to record in mnemonic rhyme their chronologies and treatises on geography, the sea, and the technics of husbandry. Henry III employed a *versificator regis* to chant rhymed chronicles, epitaphs and the like.

If Maya "books" covered fields other than those of the extant codices, we will never know, because the Spanish friars destroyed them. Says Diego de Landa flatly, "We burned them all."

It was decreed that idolatry must be stamped out. Diego de Landa himself signed the auto-da-fé in 1562. As part of the Spanish religious program, all Maya "books" were seized and brought to the town of Maní.* "We found a large number of books . . ." wrote Landa, "and they contained nothing in which there was not to be seen superstition and lies of the devil, so we burned them all, which they regretted to an amazing degree and which caused them much affliction." This is confirmed by a historian writing in 1633. In Maní, Landa "collected the books and he commanded them burned. They burned many historical books of ancient Yucatán which told of its beginnings and history, which were of so much value." José de Acosta, that learned Jesuit who traveled in Peru and Mexico in the springtime of that world, was angry at this iconoclasm: "This follows from some stupid zeal, when without knowing or wishing to know the things of the Indies, they say as in a sealed package that everything is sorcery . . . the ones who have wished earnestly to be informed of these found many things worthy of consideration."

Diego de Landa carried out this work thoroughly enough; of the hundreds of "books," only three somehow escaped this holocaust.

Maya texts are known, in the broad, and of what they generally treated. It is doubted, even by the best informed scholars, that historical events were recorded on the monuments.

This is a typical example of a Maya text found on a superbly carved stela at Tikal: "6 Ahau 13 Muan, completion of the count of 14, the completion of the tun." Its concern is calendrics. There is no mention of the name of the city, the ruler, or any historical events that occurred during "6 Ahau, 13 Muan." Such is the nature of inscribed texts elsewhere among the Maya.

How very different are the records of the Middle East, which are tautological, chatty, and informative, as for example *The Sixty-Two Curses of Easharhaddon.*[78] In Maya terms this Assyrian talking tablet is miniscule (18 by 12 inches). In style it differs not much from the tablets at Palenque: king-gods thundering down to kneeling vassals. In May, 672 B.C., Easharhaddon, king of Assyria, swore his vassals to a covenant and called down on them an awesome array of curses if they violated it. He demanded that his son Ashurbanipal be his successor. The tablet is alive with furor;

* "And . . . this witness being in the said pueblo of Maní and Homun, saw the said friars suspend many Indians by their arms, and some of them by the feet and hang stones from their feet and whip them and spatter them with tapers of burning wax, and mistreat them grievously in such a way that afterwards, at the said time, when as he has said they were given penance and brought forth in the said public auto [da-fé], there was not a sound place on their bodies where they could be whipped. . . ."

the very names clang like the crash of cymbals: ". . . may Sarantium, who gives light and seed, destroy your name and land . . . may Isthar, goddess of battles and war, smash your bow . . ." and so it goes on until sixty-two curses are uttered. Out of it come dates, history, people, character.

What is there of the Maya in those glyph-texts, such as this, that have survived? Something such as this:

> Katun 11 Ahau is set upon the mat: is set upon the throne. When the ruler is set up: Yxcal Chac sits face to their ruler.
>
> The fan of heaven shall descend; the wreath of heaven, the bouquet of heaven, shall descend.
>
> The drum of the Lord 11 Ahau shall resound; his rattle shall resound.
>
> When knives of flint are set in his mantle; on that day there shall be the green turkey; on that day there shall be Sulim Chan; on that day there shall be Chakan-putun.
>
> They shall find their harvest among the trees: they shall find their harvest among the rocks, those who have lost their harvest in the katun of Lord 11 Ahau.[79]

Such is the nature of the inscribed texts found throughout Mayadom. Only on the very rarest occasions is there anything other than this almost pathological concern with time's passage. Years were burdens carried by the gods, who were good or malign; none indifferent. The bad could be influenced by appropriate ceremonies, and it was "possible to ease the woes of Ix and apply balm to the ills of Cauac." Like ourselves, the Maya judged human actions by the pain and pleasure they caused them. That which was carved on Maya monuments was to influence the gods, but it was scarcely what we think of as literature.

In addition to the three surviving Maya codices and the vast corpus of Maya glyph-texts on the monuments, there are the Books of Chilam Balam (the Books of the Jaguar Priest).[80] There are many of these. The text is Maya written in European script. The dates of their composition vary between the first half of the sixteenth century, when the Maya conquest was a fact, and the late eighteenth century. The themes are of a similar tenor to that which has been deciphered in the Maya books. Maya priests dictated from the books that had escaped the burning to a bilingual scribe who set it down in European script in Maya. They are not chronicles in our sense. As to whether they are literature, let the books speak for themselves. The opening lines of one of them read:

> This is the order of the Katunes since [the Itzás] left their land, their home of Nonoual.

> Four Katunes stayed in the Tutal Xiu, Ahua-10 Ahua [A.D. 849–928] at the decline of the Zuyua.

In these books there is much on the "language of Zuyua," a cabalistic form of speech used by priests to determine if those of their kind were "worthy" and knew the details of rituals. One will notice how antiphonal is the text. It suggests that much of Maya literature was oral, like that of all earlier cultures.

There are few surviving chants, history chanted to meter and drum beat:

> A tender boy was I
> > at Chichén

> When the evil man
> > the army master

> Came to seize the land
> O at Chichén Itzá
> > godlessness was born

> Yulu uayano
> I Mix was the day
> > when he

> When he was taken at
> > Chikin ch'en

> > > Behold how I remember the
> > > > the song

> Godliness was favored
> Yulu uayano

We know that the Maya had dramatic presentations. Dances were many, reaching into hundreds of distinct choreographies. Rhythm was considered so important by the Maya that a drummer could lose his liberty or perhaps his life for a wrong beat.

This is one of the songs of the "Dance," which Diego de Landa once witnessed and thought "worthy of seeing":

> Take three light turns
> around the painted stone column
> where virile is tied that
> boy, impollute, virgin, man.
> Take the first; on the second
> take your bow, place the dart,
> aim to his heart; you need not
> employ all your strength to
> pierce him; not to
> wound deep into his flesh
> and so he may suffer
> slowly, as wished
> the beautiful Lord God.

Eric Thompson, that most literary of Maya scholars, has praised the mythopoetic qualities of Maya verse, calling attention to its free use of iambs and the repetitive antiphonal rhythm similar to the Old Testament. The Maya told their history in cadence. Verse is one of the most ancient of forms among all people, and was originally a clumsy artifice to aid the memory of people who could not read. If one finds it hard to believe that a mnemotechnical expedient has been transformed in the course of time into a beautiful poetry, it is enough to reflect that in Greek architecture a beam laid upon wooden pillars became the architrave of the temple and the other end of the framing of the roof became the marble triglyph, or that the simple Maya house evolved into a temple such as that of Tikal, which soars to 239 feet in height. But to liken the cadence of Maya verse to the powerful rhythms of the Old Testament goes too far. The fault belongs not to the Maya but rather to ourselves, who have labeled them the Intellectuals of the New World.

The Maya have been the subject of much romantic misconception. Ever since Chateaubriand in 1791 sat on a riverbank with some Indian girls of the Natchez tribes and, beguiled by his longings and vexations, conceived his two Floridians, Atala and Celuta, the "noble savage" theme has kept the stage. This imaginary exoticism has entered the bloodstream of American proto-history, where it ferments into an intoxicant that every new generation drinks.

Maya literature was symbolical and abstract. It was antisocial, because only the initiate could understand the value and meaning of its symbols. What has one when the glyphs are translated? The Maya says nothing of himself or his history. A mere date is fleshless; it lacks blood and passion unless it is connected with meaningful human events. Time knows its business. What is abstract and symbolical in literature disappears; all that is purely sonorous vanishes into the air.

38. Xul—The End

The Maya, first of the Sun Kingdoms to feel the weight of the white man, were curiously enough the last to fall under that weight. For there was no escaping the wave of the future, once Columbus noted the presence of a very superior people, *"Maian,"* in 1502. The Spanish persisted. The relationship was violent from the beginning. The Maya were fierce warriors; they gave no quarter and asked none. When the report reached the Spanish governor at Cuba—"we have discovered thickly peopled countries with masonry houses, and people who cover their persons in cotton garments"—more conquistadors poured over to break a lance; hundreds left their bodies on Yucatec shores.

When Cortes arrived he gave a practiced military eye to the inhospitable shore and, somehow sensing that there was little gold, remained only long enough to pick up the castaway Aguilar. In 1524, Mexico having been conquered and organized, Cortes sent Pedro de Alvarado to undertake the conquest of Guatemala and dispatched Cristóbal de Olid to Central America to sniff out the tribute channels of the Aztecs. Instead, the latter set up an independent government in Hibueras (Honduras). So Cortes set off after him, making the famed trek through quagmires and rivers and jungles. He cut a wide swath through Maya territory, meeting little resistance. It was known that the Aztecs had been toppled and that he, Cortes, was the toppler. The Maya were in awe of that small, energetic man who, undismayed by the terrible geography of the land, came down upon them replete with mistress, falcons, buffoons, and jugglers.

In 1527 came the turn of the Maya. Francisco de Montejo, who had played his part in the conquest of Mexico (it was he who had carried its treasure to Spain), used this to advantage; he emerged from an audience with the king with a contract to conquer, settle, and convert all Mayadom. He arrived in Yucatán in 1527 with 380 men, 57 horses, and high hopes. Montejo was, says one who knew him, "middle-sized and with a merry face. He was fond of rejoicings but was a businessman; and a good horseman. When he came over to Mexico he may have been about thirty-five. He was liberal and he spent more than his income warranted. . . ." The lives he would spend were even more unwarranted. The party settled at Xelha, where skirmish and sickness whittled away his forces. He then moved up the north coast, encountering one large Maya city after another. At every turn the Indians attacked, chewing up his small troop.

Even so, Montejo was attacking a people completely disunited, for they were as much at war with themselves as with the Spaniards. Even the example of Mexico had brought the Maya no unity. Mayapán, which ruled most of Yucatán, had collapsed, and the land was split up into warring factions. In 1467 came the horrendous hurricane that caused a fearful loss of lives and devastation. In 1516, in the wake of the first Spanish contact, came smallpox (*mayacimil*, the "easy death"), killing thousands upon thousands. Family rivalries caused constant intertribal wars. Despite all this the Maya routed the Spaniards. After trying to gain lodgment without success in Yucatán, the expedition sailed down to Chetumal, at the great bay of Zamabac. Here was a large city of 2,000 houses. Cacao, honey, and canoe building were its interests. At this city, which traded with Panama, the Spaniards found gold and, within days, war. They hoped to be helped by the other Spanish castaway, Gonzalo Guerrero, but he would have none of them. As a Maya *Nacom*, Guerrero prepared the thrusts and counterthrusts against the Spaniards. He soon tossed the would-be conquistadors out of their foothold in Chetumal. They then embarked and continued southward to put in at Ulua, a Maya trading post in Honduras. When knowledge of this was transmitted to Guerrero, he led a flotilla of war canoes to relieve that outpost. He was killed by a shot from an arquebus, but his death did not change Spanish fortunes. By 1535 there was not a white man left alive in the whole Yucatán peninsula. Those who had not died or wearied of unsuccessful war had heard the clarion call from Peru, where Francisco Pizarro was engaged in the conquest of the Incas.

Montejo, full of years and scars, resigned from his title and authority in favor of his son. Furiously renewing the conquest in 1542, the conquistadors occupied half of the peninsula and founded their capital, Merída, within the buildings of ancient T'ho. In 1546 they put down with terrible and indiscriminate slaughter those Maya tribes who refused the yoke of peace, and the conquest was over.

The Maya were engulfed by the waves of conquest. They had known slavery, which was part of their social system, but their new masters improved upon it. Five hundred thousand free men were sold into peonage; ancient Maya centers were destroyed; and the chieftains who did not submit were killed. The priests were disposed of and their books burned. Their learning died with them.

Still, the conquest was not complete. After the fall of Mayapán, one Itzá tribe moved, en masse, out of Yucatán into the lakes of El Petén. This was in classical territory, with Tikal only fifty miles away. There they lived unmolested until 1618. The Spaniards became aware of them soon enough. It was a Neo-Maya state and its mere existence encouraged rebellion among other Maya living under the Spanish yoke. It was similar to the Neo-Inca state in Peru that, under various Lord Incas, existed for sixty years after the Spanish conquest.

In 1622 Fray Diego Delgado, in search of martyrdom, offered to Christianize the Itzás. He was accompanied by soldiers, who, not as delicate in these matters as himself, cut a swath of destruction on the way to El Petén. Leaving the soldiers behind, Delgado and a large group of Indians he had converted to Christianity proceeded to the Itzá capital of Tayasal, on friendly invitation of its lord, Canek. But when they reached the town, Delgado and his entire party were put to death as a sacrifice to the Itzá gods. Throughout the century there were repeated attempts to enter Itzá territory: they were repulsed. Construction was begun on a Guatemalan–Yucatán highway designed to bring two economic units together. The Itzás were in the way, and that decided their fate. "I, Fray Andrés de Avendaño y Loyola . . . who had no other wish than to sow in their hardened hearts the pure grain of evangelical seed," set off to the Itzás in 1696. After years of hardship, on his second attempt he entered Tayasal alive. It had twenty temples, not unlike those in Yucatán, and numerous houses; other islands were similarly inhabited, as were the immediate shores of the lake. Avendaño, with a subtle play of dialectics—he had earlier mastered the language and glyph-writing—finally broke down the Itzás' mental resistance to Spanish contact; they agreed to come peacefully into the Spanish fold.

January 1697 found Martin de Ursua, governor of Yucatán, with his soldiers at the farthest point of the new road. On March 13, a force of Spanish soldiers crossed the lake in a large galley to accept the peaceful surrender of the island capital of Tayasal—or to make an assault on it.[81] As it made its way, a canoe flotilla of 2,000 armed Indians encircled the galley. The soldiers were under orders to withhold their fire, which they did even though provoked by accurate arrow thrusts from the Itzás. But near the shore of Tayasal a soldier, wounded to fury by an arrow, fired his arquebus at close range. At this, the other soldiers fired, and the lake soon was strewn with Itzá dead. As the troops landed, the remaining Indians fled. On March 14, 1697, the Spaniards formally took possession, in the name of the king, of the last living city of the Maya.

The Maya had endured as a cultural entity for 3,700 years.

Bibliography and Notes

The bibliography is designed for use in further reading. The first titles are more or less in historical sequence and a reading of them in this order will give one a good idea of the conquest of the Maya as it developed. The specialized titles have been selected to fill out the picture of the Maya and their world.

1. See S. E. Morison, *Admiral of the Ocean Sea*, Boston, Little, Brown and Company, 1942.
2. Knorosow has made a brief summary of the studies of the ancient Maya hieroglyphic writing in the Soviet Union, (USSR, Academy of Sciences, Moscow, 1955).
3. G. G. Healy, "Maya Murals: Great Discovery Sheds Light on Culture of Ancient Race," *Life* magazine, April, 1947.
4. *Información de servicios y meterios de Gerónimo de Aguilar . . .*, *Archivos de las Indies*, ed. Perez Martinez, Mexico, 1938.
5. P. A. Means, "History of the Spanish Conquest of Yucatán and of the Itzás," *Papers of the Peabody Museum*, Vol. VII, Cambridge, Mass., 1917; also Robert S. Chamberlain, *Francisco de Montejo and the Conquest of Yucatán*, Ph. D. dissertation, Harvard Univ., 1936.
6. Means, *op. cit.*, gives full details of the final throes of the Itzá-Maya struggle.
7. *Letters of Cortés*, 2 vols., ed. F. A. MacNutt, N. Y. and London. The originals of these letters are in the National-bibliothek in Vienna.
8. Bernal Díaz del Castillo, *Historia verdadera de la conquista de la Nueva España*. (Tr. by A. P. Maudslay as the *True History of the Conquest of New Spain*, 5 vols., London, 1908–16.) Of the numerous editions of this work, that published recently in Mexico (2 vols., Editorial Porrua, 1955) is the most complete and gives the whole of Díaz' travels with Cortes in the Maya country.
9. Published by Spanish scholars in 1898–1900, these are the reports and demi-histories written in the sixteenth and seventeenth centuries.
10. Antonio Ciudad Real was a famous Maya scholar of the late sixteenth century who wrote an account of a journey of inspection as secretary-general of the Franciscan order. His observations are of the highest order. *Relación breve y verdadera de algunas cosas de las muchas que sucedieron al Padre Fray Alonso Ponce en las provincias de la Nueva España*, Collección d eDocumentos Inéditos para la Historia de España, Vols. LVII–LVIII, Madrid, 1872.
11. Landa's *Relación de las cosas de Yucatán*, ed. with notes by A. M. Tozzer, *Papers of the Peabody Museum*, Vol.

XVIII, Cambridge, Mass., 1941. Landa wrote his *Relación*
in Spain in 1566, and took the manuscript back to Yucatán
in 1573. After his death the work was kept in the convent
at Mérida. It was first published by Brasseur de Bourbourg,
Paris, 1864. There were later editions by Jean Genet and
William Gates. Alfred M. Tozzer's is the sixth edition and
the most authoritative to date.

12. García de Palacio was a lawyer and judge of the Royal
    Audience of Guatemala. In his report to Philip II, dated
    March 8, 1576, he describes the Indians of Guatemala.

13. M. H. Saville, *Bibliographic Notes on Palenque*, Heye
    Foundation, Vol. VI, N. Y., 1928, gives a complete bibli-
    ography of books published on Palenque up until 1928.

14. Saville, *op. cit.*

15. Edward King, Viscount Kingsborough, *Antiquities of Mexi-
    co*, 9 vols., London, 1830–48.

16. John Lloyd Stephens, *Incidents of Travel in Yucatán*, 2 vols.,
    ed. with notes and introduction by Victor W. von Hagen,
    Norman, The University of Oklahoma Press, 1960, and
    Incidents of Travel in Central America . . ., New Bruns-
    wick, N. J., Rutgers University Press, 1949. See also the
    biography *Maya Explorer* by von Hagen, Norman, The
    University of Oklahoma Press, 1947; and by the same au-
    thor, *Frederick Catherwood, Architect*, N. Y., Oxford Uni-
    versity Press, 1950.

17. To mention only a few of these scholars, the work of
    Miguel Angel Fernandez on Jaina and José García Payen
    on El Tajín, in Veracruz; the fascinating work done by Al-
    berto Ruz Lhullier at Palenque, resulting in the discovery of
    the tomb under the Temple of the Foliated Cross; that of
    the artist-anthropologist Miguel Covarrubias (*Indian Art of
    Mexico and Central America*, N. Y., Alfred A. Knopf, Inc.,
    1957; *Mexico South, The Isthmus of Tehuantepec*, N. Y.,
    Alfred A. Knopf, 1946; London, Cassell, 1947.); and the
    work on the correlation of the Maya calendar by Juan
    Hernandez Martinez have given much to the literature on
    the history of the Maya.

18. F. de Waldeck, *Voyage pittoresque et archéologique dans
    la province de Yucatan (Amérique Centrale), pendant les
    années 1834 et 1836*, Paris, 1838.
    C. E. Brasseur de Bourbourg, *Histoire des nations civilisées
    du Mexique et de l'Amerique Centrale*, 4 vols., Paris, 1857;
    *Popol Vuh. Le livre sacré et les mythes de l'antiquité
    Americaine*, Paris, 1861; *Recherche sur les ruines de Pal-
    enque*, Paris, 1866.
    Jacques Soustelle, "Notes sur les Lacandon du Lac Petjá
    et du Rio Jetjá (Chiapas)," *Journal de la Societé des Ameri-
    canistes de Paris*, N. S. XXV, 153–180. *Le Totémisme des
    Lacandons*, Maya Research, II, 325–344. "La culture ma-
    térielle des Indiens Lacandons," *Journal de la Societé des
    Americanistes de Paris*, N. S. XXIX, 1–95.
    Jean Genet and Pierre Chelbatz, *Histoire des Peuples Mayas-
    Quichés (Mexique, Guatemala, Honduras)*, Paris, 1927.

19. Thomas Gage, who traveled in Guatemala between 1625
    and 1637, gave English readers their first glimpse of these

lands. See Gage's *Travels in the New World,* ed. by J. Eric
S. Thompson, Norman, The University of Oklahoma Press,
1958. Juan Galindo was the pseudonym of an Irish soldier
of fortune who wrote (1835) *The Ruins of Copán.* Captain
Herbert Caddy went to Palenque in 1840. His manuscript
City of Palenque, illustrated with 24 sepia drawings, is un-
published. He was followed by Frederick Catherwood, il-
lustrator of Stephens' books and himself author-artist of
*View of Ancient Monuments in Central America, Chiapas
and Yucatán,* London, 1844. Catherwood is followed historically by Alfred Maudslay, who wrote numerous papers and edited the journal of Bernal Díaz del Castillo.
Thomas Gann, a medico who lived in British Honduras,
made known, through his explorations and publications, a
new area of the Maya. He is author of *Maya Cities,* N. Y.,
1927. J. Eric S. Thompson, English-born and -educated but
attached mostly to American institutions, is the outstanding
figure in Maya archaeology. Among his many publications
are *Mexico Before Cortés,* N. Y., 1933, and the other studies
cited throughout these notes.

20. *Vues des Cordilleres . . . .,* published by Alexander von Humboldt in Paris, 1810, is a rare expensive folio. His was the
first, by judicious text and fine illustrations, to stress the
oneness of indigenous culture. Teobert Maler was the first
German to make explorations of Maya ruins; "Researches
in the Central Portions of the Usumatsintla Valley," *Memoirs of the Peabody Museum of American Archaeology and
Ethnology,* II (1903), 77–208. Dr. Carl Sapper, the great
geographer, delineated the land in *Das Nördliche Mittel-
Amerika,* Braunschweig, 1897. Eduard Seler made many
important contributions such as *Antiquities of Guatemala,*
Vol. III, Bull. 28, Bureau of American Ethnology, Washington, 1904. Walter Lehmann's work on Maya and Mexican languages has never been supplanted (*Zentral-Amerika,*
2 vols., Berlin, 1920). Dr. Ernst Förstemann wrote numerous
important papers on Maya writing, and there were many
Germans who followed him, such as Hermann Beyer
(*Studies on the Inscriptions of Chichén Itzá,* Washington,
1937), a tireless worker until he was betrayed by some
of his American colleagues and died in a Texas concentration camp during the late war.

21. E. W. Andrews has done much work on Yucatán's north
coast; he is now excavating the ruins of Dzibilchaltun, which
may change our concept of the Maya (see "Dzibilchaltun:
Lost City of the Maya," *National Geographic Magazine,*
January, 1959). Other important American studies, listed
alphabetically by author, include:

F. Blom and O. La Farge, *Tribes and Temples,* 2 vols.,
New Orleans, 1926–27.

Brainerd, G. W., *The Maya Civilization,* Los Angeles, The
Southwest Museum, 1954.

Brinton, D. G., *The Maya Chronicles,* Philadelphia, 1882.

Gates, W., *An Outline Dictionary of Maya Glyphs,* Baltimore, The Maya Society, Johns Hopkins University, 1931,

and *The Dresden Codex*, Baltimore, The Maya Society, Johns Hopkins University, 1932.

Goodman, J. T., "The Archaic Maya Inscriptions," *Biologia Centrali-Americana*, section on archaeology, London, 1897.

Holmes, W., *Archaeological Studies among the Ancient Cities of Mexico*, Chicago, 1895–97.

Kidder, A. V., *Excavations at Kaminaljuyu, Guatemala*, Carnegie Institution of Washington,* Pub. 561, Washington, D. C., 1946.

Lothrop, S. K., *Tulum*, C. I. W., Pub. 335, 1924.

Morley, S. G., *The Ancient Maya*, Palo Alto, Stanford University Press, 1946.

Morris, E. H., *The Temple of the Warriors at Chichén Itzá*, C.I.W., Pub. 406, 1931.

Redfield, Robert, *Chan Kom, a Maya Village*, C.I.W., Pub. 448, 1934.

Ricketson, O. G., Jr., *Uaxactun . . .*, C.I.W., Pub. 447, 1937.

Roys, R. L., *The Indian Background of Colonial Yucatán*, C.I.W., Pub. 548, 1943.

Ruppert, K., *The Caracol at Chichén Itzá*, C.I.W., Pub. 454, 1935.

Satterthwaite, L., Jr., "Thrones at Piedras Negras," Univ. of Pennsylvania, *University Museum Bulletin*, VII, 1937, 18–23.

Smith, A. L., *Archaeological Reconnaissance in Central Guatemala*, C.I.W., Pub. 608, 1955.

Spinden, H. J., "A Study of Maya Art," *Memoirs of the Peabody Museum*, Vol. VI, Cambridge, Mass., 1913.

Teeple, J. E., *Maya Astronomy*, C. I. W., Pub. 403, 1937.

Wauchope, R., *House Mounds of Uaxactun*, C.I.W., Pub. 436, 1934.

Von Hagen, V. W., *The Aztec and the Maya Papermakers*, N. Y., J. J. Augustin, 1943.

22. J. E. S. Thompson, *The Rise and Fall of Maya Civilization*, Norman, The University of Oklahoma Press, 1954, p. 4.

23. See V. W. von Hagen, *The Aztec: Man and Tribe*, N. Y., The New American Library, 1958, pp. 28–35.

24. See V. W. von Hagen, *The Realm of the Inca*, N. Y., The New American Library, 1957, pp. 203–209.

25. See von Hagen, *The Aztec: Man and Tribe*, pp. 141–143.

26. See Diego de Landa, *Relación de las Cosas de Yucatán*, Tozzer ed. p. 22 and footnote 127.

27. *The Book of Chilam Balam of Chumayel*, tr. and ed. by Ralph L. Roys, C. I. W., Pub. 438, Washington, D. C., 1933.

28. *Popol Vuh: The Sacred Book of the Ancient Quiché Maya*, ed. by D. Goetz and S. G. Morley, Norman, The University of Oklahoma Press, 1950, p. 78.

29. Walter Lehmann, *Zentral-Amerika*, 2 vols., Berlin, 1920.

30. Thompson, *The Rise and Fall of Maya Civilization*, p. 167.

31. H. D. F. Kitto, *The Greeks*, Harmondsworth, England, Penguin Books, Ltd., 1951, p. 64.

32. Lucien Lévy-Bruhl, *Primitives and the Supernatural*, tr. by Lilian A. Clare, New York, E. P. Dutton & Co., Inc., 1935,

* Hereafter abbreviated as "C.I.W."

p. 267. A superbly logical excursion into primitive beliefs and attitudes.

33. So says Rémy de Gourmont, in *The Natural Philosophy of Love* (London, 1926). This French critic, a friend of Anatole France, a defender of the symbolists, and the translator of Nietzsche into French, wrote this careful scientific inquiry into the subject of sex and its relation to man and animals. It is provocative and filled with ironical observations.

34. Huxley's observations (*Beyond the Mexique Bay*, N. Y., Harper & Brothers; London, Chatto & Windus, 1934), strictly unanthropological, are penetrating.

35. Kitto, *op. cit.,* p. 222.

36. R. Wauchope, *Modern Maya Houses*, C.I.W., Pub. 502, Washington, D. C., 1938.

37. P. Mangelsdorf, *Races of Maize in Mexico*, Cambridge, 1956, p. 19.

38. See R. Redfield, *The Folk Culture of Yucatán*, Chicago, University of Chicago Press, 1941, pp. 44 ff.

39. M. Steggerda, *The Food of the Present-Day Maya . . . ,* C.I.W., Pub. 456, Washington, D. C., 1937.

40. Von Hagen, *Jungle in the Clouds* (*Search and Capture of the Quetzal-bird*), New York, Duell, Sloan & Pearce, 1940; *The Jicaque Indians of Honduras,* New York, Museum of the American Indian-Heye Foundation, No. 53, 1943, pp. 51–53.

41. See A. O. Shepard, *Ceramics for the Archaeologist,* C.I.W. Pub. 609, Washington, D. C., 1957.

42. See M. Covarrubias, *op. cit.,* 1957; and R. E. Smith, *Ceramics of Uaxactun; A Preliminary Analysis . . . ,* Guatemala, 1936.

43. Scholars discovered in the Spanish Archives in Sevilla an important manuscript containing a narrative history of the Chontal and Acalan, fourteen generations before Cortes. See Roys, *The Indian Background of Colonial Yucatán,* p. 126.

44. *Balche* (*Lonchocarpus longistylus*) bark was steeped in the fermented honey. Elsewhere—the Amazon and Central America—*balche* was used for a stupefacient; Cattle, when they drink water containing the juice of the Lonchocarpus, will abort; *balche* in mead not only made the Maya drunk, it also must have acted as a violent purgative. The Maya regarded it as healthy; "purged their bodies . . . they vomited up worms when they drank it." Landa, who called *balche* mead "the wine of the country" admitted it was wrong for the Spaniards to prohibit it. The drinking of *balche* mead is illustrated in the Maya codices.

45. *Dresden Codex,* William Gates ed., 2nd Itzamna Section, Baltimore, 1932.

46. Landa, *Relación de las Cosas de Yucatán,* Tozzer ed. pp. 104–107. Dances are mentioned in the *Popol Vuh* of the Highland Maya: the dances of the *puhuy* (owl), the *cux* (weasel), the *iboy* (armadillo), the *xtzul* (centipede), and the one called *chitic,* performed on stilts. The Yucatán Maya danced on stilts when the New Year fell on the day of the Muluc.

47. Lévy-Bruhl, *op. cit.*, p. 24.

48. F. Blom, *The Maya Game* pok-a-tok, Middle American Research Series, Pub. No. 4, New Orleans, 1932.

49. Fr. Bernardino de Sahagun, *Historia general de las cosas de Nueva España,* 3 vols., Mexico, 1950, Vol. II, Book VIII, Chap. 10, p. 297.

50. Roys, *The Ethno-Botany of the Maya,* Middle American Research Series, Pub. No. 2, New Orleans, 1931.

51. See Tatiana Prouskouriakoff, *A Study of Classic Maya Sculpture,* C.I.W., Pub. 593, Washington, D. C., 1950. See also Juan de Torquemada, *Los Veinte y un libros rituales y Monarquia Indiana,* 3 vols., Madrid, 1923.

52. A. Ledyard Smith, *Archaeological Reconnaissance in Central Guatemala,* C. I. W., Pub. 608, Washington, D. C., 1955.

53. See Gregor Paulsson, *The Study of Cities,* Copenhagen, 1959.

54. See Tatiana Proskouriakoff, "The Death of a Civilization," *Scientific Monthly,* December, 1946, pp. 82–87.

55. Aldous Huxley, *op. cit.*

56. See T. Proskouriakoff, *An Album of Maya Architecture,* C. I. W., Pub. 553, Washington, D. C., 1946.

57. S. G. Morley, *The Inscriptions at Copán,* C. I. W., Pub. 219, Washington, D. C., 1920.

58. S. G. Morley, *A Guide to the Ruins of Quirigua,* C. I. W., Pub. 16, Washington, D. C., 1935.

59. H. F. Cline, "The Apochryphal Early Career of J. F. de Waldeck," *Acta Americana,* Vol. IV, No. 4, Mexico, 1947.

60. A. R. Lhullier, "The Mystery of the Temple Inscriptions," *Archaeology,* Vol. VI, No. 1, 1953, pp. 3–11.

61. K. Ruppert, J. E. S. Thompson, and T. Proskouriakoff, *Bonampak . . . ,* Washington, D. C., 1955.

62. S. K. Lothrop, *Tulum . . . ,* C. I. W., Pub. 335, Washington, D. C., 1924.

63. See P. Kelemen, *Medieval American Art,* 2 vols., N. Y., the Macmillan Company, 1943. A very mature work by a Hungarian-born and European-educated scholar who brings to the Maya a freshly conceived point of view on their art as art.

64. Proskouriakoff, *A Study of Classic Maya Sculpture.*

65. S. K. Lothrop, "Metals from the *Cenote* of Sacrifice, Chichén Itzá, Yucatán," *Papers of the Peabody Museum,* Vol. X, 2, Cambridge, Mass., 1952. This, done by *the* expert on indigenous American goldwork, is the belated report on Thompson's dredgings.

66. See Sir Harold Spencer Jones, "The Calendar," in *A History of Technology,* ed. by Charles J. Singer and others, New York and London, Oxford University Press, 1957, Vol. III, pp. 558–81.

67. The starting points of other world calendars are as follows:
    1. Jewish: the supposed date of the creation of the world, 3761 B. C.
    2. Greek: 776 B. C., when the first Olympiad began.
    3. Roman: the date of the foundation of Rome, 753 B. C.

4. Islamic: A. D. 622, the year in which Mohammed went to Mecca.

5. Christian: the birth of Christ.

68. See Alfonso Villa, *The Yaxuná–Cobá Causeway*, C. I. W., Pub. 436, Washington, D. C., 1934.

69. See J. E. S. Thompson, H. E. D. Pollock, and Jean Charlot, *A Preliminary Study of the Ruins of Cobá . . . ,* C. I. W., Pub. 424, Washington, D. C., 1932.

70. V. W. von Hagen, *The Coastal Highway of the Incas,* chapter on communications and *chasquis.* This study, the result of eight years of physical exploration of the Inca roads and exhaustive search in the Archives Nacionales del Peru for ancient *chasqui* records will be published in 1961.

71. R. L. Roys, *The Indian Background of Colonial Yucatán.*

72. W. Gates, *op. cit.,* 1931.

73. See J. E. S. Thompson, *Maya Hieroglyphic Writing,* C. I. W., Pub. 589, Washington, D. C., 1950.

74. See Note 2. It is unfortunate that politics have entered into Maya studies. We have all too little on the course of Dr. Knorosow's studies.

75. Von Hagen, *The Aztec and Maya Papermakers.* There are three editions of this work, the first book on the subject. The 1943 edition was limited to 220 copies and contained actual samples of bark-paper. Another edition published the following year from the same type has been better proof-read, but lacks the paper samples. A superb edition, limited to 750 copies, was issued in Mexico, *La fabricación del papel entre los aztecas y los mayas* (1945). It also contains actual paper samples.

76. See Landa, *Relación de las cosas de Yucatán,* Tozzer ed. p. 169 and footnotes.

77. See Angel María Garibay, *Historia de la literatura Nahuatl,* 2 vols., Mexico, 1953. A fascinating inquiry into the nature of Aztec literature, it shows the sensitive nature of a people renowned mostly in human memory for their massive human sacrificial rituals. Sections appear in translation for the first time in von Hagen's *Aztec: Man and Tribe.*

78. Transcribed by Donald J. Wiseman, Asst. Keeper in the Department of Western Asiatic Antiquities in the British Museum.

79. As translated by R. L. Roys, *The Book of Chilam Balam of Chumayel,* C. I. W., Pub. 438, Washington, D. C., 1938.

80. There are many different texts of the Books of Chilam Balam. For an excellent summary of them all, see *El libro de los Libros de Chilam Balam,* by Alfredo Barrera Vásquez and Silvia Rendón, Mexico, 1954.

81. See P. A. Means, *History of the Spanish Conquest of Yucatán and the Itzás.*

Index

Abbot of Cluny, 201
Acalan Province, 88, 181
Africa, 80, 201
Aguilar, Gerónimo de, 13, 165, 194, 209
Ah-cuzumil peten (Swallow Island), *see* Cozumel
Ah Xupan, 123
Alaska, 26
Alexander the Great, 71
Algeria, 67
Almuchii, 160
Alvarado, Pedro de, 209
Amazon River, 144
Ambras, 74
Ancient History of America, 16
Antiquities of Mexico, 16
Arawaks, 36
Araya Peninsula, 193
Aristobolus, 71
Aristophanes, 176
Arizona, 99
Ascension, Bay of, 192
Atala, 208
Athens, 45
Avendaño, Antonio de, 146
Aztecs, 55, 69, 95, 100, 123, 128, 135, 137, 176, 190; fall of, 13; gods of, 110; maps of, 46; and symbols, 76; use of *agave*, 77; writing of, 197

Bacalar, Lake, 180
Balam, Chilam, 34
Bat Caves of New Mexico, 62
Bernaconi, Antonio, 148-149
Bonampak, 12, 41, 50, 62, 75, 96, 114, 115, 125, 133, 143, 154, 155, 172, 173, 174
Books of Chilam Balam, 206
Brasseur, C. E., 17, 195
Brillat-Savarin, A., 56
British Honduras, 25
Buct-zotz, 191

Cachi, 90
Caddy, Captain Herbert, 17
Caesar, Julius, 176
Calakmul, 22
Campeche, 24, 80, 127, 169

Capri, 157
Caribbean Sea, 85, 165
Carlos II, 150
Carlos III, King of Naples, 15
Carlos V, 88, 200
Carnegie Institution, Washington, 18, 161
Castorp, Hans, 174
Catherwood, Frederick, 17, 124, 150, 157, 159, 165, 181
Catoche, Cape of, 167
Cehache, 127
Celuta, 208
Central America, 150, 209
Chabalam, 182
Chac Mool, 162, 164
Chacmultun, 160, 172
Chakauputún, 34
Champollion, Jean-François, 199
Champotón, 127, 180
Charles V, 74
Chaunche, 89
Chetumal Bay, 192
Chetumal Province, 135, 146, 149, 171, 180, 182, 191, 210
Chiapas, 16, 25, 138
Chichén Itzá, 25, 34, 36, 48, 54, 73, 76, 89, 90, 91, 93, 98, 99, 101, 109, 110, 120, 123, 128, 137, 144, 160, 161, 163, 164, 165, 166, 171, 172, 182, 191, 192, 194, 204
Chikin Chel, 192
Chimor, 194
China, 155
Cholula, 163
Cifuentes, Spain, 15
City-state, 45
Clouds, 176
Cobá, 32, 63, 165, 182, 185, 190, 192
Coclé, 194
Cocoms, 109–110
Codex Tro-Cortesianus, 97
Colombia, 87, 170, 194
Columbus, Christopher, 11, 13, 85, 170, 191, 193
Connecticut, 200
Conquest of Peru, 12
Copál, 120

Copán, 15, 29, 63, 64, **76**, 83, 99, 132, 147, 174, 178
Copán River, 147
Corinth, 45
Cortes, H., 74, 75, 85, 87, 88, 171, 180, 181, 190
Costa Rica, 19, 170
Cotoche, Cape, 191
Cotzacoalcos, 88
Covarrubias, Miguel, 169
Cozumel Island, 13, 48, 56, 132, 160, 165, 180, 183, 185, 194
Crete, 155
Cuba, 193, 209
Cueva de la Araña, 55
Cuzco, 121, 123, 129

D'Asterac, Monsieur, 78
Delgado, Fray Diego, 21
Díaz, Bernal, 48, 88, 89, 91, 127, 129, 135, 193, 200
Díaz, Juan, 90
Dresden Codex, 17, 36, 95, 111, 202
Dzibilichaltún, 169, 183

Easarhaddon, King of Assyria, 205
East Germany, 84
Easter Island, 201
Ecija, Spain, 13
Edward the Confessor, 84
Ekab, 24, 86, 167, 191
Ekal, 190
El Petén, 22, 28, 64, 74, 127, 144, 182, 201
Epictetus, 89
Ethnology of the Maya, 106

Fayum, Egypt, 68
Ferdinand, Archduke, 74
Flanders, 74
Förstemann, Dr. E., 200
France, Anatole, 78
Francis I, 17
Frederick the Great, 105
Fry, Roger, 169

Gage, Thomas, 17
Galindo, Juan, 17
Gates, William, 195, **196**, 197
Goodman, J. T., 200
Gourmont, Rémy de, 51
Grant, Ulysses S., quoted, 18
Great Ball Court, 98
Greece, 71
Greeks, food of, 55
Grijalva, Juan de, 86, 90, 143, 165
Grotefend, Georg, 199

Guanaja, 13, 85, 195
Guatemala, 15, 18, 25, 43, 180, 185
Guerrero, Gonzalo, 89, 135, 165, 210
Gulf of Mexico, 19

Harvard University, 18
Henry III, 204
Hibueras, *see* Honduras
Hieroglyphic Stairway, 149
Hispaniola, island of, 52
Historia Antigua de América, 150
History, 17
Holactun, 160
Honduras, 64, 74, 135, 181
Honduras, Gulf of, 181
Huasteca, 194
Humboldt, Alexander von, **17**
Huntichmool, 160
Huxley, Aldous, 48, 108, 124, 157, 159, 170

Iliad, 204
Incas, 45; laws of, 115
India, 155
Iraq, 77
Italy, 71
Itzás, 35, 121, 171; books of, 202
Itzcoatl, King, 89
Ix Azal Noh, 70
Ix Chebel Yax, 70
Ix Zacal Nok, 70
Ixil, 42
Izabal, Lake, 181
Izamal, 144, 160, 169, 179, 180
Iztapan, 181

Jaina, 40
Jamaica, 193

Kabah, 123, 159, 160, 182
Kaminal-juyu, 109
Keuic, 160
Kickmool, 160
Kiminaljuyu, 85
King, Edward, 16
Kitto, H. D. F., 45
Knorosow, Dr. Yuri, 11, 199
Knossos, 79
Kukulcan, 54, 93, 161; Temple of, 164

Labná, 159, 182, 183
Lacondon, 155
Laguna de Pom, 86
Laguna de Términos, 192
Lancaster Turnpike, 179

Land of the Turkey and the Deer, The, 123

Landa, Fray Diego de, 15, 22, 23, 37, 38, 40, 41, 47, 50, 52, 55, 60, 62, 65, 66, 67, 69, 74, 76, 80, 86, 87, 90, 91, 93, 95, 97, 98, 99, 108, 110, 115, 120, 121, 122, 131, 134, 136, 137, 138, 139, 143, 144, 163, 169, 178, 179, 195, 199, 201, 202, 204, 205

Las Casas, 182

League of Mayapán, 36, 43, 159, 167

Lehmann, Walter, 18, 42

Lévy-Bruhl, 99

Lhullier, Alberto Ruz, 151

Loche, 117

Lost Tribes of Israel, 16

Loyola, Fray Andrés de Avenaño, 211, 212

Luther, Martin, 111

Magic Flute, The, 76

Maiam, Province of, 13

Maler, Captain Teobert, 18

Malinche ("the Tongue"), 13, 88

"Mamon" pottery, 27

Mangelsdorf, Dr. Paul, 62

Mani, 88, 190, 204

Mann, Thomas, 174

Margarita Island, 193, 194

Maudslay, Alfred, 17

Mauretania, 67

Maximilian, Emperor, 18

Maya, agricultural methods practiced by, 62–70; approach to art, 171; architecture of, 140–141; basketry practiced by, 77; calculation used by, 199; calendar of, 64–65; city-states built by, 120; civilization, birth of, 29; communications of, 190–194; conquest of, 211; crime and punishment by, 102–103; culture of, 26; as curers, 104–108; cures of, 104–108; dances of, 98, 206–207; day of, 53; description of, 26; dialects of, 33, 42; diet of, 55; eating habits of, 55; featherwork, 73–76; festivals of, 91–94; games of, 99–101; glyph-texts of, 206–207; glyph-writing of, 12; gods of, 132, 137; house, Nā, 52–53; intellectual equipment of, 27; and land communications, 179–190; language of, 42–44; literature of, 200–212; lords, 112–118; as makers of pottery, 78–84; markets of, 89–91; marriage customs of, 47–48; and Mexicans, 42; monogamy among, 49; monoliths of, 168; music of, 94–97; names and naming of, 58; physical characteristics of, 38–39; and planets, 178; and prenatal factors, 58; priests of, 136; religion of, 131–139; and ropemaking, 77–78; sculpture of, 167–171; sexual liberty among, 48; slavery practiced by, 89; society of, 37, 45; and Spaniards, 129; Spanish conquest of, 13; symbol of mat, 76; and taxes, 68–70; temple cities of, 32; temples of, 150–152; and trade, 84–89; tribute demanded by, 61; use of rope by, 77; vocabulary of, 44; warfare by, 125–128; weapons of, 124, 130; weaving by, 70–73; women, 49, 50

Maya "Rosetta Stone", 195

Mayadom, ceremonial centers in, 140; Indians in, 43; leaders in, 115; murals found in, 172; phases of pottery in, 82–84; population of, 37

Mayapán, 34, 36, 120, 121, 122, 123, 124, 127, 140, 182, 203, 210, 211

"Mayathan," speech of Maya, 43

Mazalan, 180

Mazanho, 192

Mazarin, Cardinal, 100

Melanasia, 80

Mérida, 190, 211

Mexico, 132, 147, 164, 210; conquest of, 210

Mexico, Gulf of, 19

Mexico City, 174

Mico Mountains, 181

Milan, 42

Mnemosyne, 204

Moctezuma, 74, 112, 114, 115, 118, 134

Mochica pottery, 105

Monte Albán, 96

Montejo, Francisco de, 112, 117, 194, 209, 210

Morley, Dr., 19, 64, 119

Morocco, 67

Mosque of Omar, 16

Motagua River, 181

Museum für Volkerkunde, 74

Muzo, 194

Myrina, 110

Naco, 181, 182, 193
Naples, 42
Naxactum, 82
Nicaragua, 99, 192, 193
Nicaragua, Lake, 193
Nicaragua Interocean Canal, 193
Nietzsche, 61
Nineveh, 78
Nito, 85, 181, 182
Noah, 131
Numidia, 67

*Of the Very Renowned Edifices
    of Uxmal*, 143
Olid, Cristóbal de, 209
Olmeca, 195
Omoa, 191, 193
On the Things of Yucatán, 195
Otolum, 149

Palace of Sennacherib, 78
Palacio, Diego García de, 15, 147
Palenque, 16, 17, 63, 83, 88, 109,
    113, 120, 149, 150, 152, 153,
    154, 161, 169; discovered by In-
    dians, 16
Panama, 170, 193, 194
Pantagruel, 104
Pantheon, Rome, 144
Paris, 150
Peón, Simón, 159
Peresianus Codex, 203
Persia, 68
Perez, Juan Pío, 200
Peru, 73, 105, 132, 190
Petén, Lake, 87, 180
Peto, 200
Philip I, 147
Philip II, 15
Piedras Negras, 63, 83, 85, 88,
    161
Piura, 71
Pizarro, Francisco, 12, 210
Polé, 160, 180
Pollock, H. W. S., 124
Polynesia, 201
Popol Vuh, 27, 34, 82, 83, 85,
    165, 203
Potonchon, 171
Prescott, W. H., 12, 16, 150
Proskouriakoff, Tatiana, 124, 164,
    168; quoted, 160
Ptomemy, 184
Puuc, 34, 41, 48, 132, 155, 157,
    159, 160

Quetzalcoatl, 33, 124, 164, 165
Quiché, 42
Quintana Roo, 25, 193

Quirigua, 76, 149

Real, Padre Ciudad, 15, 48, 143
Reine Pédanque, 78
Relatiónes de Yucatán, 15
Rio, Captain Antonio del, 16
Rio Tacotalpa, 182
Romans, signs of good or ill for-
    tune among, 105
Royal Library, Dresden, 202
Roys, Ralph, 106
Ruppert, Karl, 124
Russian Academy, 199

Sabacche, 160
Sahagun, Bernardino de, 100
San José, 146, 147
Santa Rita, 174
Sarantium, 206
Sayil, 123, 160, 167, 182
Scott, Sir Lindsay, 80
Seler, Edward, 18
Seville, 143, 165
Sierra de Espíritu Santo, 181
*Sixty-Two Curses of Easharhad-
    don, The*, 205
Smith, A. Ledyard, 119, 124
Smith, Robert, 124
Soliman, 165
Soloson, 176
Solosuchiapa, 182
Sosigenes, 176
Soustelle, Jacques, 17
Spain, 150
Spaniards, 99, 170, 203; battle
    with Maya, 129; comments on
    books read by Maya, 201
Sparta, 45
Spengler, O., 83, 135, 136
Stephens, John Lloyd, 16, 124,
    147, 149, 154, 159, 160, 165,
    181
Strabo, 84
Stromvik, Gustav, 124

Tabasco, 25, 33, 80, 85, 88, 161,
    180, 181, 191
Tahdziu, 118
Tacab, Lake, 180
Tajamulco, Mount, 19
Tampico, 27, 194
Tancah, 165
Tayasal, 181, 201
Teapa, 182
Tehuantepec, Isthmus of, 27
Temple of the Diving God, 167
Temple of Tula, 164
Temple of the Warriors, 90, 123,
    164, 172
Tenochtitlán, 45, 123, 204

Teotihuacan, 32, 43, 85, 162
Testera, Jacques de, 17
"Testerian Hieroglyphics," 17
Thebes, 78
Theophrastus, 71
T'ho, 179, 211
Thompson, Eric, 18, 37, 42, 44, 62, 70, 78, 123, 137, 147, 164, 195, 202, 208
Tikal, 22, 25, 29, 54, 63, 64, 83, 85, 105, 120, 121, 124, 137, 144, 145, 146, 159, 161, 170, 181, 182, 183, 185, 192, 194, 205, 208, 211; pyramids of, 145–146
Tizimin manuscript, 34
Toltec-Mexicans, 27
Toltecs, 34, 155, 159, 176; invasion of Chichén by, 161
Torquemada, 101
Troano Codex, 203
Tro-Cortesianus Codex, 203
Trujillo, 193
Tula, 32, 33, 162, 163, 164, 165
Tulum, 122, 127, 140, 165, 166, 167, 169, 174
Tutul Xiu, 123
Tutul Xiu dynasty, 34
Tzeltal, 42

Uaxactum, 22, 64, 144, 145, 147, 169, 172, 182
Ulua, 147
University of Pennsylvania, 145
Ursua, Martin de, 211
Usumacinta River, 27, 34, 85, 86, 88, 149, 153, 181, 192
Uxmal, 34, 48, 123, 141, 155, 157, 158, 159, 160, 165, 182; buildings at, 155–157
Uyamil, 192

Valdivia, Captain, 13, 129
Valencia, Spain, 55
Vanderbilt, Commodore, 193
Venezuela, 109
Venice, 193

Ventris, M., 200
Veracruz, 80, 86, 90, 195, 200
Veragua, 170, 171
Verapaz, 74
Via Salaria, 86
Vienna, 76, 150
Villa, Alfonso, 184
Virginia City Enterprise, 200
Von Hagen, Victor, 75

Waldeck, Jean Frederic, 16, 17, 150, 157
Washington, Booker T., 89
Whorf, B., 200
World of the Maya, The, 19

Xamanzaná, Lord of, 13
Xaxuná, 32
Xcalumkin, 160
Xelha, 127, 165, 166, 185, 192, 210
Xilanco, 192
Xicalanco, 28, 33, 42, 72, 85, 86, 87, 149, 161, 165, 171, 180
Xkalumpococh, 160

Yache 160
Yahilan, 112
Yaxchilan, 22, 63, 88, 138, 153, 154, 155
Yaxuná, 182, 183
Yucatán, 13, 14, 15, 16, 17, 19, 23, 24, 25, 27, 32, 34, 40, 41, 43, 45, 50, 54, 56, 59, 63, 64, 65, 74, 83, 85, 86, 89, 95, 109, 116, 117, 121, 127, 132, 143, 155, 159, 163, 164, 165, 167, 170, 171, 172, 179, 182, 190, 193, 200, 201, 203, 210, 211; jungles of, 225; temple cities of, 20; water in, 25
Yum Kaax, 63

Zacapa, 147
Zamabac, 192
Zamabac, Bay of, 167
Zipaquira, 87
"Zuyua, language of," 122